The Ronde

The Ronde

INSIDE THE TOUR OF FLANDERS: THE WORLD'S TOUGHEST BIKE RACE

Edward Pickering

**SIMON &
SCHUSTER**

London · New York · Sydney · Toronto · New Delhi

A CBS COMPANY

First published in Great Britain by Simon & Schuster UK Ltd, 2018
A CBS COMPANY

1 3 5 7 9 10 8 6 4 2

Simon & Schuster UK Ltd
1st Floor
222 Gray's Inn Road
London WC1X 8HB

www.simonandschuster.co.uk

Simon & Schuster Australia, Sydney
Simon & Schuster India, New Delhi

A CIP catalogue record for this book
is available from the British Library

ISBN: 978-1-4711-6927-4
Ebook ISBN: 978-1-4711-6928-1

Typeset in Bembo by M Rules
Printed and bound by CPI Group (UK) Ltd, Croydon, CR0 4YY

MIX
Paper from
responsible sources
FSC
www.fsc.org   FSC® C020471

Simon & Schuster UK Ltd are committed to sourcing paper
that is made from wood grown in sustainable forests and support the Forest
Stewardship Council, the leading international forest certification organisation.
Our books displaying the FSC logo are printed on FSC certified paper.

CONTENTS

	Acknowledgements	1
	Prologue	5
1.	Bruges	13
2.	Flanders	19
3.	Kruisberg	35
4.	Knokteberg	51
5.	Oude Kwaremont	65
6.	Paterberg	79
7.	Koppenberg	94
8.	Steenbeekdries	115
9.	Taaienberg	131
10.	Eikenberg	145
11.	Flanders II	157
12.	Molenberg	172
13.	Leberg	189
14.	Valkenberg	205
15.	Tenbossestraat	225
16.	Muur	240
17.	Bosberg	259
18.	Meerbeke	270
	Epilogue	276
	Bibliography	283
	Index	287

'It seems that Belgium was created to torment the cyclist.'

—ALEXI GREWAL

'*De Galli Belgae fortissimi sunt.*'

—JULIUS CAESAR

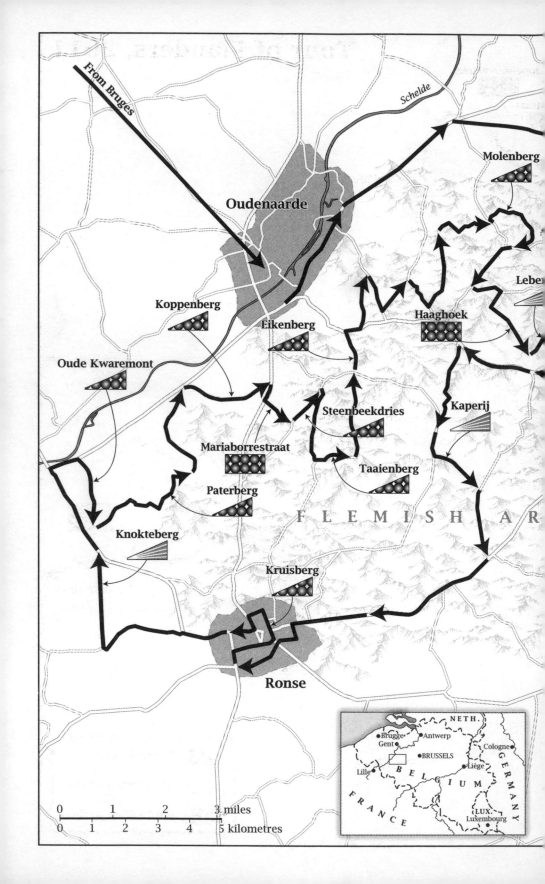

From Bruges

Schelde

Molenberg

Oudenaarde

Lebe

Koppenberg

Eikenberg

Haaghoek

Oude Kwaremont

Kaperij

Steenbeekdries

Mariaborrestraat

Taaienberg

Paterberg

F L E M I S H   A R

Knokteberg

Kruisberg

Ronse

0   1   2   3 miles

0   1   2   3   4   5 kilometres

NETH.

Brugge
Gent   Antwerp
                        BRUSSELS
Lille   Liège

Cologne

G E R M A N Y

B E L G I U M

F R A N C E

LUX.
Luxembourg

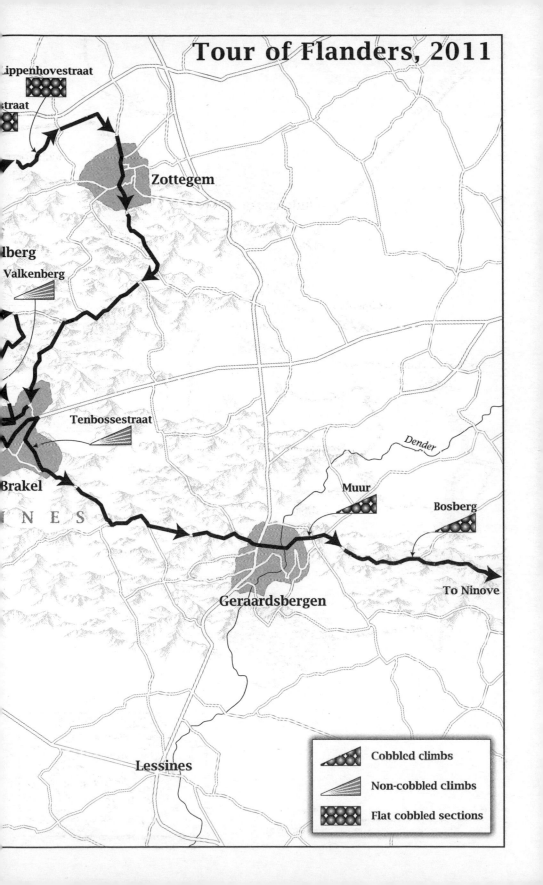

Tour of Flanders, 2011

Lippenhovestraat

straat

Zottegem

lberg
Valkenberg

Tenbossestraat

Brakel

I N E S

Dender

Muur

Bosberg

To Ninove

Geraardsbergen

Lessines

Cobbled climbs

Non-cobbled climbs

Flat cobbled sections

For James & Tommy

ACKNOWLEDGEMENTS

It is a truth universally acknowledged that a writer in possession of an idea for a book must be in want of a publisher who doesn't lean too heavily when words are spectacularly late. Thank you to Ian Marshall at Simon & Schuster, whose continued support and patience kept Ronde alive in good times and bad.

Thanks to my eagle-eyed copy editor Charlotte Atyeo, who gently but firmly curtailed my excesses, separated facts from alternative facts and made the book a better one. Also to my agent Kevin Pocklington, to whom I owe several Belgian beers.

For looking over various drafts of the text and providing advice about what worked and what didn't, thanks to Lionel Birnie, Mike Webb and Lex Webb. Lionel introduced me to Belgian bike racing and culture in the first place and I hope to share many more Leffe Blondes and La Chouffes with him, while putting the world to rights.

Thanks to the riders and team managers of the 2011 race who talked me through their experiences of the race and informed my story of it. Tom Boonen, Fabian Cancellara, Sylvain Chavanel, Juan Antonio Flecha, Roger Hammond, George Hincapie, Tristan Hoffman, Sebastian Langeveld, Björn Leukemans, Robbie McEwen, Nick Nuyens, Wilfried Peeters, Staf Scheirlinckx, Marc Sergeant, Geraint Thomas, Maarten Tjallingii and Jonathan Vaughters were all generous with their time and insight, and honest about what went right, what went wrong and why. Thanks to them, and the whole race peloton, for making the 2011 Ronde one of the most compelling bike races I have ever seen.

Thanks to a varied cast for their stories about themselves and the race in general. Baden Cooke, Roger Decock, Dirk Demol, Stijn Devolder, Walter Godefroot, Barry Hoban, Andreas Klier, Nikolas Maes, Patrick Lefevere, Johan Museeuw, Allan Peiper, Stijn Vandenbergh, Eric Vanderaerden and Peter Van Petegem were all fascinating interviewees who helped me understand more about the Tour of Flanders and how it works.

I was lucky to have some good guides to Flemish culture – Guy Fransen was a cheerful and patient source of advice, phone numbers and stories. Rik Vanwalleghem, Kevin Bruggeman and Willie Verhegghe helped me understand the race and Belgium a little better (even if to fully understand either would be a lifelong project). I was appreciative that both Father François Mbiyangandu and Tom Van Damme tolerated my doorstepping and welcomed me into their church and home respectively at short notice. Thanks also to the various innocent members of the Flemish public who answered my questions when I knocked on their doors, spoke to them in bars and accosted them on the streets.

I was lucky that cycling has had such diligent chroniclers. I mined back copies of *Winning, Cycle Sport, Procycling* and *Rouleur,* along with the well-thumbed books listed in the bibliography, for stories about the race, and I should also give special mention to the website *bikeraceinfo,* which is nerd heaven and has a comprehensive list of the Ronde's routes and results. Thanks to Daniel Friebe for his insight about Merckx and to colleagues and peers for listening to my half-baked theories about bike racing and for company on the road: Daniel Benson, Sam Dansie, Alasdair Fotheringham, Andy McGrath, Richard Moore, Sadhbh O'Shea and many more. I had help from

ACKNOWLEDGEMENTS

Alessandro Tegner, Ben Wright and Elke Weylandt in setting up interviews, and I also tapped up fellow nerd Cillian Kelly for confirmation of some of the stats in the book.

Lastly, and most importantly by a huge distance, thanks to my family, without whom writing this book would have been impossible. My wife Ellie and sons James and Tommy take up the slack when I periodically disappear into the writing cave and they provide unconditional love and support. And cake deliveries.

PROLOGUE

This is the story of a bike race.

Bike races are simple. Mostly, the riders start in one place, finish in another and the first across the finish line wins. Bike races are also complex: tree diagrams of events leading to outcomes leading to more outcomes and so on. They are possibly the best example of chaos theory in sport. They are more complex than that again. Compare the constrictive dimensions of a football field and the prescriptive tactical shape of the teams with the infinite possibilities of 200 riders on a road, out in the real world of weather, the landscape and human culture. More than most other sports, the narrative of cycling bleeds into the real world. To tell the story of a bike race is to tell the story of everything: history, geography, sociology and, in the end, a winner and losers.

For years, I thought that stage races like the Tour de France were the highest expression of sporting value in cycling. The grandeur and geographical logic of races taking in whole regions or countries were compelling to me, and my gateway drug into the sport was the Tour de France. I discovered the Tour in 1985 when Channel 4 showed edited highlights every evening during the race. I was an athletics fan, more specifically a middle-distance running fan (and even more specifically, a Steve Ovett fan); my dad was a French teacher who encouraged me into lifelong Francophilia. The Tour combined endurance sport and France, plus the mountains looked incredible. I couldn't take my eyes off it. It was immediately apparent that the race was more than just sport, though the sport alone might have been enough to hook me in the first place. However, the overlap of geography and culture with the race added multiple layers of complexity – I didn't just love the endurance side of it: it was clear that there was a depth and texture to the event that I couldn't see in any other sport.

For a couple of years, as far as I knew, the Tour de France was the only bike race that existed, and I never stopped to consider what the participants did for the rest of the year. By osmosis I learned that there was also a Tour of Italy and a Tour of Spain – the Giro d'Italia and Vuelta a España. Then I started buying cycling magazines and realised that there was an entire cycling season, stretching in those days from February to October, and that there were many more races like the Tour: Paris–Nice, Tirreno–Adriatico, Critérium International, the Critérium du Dauphiné Libéré, the Tour of Switzerland, and a couple of abortive attempts at setting up races in Anglo-Saxon countries (the Kellogg's Tour of Britain and the Tour de Trump). Some of the more obscure races were geography lessons in themselves – from these I learned where Romandy and the Basque Country were and what their relationship was to the countries of which they were part.

I also learned that there were other races in the cycling season. Dull-looking one-day races in flat countries where it pissed down with rain and the riders got covered in crap thrown up from the road: the Classics. The riders of the Tour de France danced up the beautiful mountains in bright sunshine, just like I wanted to; there was nothing particularly aspirational about watching square-headed thugs shouldering each other about on cobbled roads in northern Europe. The Tour was romance; the Classics gritty pragmatism. It was colour television versus black and white; Shakespeare versus kitchen-sink drama. The Classics were generally something I read about to pass the time between Paris–Nice in March and the Tour of Romandy at the end of

April, though my interest flickered briefly when British rider Sean Yates had a good run of results in Paris–Roubaix and Steve Bauer – a Canadian but still, at that point in cycling history, an Anglophone rarity and therefore interesting to me – was beaten by a centimetre by Eddy Planckaert in the 1990 edition of that race. Paris–Roubaix stood out, along with the Tour of Flanders, for the fact that some of the roads were cobbled.

The Tour de France became less interesting during the 1990s. It was partly the increasingly effective use of drugs, which eliminated or reduced the effect of one of the most interesting things about sport – fallibility – and partly the baleful dominance of Spanish rider Miguel Indurain, who won five yellow jerseys in a row by being a boring square. At the same time, I started to realise that the tactics in the one-day events had a lot more finesse than the stage races and, in terms of culture and belonging to their region, the Classics were every bit as rich as the longer events. Richer, even. In order to belong to all of France, the Tour has to spread itself thinly, with regions taking uneven turns to host the race. The Tour of Flanders, on the other hand, is concentrated into the same small corner of Belgium every year.

The Tour of Flanders, also known as the Ronde van Vlaanderen or more simply, de Ronde, is more than a bike race. It sometimes gets described as the Flandrian equivalent of the FA Cup final or Wimbledon, but these clichés do a disservice to the event. The Cup final may be the traditional end to the English and Welsh football season, but at heart only the supporters of the two teams involved really care. Wimbledon is closer – there's a particular strain of Englishness which the tournament represents, but still you have to like tennis to enjoy it. The Tour of Flanders has far more in common with Carnival, or with the *matsuri* of Japan – festivals that combine various elements of Shinto, fertility rites, booze, taiko drumming, fireworks, occasional violence and local pride. It's this last element which is the most important. To think of the Tour of Flanders as only a sporting event is to miss its wider significance. The Ronde is the expression of an entire culture: its geography, landscape, people, society, meteorology, politics, history and self-image. The race meshes perfectly over its host region's landscape and culture.

The first half of the Tour of Flanders, in its modern iteration, crosses the Flandrian plains, which are wide open to the prevailing west winds. These funnel up the English Channel from the Atlantic, bringing Belgium 200 days of rain a year. Then the riders, battered by the wind, come head on against the *Vlaamse Ardennen,* the Flemish Ardennes, a small ridge of cultivated hills, copses, narrow roads and quirky but functional villages. The Flemish writer Omer Wattez, who has been credited as the originator of the term '*Vlaamse Ardennen*', described it thus: 'My beautiful country, with broad horizons, a land of hills and valleys, where you can visit 10 or 12 villages on foot in one day . . . where you can see 20 villages, with their church towers, houses, homesteads and orchards, from the tops of the hills. My beautiful country with its wide vistas, strong green and long rows of trees.'

The *Vlaamse Ardennen* are a physical manifestation of the language border between Dutch-speaking Flanders and French-speaking Wallonia – the French language laps up against the southern ridge of the hills in this area of Belgium like a quiet sea. The Flemish Ardennes run east to west in a rough rectangle whose corners are formed by the towns of Oudenaarde, Ronse, Zottegem and Geraardsbergen. They are a small remnant of *Arduenna Silva*, the great Ardennes forest that existed in Roman times, though they are geologically distinct from the Ardennes region which straddles Wallonia and France to the south-east.

The Flemish Ardennes are a gentle range. The highest point

geologically is the Pottelberg at 157 metres, though since this is over the language border in what the Walloons call the *Pays des Collines*, the Hotondberg – seven metres lower but, more importantly, within the official bounds of Flanders – is considered the highest point by Flandrians.

The route of the Ronde criss-crosses the *Vlaamse Ardennen*, looping north and south, east and west, over a succession of steep, cobbled climbs: the bergs, or *hellingen* (hills). The bergs are the biggest part of the iconography of the Tour of Flanders. They're unpleasant to ride on – not only are they extremely steep and narrow in general but most of them are cobbled. Racing on cobbles is all about the fight – riders fight their bikes, the stones and each other. The cobbles (known locally as *kasseien* and to the greater cycling community by their French name, pavé) absorb the energy riders are putting into trying to propel their bikes forward and send it right back through the bike straight at them. The cobbles force the front wheel sideways in either direction, so the rider is constantly having to adjust his or her position and lean one way or the other, often right into the space occupied by another rider who is having their own private battle with the laws of physics. In the claustrophobic, sunken lanes of Flanders, the riders shout, push, grab and fall; the noise of slithering wheels on muddy cobbles and clumsy clacking from cycling shoes put to ground is a long way from the smooth and noiseless gliding of a Tour peloton cruising along a well-surfaced road in midsummer France.

The writer Robin Magowan wrote, in his book *Kings of the Road*: 'To the Flemish imagination, cobbles are to a surfaced road what poetry is to prose.' The *kasseien* are unpleasant and jarring to ride on, but they are what give the Ronde its rhythm, rhyme and metre.

However, there's more to the race than the climbs and cobbles. The wind is often strong, and the roads zig and zag around enclosed fields, which means riders need to know when to be on one side of the bunch, to shelter from the wind, and when to be on the other. The climbs are spread unevenly along the route, so riders need to know when to be near the front to reduce their chances of being brought to a standstill by a crash or congestion. Everybody therefore spends the five or ten kilometres before a climb trying to elbow their way to a position near the front, all the time trying to obey the first commandment of cycling, which is to save energy wherever possible (these two processes are exactly contradictory, so something has to give). The rider Geraint Thomas told me of some advice given to him by Scott Sunderland, a former team manager: 'Sometimes you have to spend a bit of energy to save a bit of energy.' And since the roads are narrow, moving around the bunch is harder than in most other races, which means – more than in any other event – knowledge of the terrain and the way the race interacts with it is essential. This makes the tactics very complex and the race very difficult to win. Strong riders also have to rely on their brains; clever riders also have to rely on their strength. The organisers tweak the route every season, so a lesson learned one year may not be useful the next.

In 2013, on the occasion of the 100th anniversary of the first Ronde van Vlaanderen, Belgian newspaper *Het Nieuwsblad* polled its readers to ask which was the best Tour of Flanders ever. The two frontrunners were 1969, in which Eddy Merckx won alone by five minutes in filthy conditions, and 1985, when Belgian champion Eric Vanderaerden won in even more extreme weather. It's a generalisation but I think a lot of cycling fans have two inclinations – a tendency towards enjoying the epic and heroic (weather, terrain, exploits etc.) and an idealised image of the past. So it's no surprise that 1969 and 1985 stand out as memorable editions for the photogenic misery of the protagonists. The muddied faces of the winners remind us of life's struggle – it's easy to draw a parallel between the idea of a rider setting off in a long race and the daily reality for working-class Belgians in the first three-quarters of the 20th century, of setting off to work in the fields or in the coalmines. Look at a photograph of the dirty face of a rider at the end of a long, wet bike race and the begrimed face of a coalminer after a day down the pit and there are similarities: the idea conveyed is that through work and dirt we can lift ourselves out of poverty – or at least survive to work another day.

But there's a distance between then and now. Flanders isn't some pre-industrial rural backwater; it's a 21st-century service economy. If we're going to look at the country through the prism of its most important cultural event, we have to look at more recent times. Flanders is a region with a complicated history and, while it has one foot in the past, it has the other firmly in the present. That tension between history and the future, between old Flanders and new, found perfect expression in the 2011 Ronde. This edition of the race happens to have been the last one held on the 'old' route before a new circuit-based race was introduced in 2012 (though 'old' in this case is relative – the route of the Ronde has been fluid throughout its whole existence). It wasn't epic in the way that the 1985 and 1969 editions were – the weather has been generally kind to the riders in recent years – but the 2011 Ronde was an object lesson in how bike races work. It involved complicated tactics, unpredictability and excitement featuring a broad range of characters, culminating in a 12-man free-for-all through to an exhilarating denouement. Through the story of this single edition of the race, in my opinion one of the best bike races of the last 25 years or more, I will tell the wider story of the Ronde van Vlaanderen, its history, geography and culture.

It started, as the race had done for the previous 13 editions, in Bruges.

CHAPTER 1

Bruges

Sunday 3 April 2011

Nick Nuyens is cutting it fine. While most of the 199 starters in the Ronde van Vlaanderen have already signed in and made their way to the start line on the broad expanse of the Markt in Bruges, the Belgian rider is sitting on his team bus, alone.

The impression we get, reinforced by the habit of professional bike riders to cocoon themselves inside the bus at the start of any race, is that the bus is a haven. The outside world is where autograph-hunters, fans with phone cameras and worse, journalists, lie in wait. The *raison d'être* of a cyclist is to get efficiently from A to B in the shortest possible time, and the best way to do this is to travel the shortest possible distance. This is why riders take bends on the inside. The unsolicited distractions of the outside world mean riders take a sideways step for every two steps forward, like a knight on a chessboard.

So we assume that the bus is an escape from this. But actually, team buses can also be stressful environments. Put eight or nine riders, two managers, a bunch of soigneurs, mechanics, PRs and corporate hangers-on in a narrow space like that, and at some point you'll find yourself squeezing past somebody who is getting a leg massage, trying to get to the coffee machine when somebody else is making themselves an espresso or scrabbling around for your shoes.

However, with Nuyens' team-mates all gone and the race starting very shortly, the Saxo Bank team bus is every bit the escape from the outside world, and Nuyens is making productive use of the solitude. It's a last moment of rest, he'll say later; a few minutes where he can collect his thoughts. He's been working with Rudy Heylen, a mental coach whose other clients include the Club Brugge football team; the pair met at the team hotel two days before the race to do some psychological exercises and Heylen had Nuyens write down the ten words or ideas which defined the race for him:

1. Small roads.
2. Understanding the road/wriggling.
3. Knowledge (parcours and tactics).
4. Unpredictable.
5. Attractive/thriller.
6. Very hard race.
7. Never give up/perseverance.
8. Heroic/history.
9. Good legs needed to go hard.
10. Incredible crowd/fans/arena.

Nuyens is an outsider for the Ronde. Second place in 2008 promised much, but he's followed up with a 15th place and a non-finish in the two years since. He rides for a Danish team, Saxo Bank, and is mostly ignored by the Belgian media, who divide their column inches more or less equally between stories about Tom Boonen's form and stories about Tom Boonen's private life. Boonen is a favourite for the Ronde – at this point he's won it twice. He's a thoroughbred, unlike Nuyens. A rider of class, confidence and power. Both are Belgian – Flemish in fact – but they occupy different places in the hearts and minds of the local fans and media. The fans' hearts tell them Boonen is their best chance of a home win. So do their minds.

What you need to know about Nuyens is that he wins bike races by being a weasel. This is in no way a criticism. They say that there are only seven basic plots in literature; there are even fewer ways of winning a bike race – you can be the strongest, or the luckiest or the cleverest, or more likely a combination thereof. (You can also be passive, or aggressive, in any of these three areas.) Nuyens mainly operates in the intersection between clever and lucky. He is physically strong, but the power in his legs and the efficiency of his cardiovascular system are merely conduits for his strongest assets: his brain, and an arse-coverer's instinct for flicking his rivals and looking out for number one. Some people watch bike races and get upset when the strongest rider doesn't win, as if life were that simple. Bike races remind us that life isn't fair.

A case in point: the 2011 Dwars door Vlaanderen 11 days before the Ronde. (The race's name means 'Straight through Flanders', or 'Across Flanders', although barely anybody in the peloton calls it Dwars door Vlaanderen; they prefer the more prosaic 'Waregem', which is the name of the finish town. Waregem is entirely nondescript, except for a large circular brickwork water tower on the edge of town with a moving electronic display upon which the words '*Welkom in Waregem*' rotate in kitsch and luminous perpetuity for 24 hours a day.) Nuyens and a youngish Welsh rider, Geraint Thomas, were away, just seconds ahead of the field in the final kilometre. Thomas was strong but he has a fatal weakness – a sense of fair play and a reputation for burying himself for the cause. This makes him an excellent team pursuiter but he'd never make it as a politician. To Thomas, Nuyens is an equal partner in a shared enterprise. To Nuyens, Thomas is so much expendable muscle. The most crucial difference is that you might get the impression Thomas would be happy with second place while Nuyens would not.

With 500 metres to go, Nuyens attacked. Thomas slowly came back to him. Advantage Thomas because he was now sitting in the Belgian's slipstream, saving energy for the sprint, and there was a headwind blowing down the finishing straight. If Nuyens kept working, Thomas would win and Nuyens come second.

So Nuyens started to freewheel. If Thomas didn't take over at the front, they would be caught; if he did, the Welshman could still get second in the sprint. From a situation where he would definitely finish second, Nuyens had engineered a position where either both would lose or he would win – his chances of winning had just gone from zero per cent to 50 per cent, maybe more. Sure enough, Thomas took over at the front. Nuyens slotted in behind him. Thank you very much. Nuyens won the sprint.

Nuyens thinks those two seconds of freewheeling constitute one of the best moves of his career. He didn't exactly weigh up the options; the voice of experience just told him to stop pedalling, and he'd won enough previously that he could gamble a definite second place against a possible first.

On the team bus in Bruges, Nuyens tidies up his post-race bag, eats a cake, and heads off to the Markt sign-in. The emcee is Lieven Van Gils, a television presenter and sports journalist. 'Will the last to sign in be the first to finish the race?' asks Van Gils.

'I hope so,' replies Nuyens.

*

The people of Bruges have an uneasy relationship with outsiders. The city, described variously as the 'Venice of the North', the 'City of Swans' or less edifyingly by symbolist novelist Georges Rodenbach as 'Bruges la Morte' (Dead Bruges) – has to reconcile the economic necessity of attracting thousands of visitors to its medieval streets and canals with the fact that its people just want to be left alone. Flemish cultural historian André De Vries wrote: 'If Bruggelingen are not at all pleased by the invasion of foreigners, they nevertheless do very well out of the tourist business.' (De Vries added: 'Take away the tourists and Bruges looks a great deal more attractive, and a lot deader.')

But Bruges is well used to the influx. In medieval times, Flanders hosted five fairs every year; the Bruges fair in spring lasted six weeks. So what the locals think on Tour of Flanders Sunday is anybody's guess. At least the event – the biggest bike race in Flanders – only happens for a single day every year.

People have been trading goods at the Markt, the city's focal point, since the tenth century. It is where announcements of importance were made and, in more febrile times, was the site for public executions. These days, it's a shrine to tourism: on the surface of it a functioning local marketplace but subtly geared to attracting visitors from outside and separating them from their money.

Historically, Bruges was a port, and from the start of the second millennium to about 1500 it traded with Portugal, Venice and the Genoese and was a major international cultural centre, gaining its wealth from the production of woollen cloth. Its primacy had visual representation in 'The Arnolfini Portrait' by Jan Van Eyck, though it was given much more ambiguous treatment by Geoffrey Chaucer as a den of permissiveness, gambling and dancing in 'The Shipman's Tale'. It declined in the next 400 years – its port and access to the sea having silted up – but in a very 20th-century piece of reinvention, developed a second life as a tourist destination from the early 1900s.

For one day a year, the Markt is the focal point of international cycling for the start of the Ronde. The 2011 race begins in the central square of Bruges, where Nuyens has just been the last rider to sign in and take the start line. For this one day a year, it's a nervous cauldron of pre-race excitement, and people who should know better are already on their second or third beer of the day. The previous year's winner – Swiss rider Fabian Cancellara, whose victory over Tom Boonen had been so emphatic that a corner of the internet was feverishly speculating about him having fitted a small motor to his bike, which he denied – is the centre of attention. A fan, presumably Flemish, has gone to the trouble of painting a large sign, reading 'Fabian, please have mercy' which he holds aloft in supplication.

The Markt, in a gentle warning of what is to come for the riders, is cobbled, though as the riders start, still neutralised behind a race vehicle, there is none of the fighting and straining that characterise the bergs – the cobbled climbs of Flanders. That will come in time. For the moment, the tension holds and the peloton leaves Bruges.

CHAPTER 2

Flanders

The Tour of Flanders races south from Bruges. If the prevailing west-south-west half-wind had been blowing in, this part of the race might have been difficult, but it's dry and mild and the benign weather imposes a grateful, albeit uneasy, truce on the peloton.

The terrain here, within the province of West Flanders, is flat and typically Flandrian. The riders will reach Kortrijk and then head east, covering two sides of a square formed by the towns of Roeselare, Kortrijk, Tielt and Waregem. This square is known as the Flemish Texas for reputedly having the densest concentration of millionaires in Belgium, though in the past the region has seen harder times than now.

The first notable break is a quintet of expendables who should really have been allowed to build a good lead. Koen Barbé of Landbouwkrediet, Steven Caethoven of Veranda's Willems–Accent, Skil–Shimano's Roger Kluge, Nuyens' Saxo Bank–SunGard team-mate Jarosław Marycz and Movistar's Jesús Herrada would have been the mix of chancers, self-publicists, no-hopers, journeymen and surreptitious achievers that constitutes the perfect early break. Barbé came fourth in the 2006 edition of Omloop Het Volk, a shorter Flandrian race held in February, but he hasn't bothered the top 50 in four previous attempts at the Ronde. Caethoven has won the occasional, small race but never a Classic like this. Kluge and Marycz are both second-year professionals and domestiques (the latter is Nuyens' room-mate at the team's accommodation, the Parkhotel in Kortrijk). Herrada is in his third month as a pro. Spanish riders, with one or two exceptions, have not thrived in the chilly and physical environment of the cobbled Classics any more than their tall and burly north-European counterparts have thrived in, say, the mountains of the Vuelta a España.

One of the most enduring fictions in cycling – propagated by journalists, reporters, television commentators, fans and some riders – is that the early break in a bike race is either trying to win the race or has a chance. (Actually, sometimes it does, just often enough that the fiction can continue to be maintained – it has even happened in the Ronde.) But the real function of the early break in most instances is to impose structure and discipline on the race. The dynamic between the teams represented up the road and those in the peloton provides an equilibrium that would not exist if the bunch just rode along together.

Smaller teams put riders in the break for the publicity value of having their sponsor's logo on television, on the understanding that they probably won't have their sponsor's logo on television during the finale because their riders aren't strong enough. This is why Caethoven, Barbé and Kluge are there. Barbé and Caethoven's teams are small Belgian outfits, which makes it even more important to be represented. Marycz is there to work for Nuyens. Since Saxo Bank have a man in the break, they won't have to contribute to any pace-setting in the peloton. Herrada's more likely trying to avoid trouble – when the peloton starts hitting the bergs in the Tour of Flanders, it's an absolute shit-fight. The best way to not get involved is to be up the road.

A few more things about breaks: the big teams would love to have a rider there, but they know that if they send a man up the road, all their rivals will chase him down to save themselves having to do it later when the gap is much bigger. Their rivals will also want to make sure that when it's time to chase the break, those same big teams will not be able to avoid the responsibility of contributing. If all of the big teams get a man in the break, that changes things, but it still might or might not succeed in getting away – many more riders may see the opportunity to try to join, and that will upset the feng shui. 'Big teams', in Flanders, mainly means Quick Step and Omega Pharma–Lotto, the two Belgian squads, plus maybe BMC, Garmin–Cervélo, Leopard Trek and Sky. Quick Step have Tom Boonen, and Lotto have Philippe Gilbert, who has twice won Omloop Het Volk. BMC have Alessandro Ballan, who won the Ronde in 2007, while Leopard are the team of defending champion Fabian Cancellara. Garmin are following an overly-optimistic strategy of three leaders – world champion Thor Hushovd plus sprinters Heinrich Haussler (second in 2009) and Tyler Farrar (fifth in 2010). Three-pronged strategies don't tend to work in cycling. Sky are there with the experienced Juan Antonio Flecha, a third-place finisher here in 2008.

David Millar, the now-retired British rider, described how the break formed in the 2014 Ronde, which he rode for Garmin, in his book *The Racer*: 'Certain teams [try] to get in a break while others are more concerned about preventing a dangerous group slipping away. We fall into the latter category. That means choosing two or three teams and marking them. We choose Quick Step and Lotto, so if one of their riders attacks, we go with them. We know that if those two teams aren't in the break then at some point later in the race they'll assume responsibility for chasing it down.

'By keeping it to two prominent teams it is relatively simple.

You stop thinking about individual riders and only concentrate on the jersey of those teams. If a Lotto jumps, you jump.

'The majority of big teams will be employing a similar tactic. Lotto will mark Quick Step and vice versa. Both of these teams will be marking Sky and Trek. And Sky and Trek will be marking Quick Step and Lotto and each other. So it will end up being quite a protracted shoot-out until finally a move slips away, minus the key teams and of the right size.'

Millar added that many of the riders involved in the attacks have absolutely no interest in escaping themselves, but play an important role nonetheless: 'On average after 45 minutes they're all quite fucked from marking each other out and an invisible white flag is flown and the perfect small group gets out.'

The perfect small group will consist of five to eight riders. Any fewer and there won't be enough fire-power, which means they'll get caught too soon. More than eight or nine and it will be too hard to bring back, so it won't be let go in the first place. Caethoven et al, who go after 15 kilometres, seem to be that perfect small group.

But for whatever reason, they are not. They are chased down and everything starts again from square one, except everybody is a little more knackered. Caethoven goes again. Is brought back. And then, 50 kilometres in as the race passes Zwevegem, a suburb south-east of Kortrijk, another quintet goes: Garmin's Roger Hammond, Sky's Jeremy Hunt, Caethoven's team-mate Stefan van Dijk, Kluge's team-mate Mitchell Docker and Europcar rider Sébastien Turgot. Two Brits, a Dutchman, an Aussie and a Frenchman, and not a single Belgian. The balance looks bad, and Hammond is theoretically a very dangerous rider – he's lived in Belgium his entire professional career and come third in Paris–Roubaix and second in Ghent–Wevelgem, as well as seventh in Flanders the previous season (though what most people watching don't realise is that Hammond is not on form). But sometimes the right break fails and the wrong break succeeds. The peloton chases for about ten kilometres, but while it's not ideal that Sky and Garmin both have riders up there, Quick Step and Lotto have both missed the boat. The hive mind of the main bunch decides enough is enough, somebody stops for a piss, and that is that.

I met with Rik Vanwalleghem in the café of the Centrum Ronde van Vlaanderen in Oudenaarde. Vanwalleghem is a former cycling journalist for the Flemish daily newspapers *Het Nieuwsblad* and *De Standaard*; these days he runs the Centrum, which is a museum dedicated to the Ronde. The Centrum is a functionally brutalist one-storey building just off Oudenaarde's main market square, with yellowing slabs of rain-damaged concrete arranged in wide, flat horizontals. The Markt is quaint and attractive; next door to the Centrum there's an eclectic terrace of buildings dating back to the 16th century with tall windows and steeply sloping roofs, while opposite stands the town's Sint-Walburgakerk, a gothic church whose main tower was built in the 15th century and can be seen for miles around. These juxtapositions might grate but this is the country that has spawned a Twitter account named Ugly Belgian Houses. Belgium does discordant coexistence very well.

There's a boxy Volvo permanently parked outside the Centrum − 1970s shape, 1970s orange-brown colour − with decals from Eddy Merckx's Molteni team. Inside, there's another relic from the 1970s: Freddy Maertens, one of the greatest Belgian riders never to have won the Ronde, works behind the desk, officially as a greeter, guide and receptionist but unofficially as a kind of living exhibit. The building itself might also look a bit 1970s but it was actually constructed in the early 2000s. There are displays of retro team jerseys, race memorabilia, old bikes, photographs and a computer rigged to a stationary bike on which you can pedal furiously while a video screen shows your progress up the Ronde's most famous climb, the Muur van Geraardsbergen (the 'wall' of Geraardsbergen).

I'd gone to Belgium to search for the soul of the Tour of Flanders, and this shrine to the race's history – which happens to be in the town where the current iteration of the race finishes – seemed to be as good a place to start as any. Over coffee and cake, Vanwalleghem told me what the Ronde is, or rather what it represents.

'In Flanders, when you show a bike race on television you have an audience of two or three hundred thousand people,' he said. 'For the Tour of Flanders, that doubles or triples. The two hundred thousand are the people who love cycling and know how the sport works. The other group included my mother-in-law, who knew nothing about cycling and didn't know the difference between the front and the rear wheel of the bike. She didn't know the names, except maybe Eddy Merckx. But on the day of the Ronde, she went to what we call the "high room", the salon, and she had to watch the race.

'It's a race with a big history and big names. But it's also something visceral, and you have the feeling that something important is going on. You live it and talk about it with other people. The Ronde fulfils a role of being the cement of the population.

'Every human population needs certain symbols where they can come to gather,' he continued. 'There are historical reasons that in our case it's a bike race, but in the USA you have the Superbowl, in the Middle East you have camel races on certain days of the year. It's a sociological event.

'In the first place, the meaning for the people of Flanders is that on the day of the Ronde, you have the luxury of nothing else mattering. Human beings need a totem, to acquire a social identity. It's partly an accident that it's a bike race, but if it hadn't been the Ronde it would have been something else.'

There have always been religious undertones to descriptions of the public's attitude to the Ronde in the past. The race is held on the first Sunday of April and this often coincides with Easter, which makes it easy to link the two. What could be more religious than the idea of a gathering of hundreds of thousands of people on the holiest day of the Christian calendar? Cycling revels in religious iconography, most overtly in Italy – the Madonna del Ghisallo, the apparition of the Virgin Mary at the hill of the same name, is the patron saint of cyclists; the Tour of Lombardy, one of Italy's two biggest one-day races, crosses the Madonna del Ghisallo every year. Various surveys put the proportion of Italians practising Catholicism between 80 and 90 per cent, so maybe the link between religion and cycling there is no surprise. Belgium is also a predominantly Catholic nation, albeit to a lesser extent than Italy, but for Vanwalleghem, if the people who watch the Ronde are celebrating anything at all, it's their own identity rather than something external.

'The event projects values to the population,' he said. 'The myth of the *Flandrien*. You know, we Flandrians don't complain; we go on, with the grey skies and the mud and the dreadful weather. We don't speak that much but we go on. All these things are then seen in the race, and that is our identity. That's us.'

The myth, or stereotype, of the *Flandrien* developed along with the race, and with a burgeoning sense of regional pride in the first half of the 20th century. A *Flandrien* is a rider or individual who endures pain, fatigue and bad weather uncomplainingly (there's also a French term, *Flahute*, which means the same). A *Flandrien* is unflashy, tough, ascetic and works hard. In a bike race they are aggressive and honest in their efforts. As the roots of the description go back to the Flandrian farm workers in the 1800s and early 1900s who crossed the border into France to do seasonal work in the fields or factories, there is also an undertone of class to the term – a *Flandrien* is a definitively working-class stereotype.

The archetypal *Flandrien* was Briek Schotte, who won the Ronde in 1942 and 1948. He was born in 1919 to a family of farmers who owned a smallholding of ten acres and had five brothers and sisters. At the age of ten, he watched on the roadside as the 1930 Tour of Flanders passed by and decided he wanted to be a bike racer. As a teenager he worked in a factory in Kortrijk, starting his shift at 5 a.m. and working through to the afternoon then cycling in the afternoons. Or waking up to go cycling at 3:30 a.m. before work.

The cycling journalist Adam Glasser compared Schotte's *Flandrien* attitudes with those of some of his rivals – who'd started going to the Côte d'Azur to train and who preferred to make money racing in kermis events (local races around Flanders) than to train – in *Cycle Sport* magazine in 1995:

'True *Flandrien* hard men would not go to the Côte d'Azur to train. Instead they had their own classical method. With leather crash hats over black berets, folded-up newspaper under thick jumpers, socks held up with garters, rolled raincoat under saddles they would set off in wet and freezing conditions across the endless cobbles, along canals, past windmills with their huge lumbering vanes, struggling against the blast of relentless sea winds until they reached the coast. As the light faded they would return after long hours in the saddle taking in the lung-bursting walls of the Kwaremont or Kruisberg. This was Schotte's lifestyle and it made him as hard as leather.'

Schotte had his own advice for aspiring cyclists about how hard they should be training: 'Ride until you don't know what village you're from.'

Schotte's record in the Tour of Flanders is extraordinary. He started it 20 times between 1940 and 1959, in a career of unusual longevity. As well as his two wins, he finished on the podium a further six times, twice more in the top ten, six more times in the top 25 and pulled out on the other four occasions. (The Tour of Flanders is unique among major bike races in that it continued through the German occupation of Belgium during the Second World War. The Germans decreed a 'business as usual' policy, although this was predominantly used to foment existing tensions between the Flemish and Walloon communities in Belgium and might more accurately be described as 'divide and rule'.)

Schotte himself either took being a *Flandrien* extremely seriously or played up to the stereotype. He formulated a list of ten commandments for *Flandriens*:

1. Be happy with what you've got.
2. Determination and patience get you everywhere.
3. If you're tired, go to bed.
4. Never lose your freedom.
5. Stay who you are.
6. Watch and you'll learn a lot.
7. Let yourself go and you lose yourself.
8. Never forget your roots.
9. Never believe in dreams you can't make come true.
10. Speak ill and ill will come of you.

I'd also met the current sports editor of *Het Nieuwsblad*, Guy Fransen, at the Centrum Ronde van Vlaanderen. Fransen, whose background is in news and politics, also understood the event as an expression of Flemish character: 'It's a religious day for us. It's a happening; it's everyone on the roads; it's community. It's Flanders showing its best side.

'We have the perception that the Ronde is telling our story: a bit shy, working class, working hard, in bad conditions sometimes. This is a country with a lot of rain and wind, and when you go cycling here you never have a day like you do when you are cycling in the south of France in nice weather. You have to put power into your pedals.

'It's the working guy with lines in his face. It's our land. It's us. We have success, but success never comes without hard work.'

The gap between the break and the peloton swells to eight minutes, which means that between the Hammond–Hunt–Docker–Turgot–Van Dijk group and the peloton, there are a clear five kilometres of road. Neutral observers might be thinking Hammond's Garmin team have really put themselves in a strong position: not just three leaders – Hushovd, Haussler and Farrar – safe in the bunch but another potential top-ten finisher eight minutes in front. They also have a two-time winner of the race, Peter Van Petegem, giving tactical advice from the team car.

Garmin's general manager Jonathan Vaughters has less confidence in his team. The three leaders are okay; the rest of the team less so. They have a rider on the team, Andreas Klier, who knows the roads so well his team-mates call him 'GPS'. He was instructed to move to the region by the management when he signed with a Dutch team, TVM–Farm Frites, in 1999, and he's lived here ever since, on the course with three kilometres to the finish in Meerbeke, a southern suburb of the city of Ninove. He came second in the Ronde in 2005. But he has less horsepower these days, even though the management trust him to captain the team and make the quick decisions on the road that the team car doesn't have time to process. The reason Hammond is in the break is that the team know he doesn't have the form to make the definitive selections once the Ronde hits the climbs, so giving him a head start means he'll at least be able to help the team in the third quarter of the race.

Of the three leaders, Vaughters thinks Hushovd has the best – or at least the least worst – chance. Farrar struggles on the hills so he will have to rely on the race coming back together after the final climb, which rarely happens in the Ronde, and Haussler isn't at his best.

The race follows the river Leie through Kortrijk, passing towns that are famous for bike racing and not much else: Wevelgem, finishing town of the previous week's Ghent–Wevelgem Classic; Harelbeke, home of the E3 Prijs.

In past times, the Leie was the main conduit for the flax industry that thrived in this part of Flanders. They used to soak the flax in the waters of the Leie, which gave it the nickname the 'Golden River'. These days it's more grey-brown than golden, hemmed between concrete walls through Kortrijk and beyond while huge industrial barges drift up- and downstream.

In a homage to the history of the race *helling* number one, of 18, is the Tiegemberg, not long after Harelbeke. The Tiegemberg – 750 metres long, not that steep, and tarmac – is not a hard climb, but it was the first climb the race ever used, in 1919, in the third edition. It's followed a few kilometres later by *helling* two, the Nokereberg, which is cobbled, but no harder than the Tiegemberg. It's a town-centre climb, rather than a sunken banked lane in the middle of nowhere.

After the Nokereberg, the race rattles over the cobbles of Doorn, then takes a diversion through Oudenaarde, passing the Centrum Ronde van Vlaanderen. The lull continues until Zwalm, when the gap slowly starts shrinking back from eight minutes. It's not a chase – the five riders aren't dangerous enough to justify the energy expenditure. But the peloton is stirring, as the riders head east towards the Paddestraat. The Paddestraat is a narrow two-kilometre stretch of flat cobbles built over the old Roman road which ran from Boulogne-sur-Mer in France to Cologne in Germany. The race comes here most years, and a monument has been erected: a cobblestone suspended within a circle, and the names of the winners of the editions of the race which visited the road engraved in order. The Paddestraat comes to a finish in the village of Velzeke-Ruddershove, where the route kinks right then left, and the riders hit another stretch of cobbles on Lippenhovestraat.

The run-up to the Paddestraat is where many of the big leaders start to move towards the front. Though few are as extravagantly lackadaisical as double-winner Peter Van Petegem (who was known for spending almost the first three hours of the race sitting in last position in the bunch), the aim until now has been to hide away. Nuyens prefers it at the back – he thinks that, while sometimes it's physically harder there as the accelerations affect riders at the back more than those at the front, the mental relaxation he gains from it is more beneficial. BMC's American rider George Hincapie has slowly started moving up as the race nears this section – he aims to be one of the first 40 or so rather than right at the front. He's seen the race split on the Paddestraat before, and the back half of the field is a risky place to be.

Garmin lead over the two sections of cobbles, along with Australia's Robbie McEwen. McEwen lives between Brakel and Geraardsbergen, in the heart of the Flemish Ardennes, but while his local knowledge is impeccable – if he'd turned right instead of going straight on at the Paddestraat, he'd be at his front door in 16 kilometres – he is not a specialist in this kind of race. McEwen's a bunch sprinter, a three-time winner of the Tour de France's green jersey, but this is only the second time in 16 professional seasons he's been drafted in for the Ronde, and he's on domestique duty at the RadioShack team for Grégory Rast. The Australian is a master of the dark arts of moving around a peloton and saving energy – he used to float in the wash of riders just behind the front of the peloton, then drift imperceptibly back and forward as the riders at the front rotated, to keep himself near the front but never on the front. He calls this surfing the peloton. His appearance at the front of the Ronde has little to do with any ambitious tactical plans and everything to do with saving energy by avoiding the chaos that ensues when the peloton is stretched over a narrow, cobbled road. The more energy he saves, the further into the race he can be useful, but he's fully expecting to blow up around 40 kilometres from the finish. Being at the front also gives him a clear view of the road ahead, which means he has the pick of the lines, the best of which is on the smooth pedestrian path to the right of the cobbles. McEwen, a former BMXer, bunny-hops over the gutter to the path, then back, when the way ahead is blocked by fans.

The effect of the two narrow cobbled sections is to draw the peloton out into a line two, at most three, riders wide. This is simple maths: on a wide road the bunch spreads out to six, eight or even ten riders wide, but there isn't space for that on the Paddestraat. In addition, the riders at the front are going faster, which thins the line out even more.

A peloton of 200 riders on a very wide road might measure ten riders wide by 20 riders long – so a rider at the back could make his way to the front quite easily. When the same bunch is two riders wide, it will be 100 riders long. A bike is about 175 centimetres in length, so add a ten-centimetre gap between each rider and it's now the best part of 200 metres from back to front. Needless to say, the riders at the back at a pinch point like the Paddestraat are in the race but they're not *in* the race.

At the end of the Lippenhovestraat, there's a 90-degree right turn, which slows the riders down and compresses the back end of the peloton into a barely moving traffic jam. Bernhard Eisel, who rides for HTC–Highroad, is the first round the bend. By the time the last rider, Rob Goris of Veranda's Willems – a former professional ice-hockey player who is riding with a broken hand sustained the week before in Ghent–Wevelgem and held together by six screws put in during an operation – gets round, 28 seconds have passed and there are attacks flying off the front of the peloton.

The circumstances and territory are perfect for attacking. The peloton is between two physical states, moving from strung out and fast back towards slower and bunched up, and there is a draggy curving rise which takes the riders towards the main road from Elene to Zottegem. While the momentum of the peloton slows and the climb slows the riders further, Rabobank's Maarten Tjallingii accelerates. Attacking on climbs is easy to get wrong – too early and the rider risks blowing up; too late and there isn't time to build an advantage. Tjallingii chooses a point close to the apex of the climb, which is where the bunch often decelerates slightly, to give himself a bigger differential in speed to the bunch and then to push home his advantage as the road flattens out.

He is followed by a Garmin rider, Matt Wilson. Then four more: Klaas Lodewyck of Lotto, Koen de Kort of Skil, Gert Steegmans of Quick Step and Mathieu Ladagnous of FDJ.

Then eight more. Then another quartet. As the bunch rounds the corner onto the Elenestraat, one more rider goes, and then a Sky rider, to make 20 in the break.

That's a lot of riders. Considering the effort the peloton goes to in order to ensure that no more than six or so riders get away at the start of the race, 20 is potentially dangerous even if there are still 138 kilometres to ride. It's not so much that they'll stay away but that they'll need to be chased down if they do make good their escape, and that will use up resources that teams would rather not spend at this point. Tjallingii hasn't just chosen a good spot to attack; he's also chosen a good stretch of road to hinder a chase – as the escape passes through Zottegem and Strijpen towards *helling* three, the Rekelberg, the roads narrow with roundabouts and road furniture, which bully the peloton into slowing down.

Tjallingii's move is planned. His Rabobank team have decided that since they don't have the strongest riders, they want to open up the race early and do something unexpected. But the ideal scenario is a group of six or seven, not 20.

The situation is: three Vacansoleils, two Lottos, two Garmins (including Farrar), two Leopards and 11 more in the break. One of the Leopard riders drifts back to the bunch, while the other 19 build a 30-second lead to and over the Rekelberg. Of the 25 teams in the race, 17 are represented in either the first break or the second. Of the eight outfits left behind, two are Spanish, two are much smaller teams and three have come to the race without particularly strong leaders. Only Saxo Bank has reason to chase, for Nuyens, and they don't really have the fire-power.

But it is Leopard, the team of defending champion Fabian Cancellara, who commit to the chase with three of their riders: Wouter Weylandt, Stuart O'Grady and Dominic Klemme. Three against 19 sounds like a one-sided battle, but it's not really three against 19. One of the 19 is a Leopard rider, so he won't work. The Quick Step, Garmin, Lotto and BMC riders all have important leaders back in the bunch, plus Farrar's not going to waste energy working this early, so their contribution is compromised. That already cuts the number of really motivated riders in the group down to 12, and a few others are starting to freewheel a little when it is their turn at the front. This often happens in larger escape groups where lots of teams are represented – riders start to sit in because it maximises their chances of winning, but the paradox is that if everybody thinks that way the group cannot succeed in staying away. A lot of riders working together is a force to be reckoned with. A lot of riders not working together is chaos. As Tjallingii will later reflect, the break has too many strong riders and they're thinking too much.

In this case, many of the riders who have joined the break are there in defensive roles for their team leaders – by going off the front they take the pressure off their team and force others to work. But virtually every big team has made it, which neutralises the advantage, and none of the teams quite have full confidence in the rider who *has* made it into the break except perhaps Garmin, with Farrar, but he's not going to be given the leeway to get much of a lead.

While Leopard chase, the 19-man group – initially so promising and co-operative – falls apart under the weight of its own contradictions. The whole episode has begun, taken place and finished in the space of 13 kilometres. The one difference now, apart from a few more tired legs, is that the lead of the front five, sitting at a healthy six and a half minutes when the skirmish started, has been reduced to three and a quarter.

CHAPTER 3

Kruisberg

The N8 – 145 kilometres of long straights, Flemish towns and villages and open landscapes – connects Brussels and Koksijde, on the coast, but it also provides a kind of backbone to the Ronde route. It runs east–west right over the *Vlaamse Ardennen*, linking Kortrijk, Oudenaarde, Brakel and Ninove, where the race finishes. (You'll get from Koksijde to Brussels much quicker if you take the autoroute but you'll see, and understand, the geography of the Flemish Ardennes much better if you take the extra 90 minutes – more if you get stuck behind a tractor – to go via the N8.) Much of it is *betonweg*, road constructed from sections of concrete with narrow gaps between them, which give car journeys a semiquaver percussive thud. The gaps range from a little less than the width of a cycling tyre to slightly more where the edges have eroded – no problem for the ones which run across from verge to centre, but the gap running in the direction of the road, right down the middle, can be hazardous. The *betonweg* are the furred-up arteries of rural Flanders – the single carriageways can be a slow way of getting around, and not all of them are in the best condition. Concrete surfaces are cheaper than tarmac, but they are prone to erosion because of the joins and gaps built in mainly to allow for the curing process of the concrete. The potholes caused by this erosion are easy to avoid for the riders at the front of a race, but further back in the peloton they cause crashes.

The Leopard-led bunch reaches the back of the Tjallingii group on the N8, just as the route leaves the main road for the smaller Stene road on the outskirts of the town of Horebeke. It's a typical Belgian junction: 90 degrees, narrow entrance, bumpy concrete with patches where repairs have been bodged, a drain cover right on the racing line, a narrow raised pavement on the inside and a poor surface. And just after the junction there's a patch of cobbles on one side of the road. If the contrast between old and new wasn't explicit enough, on one side of Stene there is a dairy farm and on the other is a bank. The local knowledge that is needed to win the Tour of Flanders goes far beyond knowing where the climbs come, and in what order, and it's one of the most important reasons that even the greatest Ronde champions rarely win at their first or second attempt. Corners like the one which takes the peloton on to Stene are a nightmare for the riders. Turning onto a narrower road means that effectively the racing line is single file, and everybody else has to slow down and bunch up, which means having to speed up again, with an energy cost. It's easy to know to be in front five kilometres before the Taaienberg, for example, but the local riders and those who have taken the trouble to get to know the route, beyond racing on it once a year, will also quietly drift forward in the bunch for points like the Stene corner.

Riders bunny-hop up onto the pavement to cut into Stene, or dive bomb into it, in an attempt to maintain speed but this time somebody misjudges their line, there's a small crash and Nuyens is behind it.

It takes the peloton a while to settle after Tjallingii and his 18 temporary companions are caught in Horebeke. There are aftershocks following the initial earthquake – André Greipel of Lotto, HTC's Bernhard Eisel and Vacansoleil rider Mirko Selvaggi, all in the 19-rider break, labour for a few hundred metres after the rest of their companions give up, hanging just off the front. Through the village of Schorisse, just south of Horebeke, Tjallingii gives it another half-hearted go. Then Veranda's Willems rider Bram Schmitz doesn't so much attack as carry on riding a little harder while the peloton reach an almost unanimous decision to ease off. But by the time they reach *helling* four, Kaperij, peace has broken out and a solid line of seven riders impose a blockade on the front of the peloton on the long – but by Flandrian standards steady – climb. As they follow the course of the Molenbeek ('beek' is the Flemish word for brook), the valley formed by the Maarkebeek, feeding into the Schelde river in Oudenaarde, lies behind them, a cultivated brown-green farmscape dotted with orange roofs.

The secret of comedy, and of escaping from the peloton, is timing, so Tjallingii probably thinks it's a bad joke when Andriy Grivko, a Ukrainian rider for Astana, attacks on another uphill drag and is completely ignored by the peloton. Tjallingii – a rider who rode this race 11 years in a row and never finished higher than 21st – attacked, was followed by 19 other riders and was chased down in an all-out effort by the team of the defending champion. Grivko, on the other hand, is left to do what he wants. 'Grivko is the kind of rider who attacks mysteriously with great fanfare and camera coverage,' somebody who worked for the Astana team once told me. 'And no lasting effect.'

Grivko has embarked on what is known in cycling as a '*chasse-patate*' attack – potato hunting. It describes the situation where somebody attacks from the peloton after the break has gone who a) has no chance of catching the break and b) has no chance of staying away from the peloton. Televised races tend to have three motorbike television cameras, and so with one allocated to the break, one to the front of the peloton and one to the back of the peloton, these attacks tend not even to get on television. A *chasse-patate* has little sporting or publicity value.

Three minutes ahead, the escapees continue to share the work. There's a neat historical and cultural resonance between the British pair in the break. Though Hunt now rides for Team Sky, both are remnants from the era before the explosion in interest (and therefore money) in British cycling. Their journey into the professional ranks involved a literal interpretation of the word – they physically upped and moved abroad: Hunt raced for a Spanish team and Hammond went to Belgium. Both were born in 1974 and both were prodigious in their teens – Hammond won the world junior cyclocross championships in 1992, while Hunt was the national junior road race champion the year before. In 1993 the pair shared the podium at the British amateur national criterium championships as first-year seniors (these days riders go from junior – under-18 – to under-23 and then to elite category, but back in the 1990s the transition from junior to senior happened at 19), with Hammond first and Hunt second. They were two riders barely out of the junior ranks, giving the seniors a beating. The pair raced in France together, driving out on Friday nights, racing Saturday and Sunday, and driving back again on Sunday night. They beat their own paths into the professional sport and their careers developed in parallel; the first time they ever raced together as pros, in the 1999 Ruta del Sol, there was one stage where the two Brits ran fourth and fifth. They came together for a season at the Belgian MrBookmaker.com team in 2004, diverged, then came together again for two seasons at the Cervèlo Test Team in 2009 and 2010.

Hammond rode for small Belgian teams for six years, where a series of top-ten finishes in Ghent–Wevelgem kept him in contracts, but then came third at Paris–Roubaix, which saw him sign for Lance Armstrong's Discovery Channel team, then T-Mobile. He's an unusual shape for a professional cyclist: stocky, heavy-set with a head that looks like it's carved out of granite. Even as a junior, grinning out from the pages of *Cycling Weekly* with his blond-tinted grammar-school quiff on the annual occasion of him winning the national junior cyclocross championships each of the three years he was eligible, he looked twice the width and age of the riders he beat, a man among boys.

Hunt may ride for Sky, but he's a bit of a free spirit compared with the regimented reputation of the team. His mother's heritage is Native American and he was born in central Canada but grew up in Totnes in Devon. Totnes is quite bohemian, though Hunt has a stony demeanour and an impression of detachment. The cycling journalist Lionel Birnie once told me a story of having a coffee with Hunt and a group of Australian team-mates and, even while the conversation went on around him and people were talking to him, Hunt just went to sleep. It was only when someone lifted Hunt's sunglasses off that they realised why he wasn't answering their questions. Hunt's back is a bit shot. When he rides, he actually looks like he's limping; every now and again, he'll sit at the back of the group, stand up, pull a foot out of a pedal and put it up on the saddle, then sit down, to stretch his quadriceps.

It looks like there's a truce in the race as they join the Chaussée de Ninove, the main road from Brakel to Ronse, which runs along a ridge on the southern edge of the Flemish Ardennes before descending towards the town. The lead five continue on their way; there are no more attacks from the peloton and no single team is taking responsibility for leading; Grivko is somewhere in between, and Nuyens, having filled the cleat on his shoe with mud in clambering around the crash on Stene, is off the back having it sorted out. Down the main road, he can't even see the back of the bunch. However, while the peloton looks smooth, there's a constant rotation of riders at the front, meaning there's a bit of a battle going on, and it's going very fast. Some very prominent names – Tom Boonen, Sky's Juan Antonio Flecha, Geraint Thomas and Rabobank's Sebastian Langeveld – are riding in the second row, very close to the front. The race is teetering towards a tipping point.

In Ronse: *helling* five, the Kruisberg. This is a kilometre long, first rising steadily up an urban street, then rearing up with a steep 500-metre section of cobbles, whose gradient is about 10 per cent and which takes the riders out of town and back up onto the ridge. Normally the race approaches the Kruisberg from the east and it's a dead turn into the climb, but for 2011 the parcours takes the race through Ronse, which means they have to ride up a steady rise for 500 metres before the Kruisberg even starts, though it gives them a quicker start to the climb than the usual turn. The bunch rides up fast, led by Quick Step's Andreas Stauff, and the reason for their indifference to Grivko's recent attack becomes clear as they sweep past him on the climb, ignoring him every bit as much as they did when he initially went away. The speed is high enough that riders are starting to get dropped, and another small crash forces the last 30 or so riders to slow, then accelerate again, as they are squeezed onto the cobbles by a narrowing of the road.

On the face of it, nothing is happening. The gap to the leaders when the bunch joined the main road above Kaperij had been three minutes 13 seconds. Yet, 12 kilometres later as Stauff tops the Kruisberg, it's dead on two minutes.

Ronse is a town that sits on borders and between cultures. The language border between Flemish-speaking Flanders and French-speaking Wallonia is just to the south, and perhaps it's apt that its British twin town is Sandwich. Ronse prides itself on being bilingual and welcoming to outsiders, although locals explained to me that it is a little more complicated than that. It's one of 27 municipalities in Belgium that are obliged to offer services in two languages; most of these are situated along the language border, though some are near Brussels, and some are in and around the German-speaking enclave of Eupen in the east.

Like many Belgian towns, Ronse has both a Flemish name and a French one (Renaix). Most towns are known predominantly by one or the other, but Ronse and Renaix are much more interchangeable. On a prosaic level, you could also say that Ronse – or more specifically the Kruisberg – marks the division in the Tour of Flanders between the warm-up and the main event. With 100 kilometres to go (as the climb was situated in 2011), the race proper begins here. The Rabobank rider Lars Boom said of 2011: 'You've got to be in front all the time from the Kruisberg on.'

Andreas Klier told me he didn't like the Kruisberg. 'It's a difficult and important climb. Once you are in there it's still asphalt, and you have the feeling that you have glue on your tyres – you feel like you're not really going forward,' he said. 'Once the pavé starts, the speed is already low, and to accelerate on pavé is very difficult. Riders put it in the big ring and accelerate and can make a huge gap to the guys who are already tired.'

But the Kruisberg also marks borders between tradition and progress, old and new, rich and poor and between town and countryside; even between cultures. The day I visited Ronse was cold and overcast, and I followed the route of the race from the centre of the town, where the tower of the Sint-Hermeskerk dominates the skyline, up Kruisstraat, whose signs were subtitled 'Rue de la Croix' (road of the cross) and past a small mosque to where the Kruisberg begins, off to the right.

One of the translations for 'Kruisberg' is 'Mount Calvary', but the Kruisberg's actual name is Oudestraat, or Vieille rue – the old street. The New Kruisberg continues up in a bland suburban drag to the top of the hill, en route to Oudenaarde. Just opposite the junction, on the end of a Kruisstraat terrace, there's a *trompe l'oeil* mural by the artist Jos Peeters of a bike race on a sunny street with riders cresting a hill and a pretty town in the background that is probably supposed to be Ronse but bears little resemblance to the real thing. The New Kruisberg is, of course, much newer than the Old Kruisberg. It was built in the 1950s to ease traffic on the narrow cobbled road, although these days traffic jams are common on the main road, and Eddy – a native of Antwerp who married a girl from Ronse and now runs the garage at the junction between the two – told me that well-informed locals use the old Kruisberg as a rat run to the top of the hill.

I walked up and down the Kruisberg a few times. The bottom half is a narrow canyon of small terraced houses, constructed in the main from dark red bricks offset by light-coloured mortar, with a few businesses in between the residential houses, including the Mister Drinks alcohol wholesaler, sitting back from the road, its driveway stacked high with empty crates and kegs. The road is built from concrete slabs and it has degraded in parts, while some of the houses are on the shabby side. Some were completely empty and looked derelict – number 30 had months or years of post stuffed into the mailbox, and somebody had blocked its windows with yellowing newspapers and empty cement bags. The door of number 24 was made of wood and looked rotten and brittle, with old cobwebs indicating that it had been a long time since anybody had opened it. I peered through the window and saw that plaster from the walls had begun to disintegrate, leaving thick piles of dust on the tiled floor.

But apart from these, the street looked quiet but lived-in. Many of the houses had ornate and large vases in the front windows.

I wanted to speak to the people who lived here, hoping that somebody would be able to communicate in English or French. I knocked on one door, and the young man who emerged, looking suspicious, told me in French that he didn't speak French, and that the man who lived five doors up could speak both English and French. When I knocked on that door, it turned out that the elderly man who emerged could do neither. But further up I spoke to the father of a young family called John. John explained that Ronse is one of the most multicultural towns in Belgium. 'It's not just French and Flemish here, but Turks, Poles, Moroccans and Romanians,' he said. I got the impression he neither liked nor disliked living on the Kruisberg; he told me it was nothing special. The cycling world might get very excited about roads like this, even fetishise them to an extent, but for the people who live on them on the other 364 days of the year they are ordinary, quiet thoroughfares where not much happens. (In fact, in the Kruisberg's case, it's 362 days – the E3 Harelbeke and Kuurne–Brussels–Kuurne races both regularly climb this hill.)

John also hinted that Ronse was not particularly prosperous – in fact many of the people I spoke to around the region of the Tour of Flanders pointed out that the *Vlaamse Ardennen* are relatively isolated, even though Belgium is densely populated. Of the 100 most populated countries in the world, it sits tenth in terms of population density, and second in Europe, behind the Netherlands. There is a triangle of autoroutes linking Lille, just over the border in France, Ghent and Brussels, but the Flemish Ardennes sit squarely in the middle, a picturesque region of sleepy villages, farms and crap transport links. Money tends to travel along railway lines and autoroutes, so the people who live in Ronse, for example, see less of it. This has an effect on places beyond bank balances – John complained that there's not much to do in Ronse. On the positive side, said John, the town has the cheapest housing in Flanders – what would cost 350,000 Euros in Ghent would go for 250,000 here.

Halfway up Oudestraat, the road steepened, and the cobbles began. The claustrophobic double wall of terraced houses opened out, to be replaced by trees and bushes forming a leafy tunnel describing a lazy S-bend up the hill. There was a noticeable change in the houses, too. They were detached and much bigger. One was a doctor's surgery; further up was a wellness centre called Sense of Vitality. Several of the houses had cobbled drives, and it was noticeable that the cobbles there were in a much better state than those on the road. On the drives were parked Mercedes, Audis and Skodas – many houses had two cars (further down the hill, the cars were a bit more functional – vans and small vehicles, and one had cardboard gaffer-taped in where the window was missing).

Dirk, who works in banking and moved to the town in 1989, lives in one of the houses on the top half of Oudestraat.

'Ronse is a frontier town,' he told me, though he emphasised that it was a Flemish town where the people could speak French, rather than a bilingual entity. He also described it as 'beige', meaning average, neither one extreme nor the other. Dirk told me that the town was multicultural but that life wasn't easy for most of the population. 'There are lots of unemployed people here. It used to be that Oudenaarde was a small town and we were big, but that is changing. Young people tend not to stay here. There are lots of foreigners, and hard kids.'

You get the impression that Ronse gazes north over the Flemish Ardennes to Oudenaarde with a mix of envy and inferiority. While Oudenaarde is building a thriving tourist industry, partly around cycling, Ronse is struggling to pull itself out of its post-industrial funk. When the contract Ninove had with the Tour of Flanders organisation to host the finish ended after the 2011 race, both towns bid to replace it, but Oudenaarde was chosen.

Ronse, and even the new Kruisberg, have a rich cycling history beyond the Tour of Flanders. The world road race championships took place here on two occasions, and each time there was controversy. In 1963 the hot favourite was Rik Van Looy, a very successful Flandrian rider with thighs like ham hocks who combined a huge ego with a thin skin. Approaching the finish, he asked his team-mate Benoni Beheyt – only 22 and in his second season as a professional – to work for him but Beheyt said he was suffering from cramps. Van Looy, panicking about trying to win a joint-record third World Championships, started his sprint very early, at 400 metres from the finish line. With 200 metres to go, he was in the lead, but there was a rider coming up fast on the other side of the road: Beheyt. Van Looy moved across in an attempt to block him; Beheyt reached out, and . . .

Did he grab him? Did he pull Van Looy back? Was Van Looy, in fact, the one at fault by trying to swerve across? Whichever it was, contact was made and Beheyt was the rider who crossed the line first, narrowly ahead of Van Looy. He was world champion at 22, managed one more decent season the following year, then an abrupt decline in results was followed by a slow-motion exit from the sport while Van Looy sniped from the sidelines. But the family line continued: Beheyt's grandson Guillaume Van Keirsbulck is a professional cyclist whose debut in the Tour of Flanders came in the 2011 race.

In 1988, the Worlds came back to Ronse. This time, a group of three approached the finish together: Claude Criquielion, a Walloon cyclist born just 18 kilometres away from Ronse in Lessines who'd won the Tour of Flanders the year before; Steve Bauer, an experienced Canadian who'd come fourth in the recent Tour de France; and Maurizio Fondriest, an almost-unknown Italian in his second year as a professional. The finishing straight was near the top of the new Kruisberg – the grainy YouTube footage of the race even shows the roadside mural, at the '425 metres to go' sign. Fondriest was expected to come third, and if Bauer and Criquielion had sprinted in a straight line he probably would have done. Bauer led the sprint out, switching from the left side of the road all the way to the right, because the wind was coming from the left, and he wanted to prevent anybody getting any shelter and coming round on his right. But then he moved left again, perhaps two and a half metres from the barriers. Criquielion saw the gap and accelerated into it, whereupon Bauer changed gear (in those days, gear changers were on the down tube of the frame so changing gear necessitated taking one hand off the bars) and swerved right again.

Inadvertently or not, in putting his elbow out he'd also made himself quite wide, and the two riders swung into each other. When contact was made, Bauer was hardly ahead at all, just centimetres, and so his elbow went into the crook of Criquielion's, knocking the latter's handlebars sideways. Criquielion glanced off Bauer then clipped one of the barrier's feet. The only way from there was down, and the booing started before he even hit the ground. Bauer – his momentum killed by the contact – freewheeled in while Fondriest sprinted past to win. I used to think the incident was six of one and half a dozen of the other, having only ever seen the head-on shots, but I recently came across some footage, shot from the motorbike to the side of the riders, which showed Criquielion's speed was hugely faster than Bauer's. The crash prevented the Belgian from winning, then Bauer got disqualified. Criquielion never got over it – he took an ultimately unsuccessful legal action against Bauer, while the Canadian needed a police guard at his house near Kortrijk until local heads cooled.

The Kruisberg has been a near-perennial inclusion in the Ronde. While one of the Kwaremonts (like the Kruisberg there are two – the new and old) has featured in every edition of the race except two since 1919, the Kruisberg was the third climb to be included on the parcours, making its first appearance in 1928. It has featured more than 40 times (with the New Kruisberg also figuring a handful of times).

Context is everything when you are talking about climbs in the Tour of Flanders, as in any race. Climbs are described as hard or easy, but really it depends on where they come in the race and how the riders race them. Take the Molenberg, for example. In 2007 it was the first climb of the race, 113 kilometres from the finish, and I watched from the roadside near the bottom as the riders more or less cruised up, without the slightest hint of aggression or an attack. Three years later, it was the tenth climb out of 15, and the winning break went two-thirds of the way up. Same climb, different points in the race, different effect on the outcome.

The geography of the Flemish Ardennes dictates which climbs are crucial. The Kruisberg, Oude Kwaremont, Paterberg and Knokteberg are all tucked down in the far south-western corner. During the years between 1973 and 2011, when the race finished in Meerbeke, these climbs all tended to feature early in the race and were treated more as part of the winnowing-out process than as true battlegrounds. Now that the race finishes in Oudenaarde, the Kruisberg–Oude Kwaremont–Paterberg trio have often figured as the last three climbs, and are critical. In the 2015 edition Alexander Kristoff's winning attack went over the top of the Kruisberg, but much further back the Kruisberg was also a key climb for one of the most notable historical winners. It was here that the second rider to win three Rondes laid the foundations for his first win.

The path between Italy and Belgium is a well-trodden one. Successive waves of emigrants and visitors have headed north from Italy for centuries – the Genoese sailed to Bruges in the late 13th century and Dante visited the city in the early 14th century. The Venetians, Florentines and Lucchese followed, and by the 15th century the Medici bank had opened a branch in Bruges. Giovanni Arnolfini, the subject of Jan Van Eyck's portrait, was sent to the city from Lucca. Hundreds of years later, Italians went to work in the coalmines of Wallonia. So when Fiorenzo Magni made the same journey in 1949, to compete in the Tour of Flanders and try to become the second non-Belgian to win the race, he was following a path beaten by many of his countrymen.

John Foot, in his history of Italian cycling, *Pedalare! Pedalare!*, describes Magni as the 'Third Man'. On a superficial level, this was a reference to his brilliant cycling career being eclipsed by the twin superstars of Italian cycling in the 1940s and 1950s, Fausto Coppi and Gino Bartali. It was easy to pick sides between Coppi and Bartali: traditionalist, rural and religious Italians supported Bartali, while modern-thinking, urban and secular Italians chose Coppi. The Italian fans were already split along religious and cultural lines as well as sporting ones by Coppi and Bartali, so Magni fell between the gaps. 'To date, only one book has been written about him, and even that is short and not very good,' wrote Foot, crushingly. Magni had neither the compelling character of Coppi or Bartali, nor was he as good at cycling as them. Coppi and Bartali were riders of class; Magni relied on grit, though when I emailed the Italy-based cycling writer Herbie Sykes for a character reference, he wrote back, 'I'd sum him up as the hardest, bravest, most relentless cyclist of his or any other age. He was simultaneously an absolute bastard, a visionary and a truly great rider.'

But there's more. Magni illustrated perfectly the complex cultural and political realities of European life in the late 1940s. Foot euphemistically and knowingly describes Magni as having fought in 1943 on 'the wrong side' in the civil war between the Italian Fascists and the Resistance; Magni himself said that he'd been conscripted and obeyed orders. Most damningly, eyewitnesses alleged that Magni had been involved in an armed clash between Fascist militia and partisans near Vaiano, an incident which has become known as the 'massacre of Valibona'. Magni, for his part, never denied nor apologised for his far-right views, but he claimed not to have been involved in the killings that took place. After the war, Magni was sent for trial, facing a sentence of 30 years in prison. Fellow professional Alfredo Martini provided witness testimony for the defence, but it was the faintest of praise: 'Magni is a cyclist who seemed to me to be a very good person up until 25 July 1943.' However, the prosecution was unable to prove that Magni had participated in the massacre and he was acquitted. Foot reports that in 2010, letters which showed that Magni was involved in helping the cause of the anti-Fascists surfaced, adding an extra layer of complication and ambiguity.

Either way, Magni's lack of popularity was partly due to the fact that many in Italy weren't ready to forgive those who'd been involved with the Fascists, and partly to the collective amnesia that others needed to move on. In any case, he wasn't Coppi or Bartali.

Magni did the sensible thing and moved north to Monza after hostilities ceased, which kept him away from a brief period of post-war bloodletting as old scores were settled; then he headed north again, setting his sights on the 1949 Tour of Flanders.

Historically the race had been dominated by Belgians at that point. A Swiss rider, Heiri Suter, had won in 1923 but apart from that there had been 31 Belgian – or more specifically, Flandrian – wins in the 32 editions thus far. As if to underline the home dominance, the reigning champion was Briek Schotte, the archetypal *Flandrien*.

Magni travelled to the race with one other Italian rider, Tino

Ausenda, and a journalist from *La Gazzetta dello Sport*. They took the sleeper train to Brussels, recruited the owner of their hotel in Ghent, César Debaets – a former racing cyclist who'd won Six Day races in the US – to their cause and set about ambushing the Flandrians. On the Kwaremont, Magni left most of the field behind, and his surge on the Kruisberg got rid of everybody except the Frenchman Louis Caput. Five kilometres from the finish a combine – a temporary alliance – of Flemish riders including Schotte caught Magni, but on the uphill cobbled finish in Wetteren Magni was the fastest sprinter.

The next year saw a toughening of the route – for the first time, five climbs were put on the parcours, including the first ever appearance of the Muur van Geraardsbergen – and the weather was apocalyptic, with snow, hail and strong winds. This time Magni beat runner-up Schotte by two and a quarter minutes and third-placed Caput by more than nine. In 1951 his win was even more impressive – five minutes 35 seconds ahead of the runner-up and over ten minutes clear of third. Magni arguably achieved more popularity in Belgium – a country one of whose founding principles is pragmatic realpolitik – than in Italy, where passion and partisanship abound. He was dubbed 'il leone delle Fiandre' – 'Lion of Flanders' – albeit by an Italian journalist, and his record of three consecutive victories has never been matched. 'You can win one race in Belgium by coincidence; the second is more sensational,' Magni once said. 'But a third win is practically impossible.'

CHAPTER 4

Knokteberg

The Kruisberg spits the riders back out onto the New Kruisberg at the top. It is three lanes plus a couple of bike lanes wide but the peloton, already drawn out to single file by the climb, is getting squeezed on both sides by a crowd of several hundred people in solid two- or three-deep rows. Large crowds in random, rural places are a peculiar quirk of the Ronde. In most other bike races the fans congregate on the climbs or in the towns, but the top of the Kruisberg is neither – we're off the climb and out of town, on an innocuous stretch of B-road.

As the front of the bunch pushes through, the crowd widens then comes back in again, the bulge following the main part of the peloton up the road. The riders turn left on to Zandstraat, which gently curves through a small wood and drags up around the Hotondberg, the highest point in the *Vlaamse Ardennen* on the Flemish side of the language border. If the riders turned right, to the north, they could descend the Hoogberg which, according to the official statistics, is the longest climb ever used in the Tour of Flanders at 2.98 kilometres. (What it has in length, it loses in gradient and surface – it's a hardly-there three per cent average, albeit with varying pitches, and a mix of *betonweg* and tarmac.) To the left: a sweeping view beyond the language border to Wallonia.

Marco Marcato of Vacansoleil accelerates on the drag through the forest. It's a good place to attack, a very similar spot to that on which Tjallingii went – a drag following a hard section. When there has been a climb – or in Tjallingii's case, a long section of cobbles – and the bunch has been stretched out, the internal gravitational force of the peloton tends to react afterwards by decelerating at the front and pulling the riders back together. So by hitting rivals hard when this process begins, a rider may achieve escape velocity.

Marcato is immediately tracked by many of the usual suspects: an opportunistic Skil rider, Koen de Kort (who'd also followed Tjallingii), and defensive-minded members of the bigger teams: Saxo Bank, Sky, Lotto, Leopard, Quick Step and BMC, who have no ambition except to crush the ambition of others. Then more opportunists: Astana, Lampre and Europcar. It doesn't look to have much momentum – Marcato eases off to let De Kort come through, but he doesn't look much interested and already the momentum starts to falter. Leopard have a man up there but they chase the group down anyway (when attacks go, it always seems to be the Leopard team doing the chasing) and the peloton is all together again, now one minute 40 seconds behind the leaders, and taking up the entire width of another three-lane road on the sweeping descent to Klijpe, a western suburb of Ronse. In fact the course has just covered three sides of a square – north from Ronse up the Kruisberg, west to skirt the summit of the Hotondberg, and south back down the hill. This episode in the race – from Marcato's attack to the peloton catching the 13-strong group he pulled away – lasted less than a minute. Other than to chip away another dozen seconds from the escapees' lead, its effect on the race is negligible, just one more abortive attack which half the bunch won't even have seen happen; most riders will just have inferred it from the 60 seconds or so of acceleration.

The odds on winning a bike race are long. The 2011 Ronde has 25 teams and 199 starters (Lampre, starting with seven riders, are a man short of the full complement of eight). Realistically, a handful of men have a chance to win it. In his autobiography *A Peiper's Tale,* former Australian rider Allan Peiper quoted Eddy Merckx on the Tour of Flanders: 'There are probably only ten guys at the start of this race who are thinking about winning, and all the others are just riding to get to the finish.'

A generous assessment for 2011 would be that around 12 riders have started with a decent chance of victory, which means that 187 riders haven't. Assuming these 12 riders are each sole team leaders, that's 12 riders plus their 84 team-mates who are in the race to try and win it. That leaves just over 100 riders at a loose end. Some will be trying to aim for the top ten, there is a perennial chase for WorldTour points available for those finishing down to seventh place, and some will be hoping to get into the early break. That leaves a lot of riders in the race who aren't doing anything other than making sure the peloton is quorate for the sign-on and surviving as best they can, or helping their team leader do the same.

There are four previous winners in the race, and between them they have won the previous six Rondes: Boonen (2005 and 2006), Alessandro Ballan (2007), Stijn Devolder (2008 and 2009) and Cancellara (2010). But they are not all the biggest favourites. Ballan, for example, was the strongest in the race in 2007, when he won, but there have been two complications since – a tailing-off of form in the last season or two, and a persistent miasma of doping scandal, which will eventually solidify into a two-year ban. Both times Devolder won he was riding for Boonen's Quick Step team, and as he rode off the front Boonen's rivals sat tight and watched him while Boonen sat equally tight and watched, more grimly the second year than the first. Now Devolder is riding for a different team, Vacansoleil, it's unlikely Quick Step will allow him the leeway to attack as he did when he won the race.

On the other hand, Cancellara is the outstanding favourite. He won the 2010 Ronde. He also won E3 Prijs, held eight days before the 2011 event. In the E3, he suffered a puncture, got back on to the peloton, dropped the peloton on the Oude Kwaremont and caught the escape group, then rode straight through them, attacking so hard that a Dutch rider who tried to follow him, Bram Tankink, visibly cramped up – not just a leg cramp, a debilitating whole-body cramp which caused him to seize up and stop pedalling completely. By the finish line, 16 kilometres later, Cancellara was a minute ahead. There's a good argument that the Swiss is the best cyclist in the world, though this pub debate is no less winnable than trying to decide on the world's best track and field athlete. Or even just the world's best runner.

Boonen is the second-favourite this year. His two previous wins came from being the best in the field and in 2010 he was second behind Cancellara, so he has the track record. However, confidence is another question – the Swiss rider had crushed him the year before. And then there is a gaggle of ambitious third-tier favourites which includes Ballan, plus Philippe Gilbert, Juan Antonio Flecha, Hushovd, perhaps Nuyens. And behind this group, another ten or so riders who could realistically hope to crack the top five and therefore – why not? – win.

The teams can be divided into seven loosely separated categories in order of their likely impact on the race:

1. Strong teams with one big leader
2. Strong teams with multiple leaders
3. Good teams with good leaders
4. Weak teams with good leaders

5. Strong teams with no big leader
6. Good teams with no big leader
7. Weak teams with no big leader

Category one consists of Leopard–Trek with Cancellara and Lotto with Philippe Gilbert. Quick Step falls between category one and two – Tom Boonen is the leader but they also have Frenchman Sylvain Chavanel, a multiple Tour de France stage winner, former Dwars door Vlaanderen champion and achiever of top tens in Paris–Roubaix and E3 Prijs. (Quick Step have had a tendency over the years to demonstrate that having the strongest eight riders on paper doesn't necessarily equate to being the strongest team, and their defeats are dissected forensically in the Flemish press in the days afterwards.)

The other teams in category two are Garmin, with Hushovd, Haussler and Farrar, and BMC, with Ballan and Hincapie, five times in the top ten. Sky have Juan Antonio Flecha but also Norwegian Edvald Boasson Hagen, a former winner of Ghent–Wevelgem, and Geraint Thomas, fresh from his second place at Dwars door Vlaanderen.

Saxo Bank, with Nuyens, and Rabobank, with Dutchman Sebastian Langeveld, are in the next category and paradoxically they have no less a chance in the race than the teams who are supposedly stronger on paper. Saxo Bank, especially, have gone into the race with a single leader – seven riders are devoted to the cause of giving Nuyens a chance to win – so even if they are not as strong as some of the bigger teams, their aims are not diluted. Garmin, with their three leaders, only have five more riders on the team to do the unseen, tiring work of fetching bottles and looking after the main riders (four, actually – Hammond is up the road in the break). Rabobank have hedged their bets a little more – their rider Lars Boom is also protected for the Ronde.

Category four includes Vacansoleil and the Russian-owned Katusha team. Vacansoleil have their two-time winner Stijn Devolder and a very strong specialist in the cobbled Classics, Björn Leukemans, but they are a ragtag collection of second-string sprinters and half-decent one-day cloggers. Katusha are led by Leif Hoste, a lugubrious Flamand who has the unfortunate distinction of sharing the record for the most second places in the Ronde without winning, which stands at three. The last time was 2007, and you don't have to know much about cycling to know that he's not going to match that this year. Hoste used to be a rider who popped up, rode well in the Classics, then disappeared for the rest of the season. Now he's more or less invisible all year long.

Three teams, HTC, Liquigas–Cannondale and RadioShack, occupy category five. They are strong outfits but the teams look thrown together, as if the Tour of Flanders is not a priority. HTC, for example, have been the most successful team in cycling over the last few seasons but, apart from Bernhard Eisel, none of the HTC riders has ever finished in the top 60 of the Ronde, and Eisel has never been in the top ten. At Liquigas, only one rider has ever finished in the top 70.

The biggest number of teams falls into category six: Ag2r La Mondiale, FDJ, Cofidis and Europcar from France, plus Astana, and the three Belgian ProContinental teams – Veranda's Willems, Topsport Vlaanderen–Mercator and Landbouwkrediet – who may not have strength in depth but are specialists in their home races. And the weakest teams, in category seven, are Movistar and Euskaltel–Euskadi from Spain, along with Lampre and Skil. The first three are WorldTour teams and therefore obliged to be here but it's fair to say a few of their riders would rather be anywhere else.

From Klijpe, the race turns west towards the village of Russeignies and skirts the southern edge of the *Vlaamse*

Ardennen, with the peloton very fast and cohesive but restive. The road here is given extra width by bike lanes separated from the road by a narrow band of cobbles. Riders move up fast on the bike lanes then, when they are level with the arrowhead at the front of the peloton, they bunny-hop over the cobbles to position themselves exactly where they need to be – at the front; but others have the same idea, and each new set of riders at the front is swamped and pushed backwards into the bunch. It's difficult for a rider to stay ahead of this constant roiling rotation. In theory, it's easy: just stay ahead of it by pedalling harder, but that is physically expensive. Even the domestiques whose job it is to ride at or near the front of the peloton through the first two-thirds of the race can't do this for long.

The escapees, followed 85 seconds later by the bunch, sweep into Russeignies. Opposite the red-brick church that dominates the village, they turn right then bear right again on to a narrow strip of *betonweg,* facing right up against one of the most southwesterly outcrops of the Flemish Ardennes, the Mont-de-l'Enclus. This road is part village, part farmland – as the houses peter out, the countryside opens out into large fields with old baths downcycled into drinking troughs sitting lopsided near the gates. The road narrows again at a junction a few hundred metres later. At the side of the road a warning sign imposes a ten-tonne limit on traffic, with a further piece of advice: local traffic only. This is the Knokteberg, or Côte de Trieu: *helling* number six.

The Knokteberg is one of the few climbs in the Tour of Flanders that also goes by its French name. The 3.5 kilometres of the 2011 Ronde, from just east of Russeignies to the top of the climb, are in Wallonia, in the province of Hainaut. The race also crossed the border once previously, just after Kaperij. Another 3.5 kilometres of the main road between there and Ronse are also over the language and administrative border, although if you look closely enough at the map the border runs right along the north side of the road, so it's not immediately obvious the riders are in a different part of Belgium.

The anticipation of the Knokteberg, as with the Kruisberg, is far worse than the reality. The peloton have spent several kilometres at high speed; suddenly a three-team blockade – Europcar, Lotto, Garmin – is forming at the front of the peloton and the pace slows. This is not uncommon on the Knokteberg – in 2010 Cancellara's Saxo Bank team had all eight riders in an unbroken line across the front. Tom Veelers, a Dutch rider from Skil, attacks and is let go. One kilometre or so later, as the road starts to rise between low banks and open fields, the Australian rider Simon Clarke from Astana attacks. The peloton – or rather the five riders spread across the front of it – couldn't look any less concerned as the climb rears up for a final steep curving ramp through a forest, where rain has washed a more or less permanent ridge of mud down the centre of the road. The gap from the Hammond–Hunt group goes back out to two minutes.

There's a junction at the top of the Knokteberg. The shortest and also most logical way for the route to continue, on towards the Oude Kwaremont, would be to go straight. Instead, the race tends to take a right turn here and then a left. The Ronde is full of diversions like this – it would have been quicker for the 2011 race to go straight through Ronse to Klijpe just a few kilometres before the Knokteberg, for example, but that would have meant missing out the Kruisberg. There's another reason for this diversion. The second turn after the Knokteberg takes the route on to Ronde van Vlaanderenstraat. It's apt that there should be a road named after the Tour of Flanders – what better shrine to the race than a stretch of anonymous *betonweg* curving between two of its climbs? It's more than a road, however, as

Ronde van Vlaanderenstraat is also the location for a monument to the race's founder, Karel Van Wijnendaele.

I doubt the riders even know it's here. I drove past it before realising that I must have missed it, and had to double back before I saw that what looked like a short driveway next to a small house was actually the memorial.

It's a nice spot: a small square of crazy paving with leylandii hedges lining two sides, partly sheltered by a wind-blown old blue spruce. There is a bench for cycling fans to sit and contemplate the 100-plus years of the race's existence, and a breeze-block wall with a shelf for a bust – once copper-coated but now oxidised into a dull green and black – of Van Wijnendaele wearing a suit and tie. Van Wijnendaele's name and years of birth and death, 1882-1961, are mounted in similarly green-tinted letters to the left of the bust. It was put up in 1964.

When I knocked on the door of the house next to the memorial, an elderly lady called Georgette answered.

'He's a good neighbour,' she joked of Van Wijnendaele's bust. Then she said something very surprising: 'I knew him quite well.'

Georgette used to run a café just down the road back towards the Knokteberg, called Le Marticot. When she was young, her parents ran another café, called 'A la Station', and she can remember Van Wijnendaele coming in often for a drink, especially when he was fixing the route for the following year's race. 'He was very famous in Flanders,' she said. 'Very friendly, a big, strong man.'

Karel Van Wijnendaele was a journalist, compulsive pseudonymist and polymathic dilettante who escaped the obscurity into which he was born and rode the breaking waves of both the Flemish independence movement that gathered pace at the turn of the 20th century and the burgeoning popularity of bike racing at the same time. He sensed the potential in both movements and saw how the strength of both could be harnessed in a bike race: the Tour of Flanders.

He was born Carolus Ludovicius Steyaert in 1882, in Torhout, south-west of Bruges, the fifth son of a flax worker and café-owner who died when Carolus was only 18 months old. His mother remarried, to a farmer, and the family moved to the countryside just north of Torhout, to Wijnendale, which he later took as his name. He made enough of a good impression at school to be allowed to gain special dispensation to stay on until he was 14, which wasn't the norm in those days. He said that school awakened in him the desire to learn more, and he was most taken by his studies of literature, carrying on reading and studying after he left school. At 14, he was sent to work as a cowherd but he hated it and his mother encouraged him to go to Ostend to find work. He worked there in a pharmacy as a delivery boy, earning five francs a month plus his room and board. That lasted seven months, before he returned home and discovered that his parents, with more children to support (in total he had 14 brothers and sisters), could not put him up and so he returned to Ostend. He worked in more shops, then in a theatre, selling programmes.

During this period, he went to a velodrome for the first time, to see an event in which the famous American track rider Major Taylor was competing. This also coincided with a general awakening resentment of the discrimination that existed in Flanders through the 19th century and beyond against the Flemish language and culture by francophone interests.

Steyaert moved to Brussels in 1899 and read Hendrik Conscience's *De Leeuw van Vlaanderen* (The Lion of Flanders), an 1838 novel that galvanised the nascent Flemish independence movement and was a seminal moment in the self-esteem of the Flemish people, and perception of literature written in Flemish. (It wasn't, however, very good. The writer and critic Luc Sante described it as a 'semihistorical contrivance executed in the broad strokes of Sir Walter Scott'. He went on to say, 'despite its conspicuous lack of literary merit it established Flemish literature.') Although there was a healthy and thriving Dutch literature scene in the Netherlands that went back many hundreds of years, there was significant prejudice against the language in Belgium (Flemish is essentially a dialect of Dutch, with enough overlap that they are extremely similar to each other). The Belgian constitution, drawn up when the country was founded in 1830, guaranteed 'freedom of languages', but the reality was that the legal system, education system and public institutions were effectively run in French, marginalising Flemish speakers. It wasn't until the Coremans–De Vriendt law of 1898, also known as the Law of Equality, that Flemish was officially given equal treatment. Writing *De Leeuw van Vlaanderen* in Flemish was a scandalous decision by Conscience – his father threw him out of the house because of it. The language in which the novel was written wasn't the only provocative thing about it – the story was about the battle of the Golden Spurs, a 14th-century fight between France and Flanders near Kortrijk in which the French were routed and which has been a common trope in Flemish nationalist sentiment ever since.

Steyaert's next job was as a notary's clerk back in Torhout. He hated it. He tried writing for the theatre and acting, mainly in comic roles, but he still hadn't found his calling. In 1902 he competed in his first bike race and decided right then that he would give up being a notary's clerk and be a racing cyclist. That lasted three years, and in 1905 he made another career choice: 'I tried to do with the pen what I could not do with the pedals,' he later said. He started writing for a magazine called *De Torhoutenaere* under the pseudonym 'Thourout-Sport'. He also occasionally dabbled in racing, using the pseudonym 'Mac Bolle', primarily to avoid trouble with his wife, who had banned him from wasting his time competing on the bike. He was also heavily involved in the construction of a velodrome in Torhout, and took teams of Flemish riders he called the 'Flandriens' to the United States to race on the track there.

The victory of Flemish rider Cyrille Van Hauwaert in the 1908 edition of Paris–Roubaix, then probably the biggest one-day race in the world, was a seminal moment for Steyaert. He described Van Hauwaert, the first Belgian to win Paris–Roubaix, as a 'Leeuw van Vlaanderen'. The rider had been part of an early wave of enthusiastic Flemish cycling fans, become a racer and gone on to win both Milan–San Remo and Roubaix, and he was an early muse for Van Wijnendaele. There had been a flowering of cycling races and fandom in Belgium in the 1890s as Liège–Bastogne–Liège was first run in 1892, and Paris–Brussels the following year. This early interest had waned but Van Hauwaert's success in 1907, when he won Bordeaux–Paris, and 1908 saw Belgium – or rather Flanders – quickly become the third power in world cycling after France and Italy. In 1912 a Belgian rider, Odile Defraye, won the Tour de France.

Van Hauwaert's victory coincided with Steyaert doing more and more writing under the newly adopted pseudonym of Karel Van Wijnendaele for *Sportblad, Sportman* and *Onze Kampioenen* (Our Champions) and most importantly for *Sportvriend*, a publication set up in 1909 and based in Izegem, a town between Roeselare and Kortrijk. *Sportvriend* started with a circulation of 15,000 and was distributed across East and West Flanders, along with Brussels and Antwerp. Van Wijnendaele wrote in a heroic, florid style, which went down very well with his readers.

Also in 1912, a publishing company called Patria saw a gap in the market for a sports newspaper catering for the Flemish language. Most of the papers had hitherto done a bit of pre-race coverage and results but almost no reporting on events, but Van Wijnendaele had started to exploit this. The new title would be called *Sportwereld* (Sport World), and their starting point was to poach a considerable number of writers from *Sportvriend* including Van Wijnendaele. The first edition appeared in September 1912.

The story goes that Van Wijnendaele – inspired by the success of the Tour de France in promoting the organising French newspaper *L'Auto*, and the Giro d'Italia in promoting *La Gazzetta dello Sport* – wanted *Sportwereld* to benefit from a similar event in Belgium. It's true that Van Wijnendaele's passion, personality and writing skills were a huge part of the organisation of the early editions of the race. However, more recent research suggests that, while Van Wijnendaele was an effective propagandist for the event, the organisational nuts and bolts were at least shared if not wholly taken care of by another *Sportvriend* alumnus, Léon Van den Haute. It was the latter who scouted out the route of the first Tour of Flanders, organised the finances and placated the restive burghers of some of the towns en route who didn't want the disruption.

The first edition of the race, in May 1913, was huge in its ambition and its distance. The 324-kilometre parcours was the longest ever, and the intention was to pass through as many of the big towns of West and East Flanders as possible in a statement of unity and regional pride. It was to start in Ghent, then pass through Sint-Niklaas, Aalst, Zottegem, Oudenaarde, Kortrijk, Ypres, Ostend, Roeselare and Bruges, before going back to Ghent. The race skirted the *Vlaamse Ardennen* but didn't use any of the climbs. What also wasn't epic was the startlist: 37 Belgians. The French stars of the sport had better things to do than show up for an obscure race in Belgium. Worse, the big Belgian riders who rode for French teams were absent too.

Van Wijnendaele summoned the riders to the start and said, '*Heeren, vertrekt*' ('Gentlemen, be on your way'). Twelve hours later the winner, Paul Deman, crossed the line to take the

500-franc first prize ahead of the other 15 finishers. The following year was better: a shorter race, ten more starters, three more finishers and, most importantly, a more prestigious winner in Marcel Buysse, who'd come third in the previous year's Tour de France and rode for the French Alcyon–Soly team. Alcyon didn't approve, but Buysse rode anyway, correctly figuring that Alcyon needed him more than he needed Alcyon. The Belgian's family was cycling royalty – his brother Lucien would go on to win the Tour de France.

The First World War prevented any more Rondes until 1919, but the most important thing was that it was up and running.

The journalist Guy Van Den Langenbergh, in his book *100 Keer Vlaanderen* (100 Flandrian Occasions) co-written with Nick Nuyens, described Van Wijnendáele as 'the archetypal hardworking West Flandrian'. Van Wijnendaele was one of the early architects of the Flemish ideal of the stoic, hardworking *Flandrien*, and between his race, his promotion of the Flemish language and the awakening of regional pride inspired by the race and the Flemish riders who did well in it, he had a profound effect on the region.

Van Wijnendaele's monument sits just on the Flemish side of the language border, albeit facing north-east towards the *Vlaamse Ardennen* and beyond to Oudenaarde and Ghent. After I'd visited the monument, I read Les Woodland's history of the Tour of Flanders, in which he describes how the monument came to be put up. After Van Wijnendaele died, his son Willem, who also wrote about cycling, met with Baron Behaeghel, a landowner. They drank a beer together at a local café and signed an agreement written on a beer mat that the memorial would be built on the southern approach to the Kwaremont. The name of the café was Chez Georgette.

CHAPTER 5

Oude Kwaremont

Sometimes, at the junctions where minor roads meet bigger roads in Belgium, the tarmac on the surface of the road gets gradually chipped away by the erosive action of car tyres, grit and water, revealing the original cobbles beneath. The new roads are not always exactly laid over the cobbles and, where the tarmac has not been laid, there is a lining of cobbles between the road and the verge. You know that old Flanders lies not very deep under the surface of new Flanders; if you know where to look, old Flanders is visible where the modern world has worn away.

Few editions of the Ronde are the same as each other. The organisers tweak the route every year – one year they'll approach the Molenberg from the north, the next from the south; another year they'll put in the Kruisberg and then turn towards the Hotondberg but, instead of turning left and descending to Klijpe and Russeignies, they'll go straight on and go to the Oude Kwaremont. The Tour of Flanders is a palimpsest: each new race is overlaid on the geography and history of the previous editions. And the history often shows through. Fabian Cancellara might be a modern Swiss but his long-range attacks in the race have something in common with Eddy Merckx's wins or, further back, with the exploits and tenacity of the original *Flandriens*. Tom Boonen, the modern hero of Flemish cycling, was compared physically and in his riding style to Rik Van Steenbergen, the double winner of the race in the 1940s. Sometimes the link between past and present is literal and explicit – 1988 winner Eddy Planckaert is the brother of 1976 winner Walter Planckaert, for instance. Just as Guy Fransen, the sports editor of *Het Nieuwsblad* can work in a modern, dynamic, multimedia journalistic environment and still, over a coffee and apple tart in a Flemish café, explain to me that the national psyche has always been and still is based on the characteristics of taciturn stoicism, uncomplaining hard work and a zen-like acceptance of shitty weather, we can look from the modern Tour of Flanders to the old Tour of Flanders and see that they are different yet the same.

Sometimes old and new Flanders sit literally side by side. The Kwaremont has been almost ever-present in the Ronde since the third edition in 1919. It was skipped only in 1955 and 1966. The climb's history is somewhat convoluted but the race used to head up the cobbled main road between Kluisbergen and Ronse. Barry Hoban, who took part in the race in the 1960s and 1970s, told me that the main road used to be a very hard part of the race. 'Out of Berchem, at the bottom, you went over a railway crossing and you had cobbles with a cinder cycle path all the way up. When they resurfaced it, they cut off the top of the hill by redirecting the road, but in our day it then went right on to Ronde van Vlaanderenstraat, over the top and then it was cobbled all the way down into Ronse – seven or eight kilometres of cobbles. Then we went straight up the Kruisberg,' he said.

When the main road was tarmacked and lost its sting, an alternative parallel route was found that passed through the centre of Kwaremont village, halfway up the gently sloping north-east side of the Mont-de-l'Enclus. The 'new' climb – formed from the Broektestraat at the bottom and the Schilderstraat above the village – became known as the Oude Kwaremont (the 'Old' Kwaremont) and has been a permanent fixture in the race since 1974. These days the race descends the long, wide sweeping schuss of the main road – now known as the Nieuwe Kwaremont – either from the Kruisberg or Knokteberg, then takes two right turns at the bottom to come straight back up through the village. At the top, two and a half kilometres later, the race rejoins the main road it just descended and heads back in the direction of Ronse, before peeling off to tackle the Paterberg. The old and new Kwaremonts sit parallel to each other and almost touching in places, one providing a conduit for goods, people and services between Ronse and Kluisbergen, the other providing a conduit for the world's longest continuously running Classic bike race, and both serving as a reminder of the Ronde's past and present.

The Oude Kwaremont's phenotype is slightly different from most of the cobbled bergs of the Tour of Flanders. There is one banked section of steep cobbles, about a quarter of the way up, but in general it's a draggy, open climb. It starts in open fields – it's very narrow, just wide enough for one car or four bike riders; there's an abrupt 90-degree right-hand bend, then a more gradual left, and the road starts to climb. A few hundred metres in, the cobbles begin and it steepens some more. The cobbles are quite deformed so this is the hardest part of the climb, as well as the steepest section, and there is one good line on the ridge in the middle. The wheels of heavy vehicles have driven the cobbles on each side down into the ground over the years and left them higgledy-piggledy with unpredictable gaps and protruberances, so the middle is higher than the left and right sides. Fine when the peloton is single file, but riders who want to pass have to go the long way round on a rougher, energy-sapping line.

The gradient gets shallower into Kwaremont village, then above the houses the road is very open to the fields on either side, before the final drag up to the main road. There are flat sections, which reduce the average gradient to an unintimidating three per cent, but there's nothing easy about the Oude Kwaremont. There's a huge fight to get to the bottom in front, which generally kicks off somewhere around Ronde van Vlaanderenstraat and carries on in the manner of a saloon-bar scrap in a Western down the Nieuwe Kwaremont, around the two corners on the outskirts of Kluisbergen and right to the bottom of the climb. As often happens in Flanders, once on the climb the riders at the front have a tendency to sit up, which blocks the road and allows them to choose when they subsequently start to ride hard and stretch the bunch out to breaking point. What might have been a fast-moving but cohesive peloton at the bottom often ends up being several disparate groups by the top, and even then the ordeal isn't over.

It generally takes the peloton around five minutes to climb the Kwaremont (the online Strava record is currently four minutes 27 seconds, by Dutch professional rider Niki Terpstra in the 2016 E3 Harelbeke), and that length is the reason it does such damage to the riders. By comparison, the Paterberg takes the riders around a minute and a quarter; the Koppenberg is two minutes, bottom to top. The Kwaremont suits the more powerful engines – the biggest favour the Tour of Flanders ever did Fabian Cancellara was to alter the course to make the Kwaremont–Paterberg combination the crux. The modern Ronde makes three ascents of the Kwaremont, with the last coming in the final 20 kilometres, and the Swiss rider is so perfectly suited to this climb that he could just wait until the race got there, then use it to drop almost everybody.

A lot of riders told me the Oude Kwaremont was their favourite climb. Nuyens, Devolder, three-time winner Johan Museeuw and Klier all told me they had a soft spot for it: Nuyens said of it in *100 Keer Vlaanderen* that it was 'love at first sight'.

'It's a beautiful climb,' Klier told me. 'We did it up, down, left and right, again and again through my whole career. There are several stages to it – you have the slow run-in, then you hit the pavé and basically 30 metres later it's the steepest part, towards the village.

'You could bridge to another group on the climb because it takes a long time to ride the whole climb from bottom to top. You have to see it like maths – if it takes long, you can gain more on the others. But you can also lose more.'

The top part of the climb, according to Klier, has lost a bit of its impact. It used to be that the scything wind – with nothing between the plains of Flanders and the exposed upper reaches of the Oude Kwaremont – could crowbar groups apart, but that was before the organisation placed a temporary village of marquees, tents and VIP enclosures in the fields either side.

'The tents take the wind. When I was racing, back in '03 or '04, 80 per cent of the year you had a west wind there, so it was coming from the right side. If you look at the old videos, you see everybody on the flat section riding on the left side of the road or even in the grass so nobody could sit in behind them. That's gone now, because of the tents, and it has changed the climb.'

But like every one of the Ronde's *hellingen*, Kwaremont has a life beyond the race. The marketing may be compelling to cyclo-tourists and fans, but I wanted to explore the distance between what we see on the television and the reality. I'd suspected things were getting out of hand when I read that Kwaremont beer, a popular but recent invention (it was first brewed in 2010) wasn't made in the village but in Bavikhove, a small town halfway between Kortrijk and Waregem, half an hour away by car. And when I'd met Rik Vanwalleghem at the Centrum Ronde van Vlaanderen, he'd pointed out the drawback for the locals of having such an illustrious and popular climb passing through their village. 'You know, there are something like 65 races a year over the Kwaremont,' he said. 'The people who live there are sick of it because every weekend from March to October, not only professional but amateur races go up it.' In De Zon is a small café on the well-maintained and neat central square in Kwaremont. The day I went was a mid-week mid-afternoon in December, but it was quite full – from my seat at the bar I could see at least 15 people. It was warm and smelled of spiced wine. The walls were covered in reminders of the village's heritage – old black-and-white framed photographs of cyclists retouched in colour and an aerial photograph of Kwaremont, along with adverts for Stella, Kriek, Carolus, La Trappe and various other beers, plus a certificate from *Het Nieuwsblad*: 'Het beste café van Vlaanderen'. On tap: Brugse Zot, Ename, Kwaremont and Stella Artois. Mindful of the fact that Kwaremont is not authentically from Kwaremont, and that Stella Artois is psychosomatic lemonade, I opted for the Brugse Zot, ignoring the chalked sign reading 'suggestie bier: Hoegaarden Grand Cru'.

There may be dark rumours of the locals not appreciating bike racing slowly taking over their town, but that doesn't include the barman, whose name is Frank. His estimate is that two or three thousand people pack themselves into the village on the day of the Ronde. They don't even bother to open up the café on race day – it's too small. Instead they set up a longer, more accessible bar outside and sell more beer on that one day than they do for the rest of the month; I suspect maybe not even far off their volume for the rest of the year. As Frank said, 'It's good for me, and for everyone who has a bar or café.'

Frank has been in Kwaremont for four years, which means he

took over the bar just before the route of the Ronde changed and became centred on the climb. He's from down the hill in Berchem, which is the main part of Kluisbergen. He ran a bar there, then worked as an insurance broker, before returning to pub life in Kwaremont. 'I prefer it now,' he said. 'It's a happier life.'

But he's noticed changes in Kwaremont. For many years from the 1950s, Kwaremont was an artists' colony: nothing particularly avant-garde, but many landscape painters were drawn by the elevation and the views across the rolling hills on all sides. In style they tended towards luminous washes of open landscapes, big skies and trees providing vertical structure. Yuppies followed the path beaten by the artists, and then house prices went up along with the average age of the locals. 'There used to be lots of studios, with mostly landscape painters and abstract artists along with a couple of glass makers,' said Frank. 'But they are not being replaced.'

The reason for Garmin and Lotto's blockade of the peloton on the Knokteberg, save for the egress of Veelers and Clarke, becomes clear at the top of the climb. Both teams immediately ride hard, and for Garmin it is a pre-planned move – they're not trying to win the race here, but they hope the combination of strong riders and the element of surprise will put them right at the front of the race for the Oude Kwaremont, therefore at the front for the Paterberg, since the two climbs are so close together. Klier gives British rider Daniel Lloyd a signal at the top, and Lloyd surges before he takes the right-hand bend at the top too fast, or at the wrong angle or over a patch of dust or gravel, and crashes, his front wheel disappearing from beneath him. 'One second, I was imagining the commentators singing my praises, the next, I could only imagine the number of people in hysterics in front of their TV screens,' he would later say.

Lotto and the rest of the Garmin team press on without Lloyd, lining the peloton out again on Ronde van Vlaanderenstraat and on to the N36: the Nieuwe Kwarement. They hit the road on its left – in ten minutes' time they'll be exactly at this same spot but heading in the opposite direction on the right-hand side of the road, as the junctions of the Oude Kwaremont and Ronde van Vlaanderenstraat are directly opposite each other.

The descent is lined on both sides by the parked cars of spectators, some of whom will drive as fast as they can from here to another spot (there's an unofficial competition about who can see the race at the most different places; a colleague once managed seven, though it would be possible to see many more). This practice is frowned upon by the police and one of the reasons given for moving to a circuit from 2012 was to consolidate the spectators into more manageable locations. The descent is taken fast, with the peloton consisting of a small ball of riders at the front, then a single long line with small fissures appearing under the pressure being applied by the leaders. If the riders looked right across the field, they'd see the Oude Kwaremont coming back up the hill in the opposite direction.

Other teams join in at the front. They're going at around 80 kph; the road surface is good on the main road, even though it's not that steep a descent. Wouter Weylandt and Stuart O'Grady for Leopard, Bernhard Eisel for HTC, Klier for Garmin and Jonas Jørgensen for Saxo Bank all swap turns, with Cancellara, Boonen, Flecha, Ballan et al tucked in behind. But not Devolder or Nuyens. Nuyens, back on after his hold-ups before Ronse, got delayed again over the Knokteberg – not significantly but just enough to have to pull his foot out of the pedals, stop and get going again.

Nuyens is on Devolder's wheel as they ride down, but Nuyens thinks it's strange – Devolder, who is wearing the red, yellow and black colours of the Belgian road-racing champion's jersey, seems to be struggling to hold the wheel in front, which means he's probably not on top form. Still a rider to watch, but he's not as strong as in other years. Devolder's not the kind of rider who'll wait for a team-mate to pace him back on, however. When the peloton briefly splits into at least three parts on the descent, it's Devolder who leads the second group back up to the first.

The first right turn, in Berchem, is 90 degrees and treacherous. There's a drain cover on the main road, just at the point riders will be starting to lean in to the bend, and though riders try to cut it on the inside, a traffic sign sits on the corner of the pavement, right on the perfect line for this. Robbie McEwen gets round cleanly; not many other riders do, and – through sheer momentum and technique – the Australian takes a 15-metre lead on to Parklaan, the side road which eventually leads to the bottom of the Oude Kwaremont. He seems bemused at the sluggishness with which the others have cornered and slows down, and the peloton, led by Quick Step's Gert Steegmans, envelopes him; he tucks in behind Steegmans, and for a brief moment there is a flashback to the 2006 Tour de France, when Steegmans had been hired by McEwen's Davitamon–Lotto team as his final lead-out man in the Tour de France sprints.

There's another crash: Nuyens is now in the wheel of BMC's Karsten Kroon, and coming on to the back of the bunch, when Kroon hits a lamppost, goes down and stays down. Collarbone. Nuyens has to sprint for the back of the peloton for the third or fourth time, but this time he's lucky – a motorbike with a photographer is in front of him and he has a bit of shelter from the wind. Nuyens now has a choice on the Oude Kwaremont – he knows that the bunch will slow at some point but he can't push too hard to try to get to the front because it will use energy he needs for later. *Don't panic,* he tells himself, *it will come back together.*

The peloton hits the bottom of the Oude Kwaremont and again they slow. Mat Hayman, an Australian riding for Sky, Garmin's Belgian rider Sep Vanmarcke and his compatriot Greg Van Avermaet from BMC are in the front line, and that is all the road is wide enough for. BMC's Hincapie and Ballan are just behind, as is Farrar on Vanmarcke's wheel. Boonen, Steegmans and Chavanel are all there for Quick Step. Saxo Bank rider Baden Cooke is also in the second row, blissfully ignorant of Nuyens's travails at the back of the bunch. He's not getting the information on the radio. Cooke's part in the team's plan is to be more of a wild card: his instructions are to take any opportunity that arises in the third quarter of the race.

The early, steep section of cobbles breaks the cohesion of the early break. Van Dijk and Hunt are tailed off, leaving Turgot, Hammond and Docker in front. Just over a minute later, Vanmarcke and Van Avermaet accelerate on the same piece of road. Hincapie thinks that his team-mate Van Avermaet is one of the strongest riders in the race and, while the American and Ballan are the nominal leaders of BMC, Van Avermaet has a similar free role to Cooke.

The early break in a race like Flanders may have tactical ramifications for later on, but its members know full well they are on a suicide mission. Television viewers who watch Tour de France stages are used to the early break getting caught in the final 20 minutes of racing before the race ends in a bunch sprint. However, Classics like the Tour of Flanders are long enough that there is often a second phase of attacks, usually between 80 and 20 kilometres to go (these figures vary wildly according to the race and circumstances). The riders capable of going for these breaks tend to be potential winners – maybe a few per cent short of the fire-power needed to win a big one-day race by brute strength alone, like Cancellara or Boonen, but dangerous riders nonetheless. Van Avermaet and Cooke both have leeway from their teams to go for an attack like this. So do Lars Boom of Rabobank, Björn Leukemans of Vacansoleil and Sylvain Chavanel. Stijn Devolder won two Rondes by being this kind of rider.

It's on the final part of the steep section, just coming into Kwaremont village, that Chavanel goes. Hincapie sees him but his job is to be there at the end of the race, not to chase down attacks, so the American lets him go. Van Avermaet and Vanmarcke either can't follow or decide it's not the right time, and then Steegmans and Boonen, Chavanel's team-mates, move to the front to try and slow down the chase. It gives Chavanel enough time to build up a lead of 50 metres or so. Sky's Hayman is awake to the danger and tries to chase, but he does so with the heavy weight of two Quick Step riders sitting on his wheel, which dissuades him. If he chases down Chavanel single-handedly, any counter-attack will be instant and he won't be able to chase down that one as well (or if he can, the third counter-attack will definitely be successful). If he lets him go, at least there is now a known quantity up the road.

If more than one team had co-operated to chase Chavanel, the race might have come together again. Instead, Quick Step have got a dangerous rider off the front and changed the shape of the race. Chavanel puts his head down and the real work begins.

Friday 29 September 2000. A 21-year-old first-year professional for the small French Bonjour team leads on the first stage of the Circuit Franco–Belge, which finishes on Enclus du Haut, the road which leads to the summit of the Mont-de-l'Enclus. He's 20 seconds clear of three other escapees on the climb, which is known on the Flemish side of the language border as the Kluisberg, while the bunch is almost a minute and a half behind. The Kluisberg and Mont-de-l'Enclus climbs (there are north and south faces, one Flemish and one Walloon) make occasional appearances in the Ronde. They are tucked on the very tip of the Flemish Ardennes, just a few kilometres west of the Knokteberg. Sylvain Chavanel took his first professional win atop the Mont-de-l'Enclus, defended his lead in the time trial and third stage, and only got pushed out of the race lead by a long and damaging break on the final day.

It took Belgium a full 25 years to really understand there would be no second Eddy Merckx. So it's ironic that Sylvain Chavanel found himself going to a Belgian team to avoid the pressure of the French, for their part, not having quite yet realised there was going to be no second Bernard Hinault. Chavanel's results as an amateur were superb – he was one of a golden generation of riders who came through the Vendée U team on the west coast of France around the turn of the century. Expectations were high. But while his results were good through the first eight years of his career, they weren't spectacular and the perception was that attacking verve and talent were enough to get him results in the amateurs but not in the longer, harder professional races. He had the column inches of Bernard Hinault but not his results, although anecdotal and tangible evidence points largely towards a situation where French riders were generally doping a lot less in the early 21st century than their rivals from Italy, Spain and the USA, among others.

There was a single moment in the 2003 Tour de France which summed up the gulf between a rider like Chavanel and the riders at the front of the race when the hapless Frenchman – at one point ten minutes ahead in a break on the Pyrenean stage to Luz Ardiden – was caught by a motoring Lance Armstrong with four kilometres to go. The Texan gave Chavanel a pat on the back as he sped past, a gesture which was not appreciated by the young Frenchman but which summed up the balance of power at that point between two very different interpretations of sporting ethics.

There's a further irony in Chavanel not being the second Bernard Hinault – he often tells journalists the story of when he organised play races between himself and his friends as a young child. Chavanel would invariably take the role of Greg LeMond, Hinault's nemesis in his final Tour de France. Even at the age of eight, Chavanel instinctively knew that trying to be Bernard Hinault was not for him.

Chavanel is a rider of immense pedigree and class, though this is allied with fragile morale and a tendency to place highly and often, rather than win, as a professional. He's not exactly temperamental or mercurial – away from the bike he's reassuringly average – but there's a mysterious distance between his ability and his results. He outgrew his first team, Brioches La Boulangère, then his second, Cofidis, and moved to Quick Step in 2009 in order to be a decent rider who could take his opportunities rather than the out-and-out leader he was at Cofidis with all the expectation that came with that position. He also got a pay rise. Chavanel's pay packet was a perennial fascination of the French public – the perception was that he was overpaid, overrated and over here, of which only the last changed when he moved operations to Belgium.

He has an affinity with Flanders, as demonstrated by that first professional win, though he has defied classification as a rider throughout his career. He's been, at various stages, a time-triallist, a Tour contender (by reputation and ambition rather than results), a force in the week-long stage races that run throughout the year, a stage hunter, a rouleur, a Classics specialist and even, as long as the circumstances are right, a sprinter.

But in 2008, he discovered the cobbles. Before the season he bet his Cofidis team manager that he could do a good ride in Dwars door Vlaanderen. He made the break along with then team-mate Nick Nuyens, who had already come second in the first Belgian race of the season, Omloop Het Volk, and would go on to come second in the Tour of Flanders. Chavanel attacked the break and, with Nuyens covering any efforts at chasing him down, held on to win alone. Though the French would still see him as the prodigal talent who never won the Tour de France, his ambitions from that spring on were centred on the Classics, especially the Tour of Flanders and Paris–Roubaix. And at Quick Step, he was in the perfect team both to follow his dream of winning a cobbled Classic and – with Tom Boonen attracting so much attention from the Belgian press – to avoid the pressure of team leadership.

CHAPTER 6

Paterberg

Bavikhove is an anonymous town of 3,000 souls next to the Leie river a short distance north-east of Kortrijk, where the only building taller than two storeys is a church and not much happens. It's where Stijn Devolder, the Ronde winner in 2008 and 2009, was born and grew up, the son of a steelworker father and a mother who worked in the textile industry. Devolder's a homebody and he now lives just down the road in Deerlijk with his wife, who is the niece of the 1962 Tour de France runner-up Josef Planckaert (who in turn is no relation to either Eddy or Walter Planckaert). Coincidentally, the 1988 Paris–Roubaix winner Dirk Demol and three-time Ronde runner-up Leif Hoste are also from Bavikhove. Demol coached both riders when they were young and was Devolder's manager at the US Postal and Trek teams.

The first time I became aware of Devolder was at the 2004 Tour du Haut Var, a one-day race held in Draguignan in February, just inland from the Mediterranean coast. I'd been in the area to interview some of the old boys who are perennial fixtures at smaller French races and are brought along officially to glad-hand the sponsors and fans but unofficially because they like getting together to have a drink and a reminisce about the good old days. I'd caught up with both Raymond Poulidor, who'd been known as the 'Eternal Second' at the Tour de France for finishing on the podium eight times without winning in the 1960s and 1970s, and Raphaël Géminiani, who rode all three Grand Tours in 1955 and finished in the top six each time. I wasn't really there to see the race, but I stuck around to do a report for *Cycling Weekly*.

So much for the Riviera. The weather was absolutely apocalyptic. Not only had a massive storm moved up from North Africa and across the Mediterranean, in freakish climatological circumstances it had picked up a dust storm en route and it proceeded to dump muddy, sandy rain from strange yellow-tinged clouds all over the peloton for the entirety of the race. It was cold, wet and horrible, and when a group of five escaped with about an hour to go, they were more or less left to get on with it, while most of the rest of the bunch packed. A Dutch rider, Marc Lotz, won the sprint but I was more interested in Devolder, who'd done a lot of the work in the lead group and came in third. I'd never heard of him before so I went to his hotel afterwards to interview him in the lobby. My first impression was that he looked and acted like a boy – very fresh-faced and awkward. I was struck by two things. First, he was very matter-of-fact about his strength. Second, he really was extraordinarily hard work to interview. It was like getting blood from a stone.

And that was the last interaction I had with him until late 2015 when I met him at a Trek team training camp in Alicante to try and find out how two Tour of Flanders wins – one of which was taken while wearing the Belgian champion's jersey – had changed his life in the interim. The press officer warned me: 'He's quite quiet ... '

Devolder's first memory of cycling is watching the 1988 Tour of Flanders, won by Eddy Planckaert, who quickly became his hero. He started cycling but wasn't good immediately – it was four races before he even finished one. But by September of his first season he was winning, and the next year he won 15 times. He won the junior edition of Flanders twice. As well as his two senior wins in the Ronde, he's also a habitual winner of the Belgian national championships (three times) and the Tour of Belgium (two times). He's a Flanders specialist and has ridden the race every season since 2002 and, though he dropped down a division for 2017, I suspect he's got two or three more editions in him even if the days of winning it are over. But strip out those two wins and he's only achieved one more top 20 – a 13th place in 2013. Discounting wins and withdrawals, he averages around 59th place, which is nothing special, yet you don't take two wins from two long solo breaks off the front in the Ronde without being extremely resilient.

His two Flanders wins were remarkably similar, and I watched them both from the same vantage point – the town square in Geraardsbergen, where you could both enjoy the atmosphere created by thousands of Belgians and watch the race on a big screen. The first victory was a gift, unwitting or otherwise, from his team leader Boonen. With 47 kilometres to go, on the Leberg, Devolder was on the front of a lead group that was dwindling in size with team leader Boonen in his wheel, and Boonen sat up and simply let him go, forcing other riders to chase. Groups attacked, formed, broke up, reformed and broke up again, but the one constant seemed to be that Devolder was at the front. When he was in a group of five, with 25 kilometres to go and about to be caught by the peloton, he attacked again, alone, and managed to build a 30-second lead that he defended over the Muur van Geraardsbergen and Bosberg, and all the way to the finish in Meerbeke, while Boonen sat on his pursuers. Boonen's pursuers knew full well that if they chased down Devolder, Boonen would win, and if they didn't chase him down, Boonen's team-mate would win, so they chose the latter. If they couldn't win, at least they could piss Boonen off a little.

The second victory was a little more contentious. Devolder's team-mate Chavanel was away and Devolder counter-attacked behind, which is generally inadvisable because it could very easily damage the chances of both riders by bringing the peloton up. However, nobody followed, and Devolder made the junction then attacked on the Muur to solo in to victory a second time. 'There's no other race I feel the same motivation for,' he told me in Spain. 'My season stands by this race. At other races you can have other things on your mind, but in the Ronde I have only one thing on my mind.'

Devolder is very softly spoken. I learned later that his team-mates at Quick Step used to call him 'Briek' after Schotte, for his uncommunicative nature. I was surprised to see that he has a Twitter account, though when I looked at it in December 2016, there was one single tweet, from two years before: 'No time to tweet. Out riding my bike.'

We spoke for 45 minutes or so, and he was quiet throughout, but the quietness was in no way indicative of a lack of confidence or self-belief, just as with our meeting almost 12 years previously. I've watched the footage of both his wins again, and after the first he let out a huge roar, which didn't seem at all typical of him but probably expressed his emotions in a freer way than he would in an interview. 'The first one, the way I won it was very special, and the way I won it, I rode 25 kilometres with no more than ten seconds on the group behind me. The second time was more comfortable. For everything else, it's just like the other years. You start in Bruges, you are concentrated, you dream of the victory but you don't dare to think about it.'

And what about Boonen? Did he attack his own leader? He was the team leader, but in my mind I was thinking I can win also. I won because I did my job. My job was to react to everything in the final. There were a lot of attacks and I was there every time. I had good legs and attacked. 'I was thinking on the Muur that they were coming back, but I looked and they weren't there. On the Bosberg, when you look behind, even when they are 30 seconds behind they look very close. I just kept on going. The top of the Bosberg was the toughest moment for me. When I came round the last corner, that was the first moment in the race I realised I was going to win. Those last 200 metres were . . . fabulous. It was an explosion of happiness. In that moment, I changed. Like I was a different person. The next year I had more confidence and the will to win. I wanted to prove that I could win not only once but two times. That day there was no other option but to win. I knew in the morning that I was going to be the winner and nobody else. I didn't tell anybody. I only knew it for myself.'

Later on, I asked the Quick Step manager Patrick Lefevere whether it was the team's idea for him to attack and win the Ronde, or Devolder's himself. 'If you have a bunch of 30 riders waiting for Tom Boonen to move, that's good for us. It's a tactic; Stijn anticipated it and he won,' he said. 'The second time we were not very happy at the time because Chavanel was in the breakaway. Devolder rode after his own team-mate. But on the Muur, he dropped everybody, so no comment. If you drop everybody you win, and the winner is always right.'

But Lefevere didn't find him easy to manage. 'He's not a team player; he doesn't speak at the table. When he was 16 he was winning everything and we were saying he was the new Eddy Merckx. He's strong and the team liked him because he was a good boy but he was not a team player and you can do that for one or two years, but not for seven, so we let him go.'

Devolder's results in the Ronde are inconsistent – he's either first or nowhere. It has always been this way, his team manager and childhood mentor Dirk Demol told me. Demol retired from racing in 1995, and became the manager of the Kortrijk Groeninge Spurters junior cycling team, for which Devolder rode along with Tom Boonen, one year his junior. Later on, he was a directeur sportif for Devolder at US Postal and Quick Step. 'I've known Stijn since he was a kid. His parents were fans of mine,' Demol said. 'I saw as a young rider and an amateur that he was blowing everybody away, and it was like, fuck, this guy is going to be a big champion. But with Stijn you could also see ... he was, ach ... I don't know how to say it.'

Demol paused. Then he said, 'Sometimes it was hard to believe how bad he could be. He could be the first guy to be dropped from the peloton. That was when he was not focused. But when he was focused then it's different. When we get closer to the Ronde van Vlaanderen, he is a different person. He gains confidence. For another race, maybe a one-day race in Italy, he'll participate and do his job, but his motivation is far away from Flanders. I used to see him winning a race two or three minutes ahead of everyone; even against the best young riders of Belgium and Holland he was just going away solo for 40, 50 or 60 kilometres no problem. Then the next race you saw him getting dropped. With his talent, he should be easily surviving in a peloton even when he has a bad, bad day. Strange, huh?'

It was the same when he turned professional. His inconsistency meant not many teams were interested, but Demol pulled some strings and persuaded the Vlaanderen team to take him on. He had a poor first year, and Demol recalls being in the convoy in some races and seeing Devolder being the first rider to be dropped from the peloton. Even Demol started having doubts, but in Devolder's second year he finished third in E3 Harelbeke. Then came the Tour of Flanders. 'He was really good. He punctured twice in the last 70 or 80 kilometres, and his team car was a long way behind so he lost minutes. I couldn't believe it when I looked in my mirror and saw Stijn coming back. Stijn is tough. He never cancels training. If it's cold and raining and he has to do five hours, he goes. But sometimes there's nothing you can do with him, and he does his own thing. It keeps me awake at night.'

I'd asked Demol if there was any friction between Devolder and Boonen about the two Ronde victories. It seemed strange that Quick Step got shot of the former at the end of 2010. He answered with a very long, drawn out 'ummmm . . .'

He thought for a moment, and said that there was more of an issue with the team's directeur sportif Wilfried Peeters. Boonen was Peeters' favourite – both come from the same town in the east of Belgium, Mol. 'I remember the first time he won, I almost had a fight with Peeters because you could see from 50 or 60 [kilometres] to go that Tom was not capable of winning. I wasn't supporting one or the other; for the sponsor it was best that Tom won for the publicity, but at a certain point I realised he could not win and that Devolder was riding easily. Tom was good but I could see Devolder was super, so I said maybe it was good to send him up the road, and that would also be good for Tom because he would only have to follow, but they said no. They only had one plan: Tom. Tom. Tom. The second year he was going against the team tactics, eh? He attacked and was alone, and that gave him the right to bridge up. Maybe Chavanel could stay with him on the Muur, but he knew already that he was going to win when he was bridging. You have to be a bit . . . a bit selfish at moments like that.'

Devolder's a two-time winner of the Ronde. It's a rare achievement and it's a little unfair that there is always a caveat, that he won because Quick Step's rivals were all watching Boonen. Demol said, 'Sometimes they say he won the race twice because the pressure was on the shoulders of Tom. I agree, but not 100 per cent. In the last 100 kilometres of his first win, he was bringing Tom into position for all the climbs and was still capable of going away with 25 kilometres to go. Once he is in the race to win, he can ride through a wall.'

I get the impression that Devolder has more in common with the winners and riders of the early Rondes than any of the other winners in the last 30 or 40 years, and that Karel Van Wijnendaele would approve of this stoic, tough rider. At the end of our interview I asked Devolder to describe his character, and he told me he didn't know, followed by a long, long silence. 'It's a difficult question. I never thought about it. Just . . . I don't know.'

Are you a *Flandrien*? 'It's just a word they use. It's something that doesn't exist. What is a *Flandrien*? They can call me that, but it doesn't mean anything to me.'

When I visited the Paterberg, I parked at the top then walked on to the climb and looked at the view for a while. If you want to understand or get a real sense of the *Vlaamse Ardennen*, this is one of the places I would suggest going. I could see the road that leads into the Kwaremont climb then, further up the hill, the houses of the village perched on the ridge. Beyond the gentle green slope of the hill across the valley below me stretched the Schelde river and wide plain of Flanders. The rolling hills either side, though cultivated and organised into fields and enclosures, seemed to breathe with life and freshness. This part of Belgium might be comparatively sparsely populated, but between the stretches of rural space and bare brown trees, which look like they have come directly out of a Dutch landscape painting, there were signs of industry and habitation everywhere: towns, villages, the two huge cooling towers on the edge of Kluisbergen and the movement of cars along the roads, made tiny by the distance. Somebody was driving a tractor or other heavy vehicle in the fields behind me and the wind carried the faintest hint of faraway work from the plain.

The Paterberg wears its contradictions openly. It's a steep cobbled climb in the tradition of Flandrian bergs – only 375 metres long, but extremely steep, with an average gradient of 12.5 per cent and a much steeper pitch at the top. However, it's entirely artificial. The story goes that the farmer who owns the land was envious of his friend who lived close to the Koppenberg and could enjoy the passing of the Tour of Flanders. So he built his own version, an ersatz *helling* which has, artificial or not, become the absolute crux of the modern Ronde. It's a real-life representation of the complexity of any debate between the forces of tradition and modernity.

Andreas Klier loved and hated the Paterberg. 'I don't like it as a cyclist. It must be nice if you are Peter Sagan and you can basically drop everybody on the Paterberg. But to ride up there was nice in that you could see the spectators one by one. You can see, and smell, the atmosphere,' he told me. In late 2011, the owners of the Tour of Flanders announced significant changes in the route. The start city, Bruges, would remain the same but the finish would be moved from Meerbeke to Oudenaarde, and the course would be based on three laps. The first year, the Kwaremont–Paterberg combination was tackled three times and it was too hard, but in the most recent races it has still appeared twice. Traditionalists were outraged because the established Meerbeke finish, which incorporated the climb up the Muur van Geraardsbergen, had been ditched for what they perceived to be an inferior alternative. The idea of laps was also criticised.

The problem with the traditionalists' argument – as is often the case – is that if you look back far enough 'traditions' aren't that traditional. The Ronde started in Ghent from 1913 to 1976, in Sint-Niklaas from 1977 to 1997 and in Bruges from 1998 to 2016. In 2017 it started in Antwerp. There have been more finish locations: various suburbs of Ghent, including Mariakerke,

Evergem, Gentbrugge and Wetteren; then Meerbeke from 1973 to 2011; and finally Oudenaarde. Bruges to Oudenaarde is just one more permutation in an occasionally shifting framework for the race. On the other hand, the Kwaremont and Paterberg are no Muur.

The battle over the soul of the Tour of Flanders rages on. Some fans think there's an obsession with money at the expense of the racing and atmosphere – the Kwaremont used to be a joyful free-for-all for thousands of spectators; now large parts of the climb are fenced off for expensive VIP enclosures. This is happening across the sport – MBA graduates and marketing experts are coming up with various new business models for cycling, with a common although curiously non-specific theme behind their ideas: the sport needs modernising. So when a man in the café in Kwaremont told me that the president of the UCI's road commission actually lives in a house near the top of the Paterberg, I thought there could be no better place to go to ask how the Tour of Flanders can maintain its traditions in the face of encroaching modernity.

Tom Van Damme was born in Ronse and worked in communications before getting into cycling administration and working as the director of Belgian Cycling from 2009. He's been on the UCI's Management Committee since 2013, the same year he was made president of the UCI Road Commission. It's a powerful position – two of his predecessors are Pat McQuaid and Brian Cookson, both of whom became UCI president. I'd called and left a message, and he texted to invite me over for an interview. He has lived near the Paterberg since 1996 – well before it became the final climb of the Tour of Flanders – but he's invariably busy and away on the day of the race so he rarely gets to stand and watch. We sat in his kitchen and I asked him, as both a native of the *Vlaamse Ardennen* and a high-powered official in the sport's governing body with a close interest in its marketing, what the race represented to him. 'It represents the history of cycling. It's tradition and modern racing in one race,' he said. He approved of the new course, despite his acknowledgement of the importance of tradition. The new architecture of the race made it more modern. You have to respect the Monuments, and of course the Muur was not in the race any more, but you also have to respect the geography. If you make a new final with Oudenaarde, which is a historic city of Flanders and also very close to the Ardennes, then you have to make choices. At a certain moment, you have to organise it; you have to make sure it's safe for the riders and public so it costs money, and if you need a budget of three or four million Euros then you need to be smart in a business way, and you need the VIPs and the sponsors to survive and develop the race for everybody's benefit. It's for the benefit of the teams, the riders, the public, and if you want a good television and media product, you also need the investment. It's a business, but it must still stay as a sport. In the future, maybe there will be another start or finish, but it will always be the Tour of Flanders, with the final 100 kilometres always in the *Vlaamse Ardennen*.'

Van Damme may be embracing the modern Ronde, but his childhood memories of watching the race and his nationality mean that he understands its position in the culture of Flanders. 'Everybody went to see it. Everybody who loved sport was going to watch the race and talk about it; you go and have a beer in a bar before they arrive, then you go back home and watch the television for the final, but you have to go and see it; you have to feel it. It's tradition, probably sort of a religion and it's folkloric,' he said.

I asked him why that is, and he paused, shrugged, and said he didn't know. 'Why does anybody go to a cricket match?' he asked.

*

At the top of the Oude Kwaremont, there's a left-hand turn back onto the main road at the top of the Nieuwe Kwaremont, and opposite Ronde van Vlaanderenstraat, where the riders passed just ten or 12 minutes ago. Hammond, Turgot and Docker are first through. Then Van Dijk of the early break, Veelers and Clarke, who attacked separately before and on the Knokteberg, then Chavanel and finally Hunt. The peloton, led by Hayman, comes next, a minute behind the leading three.

This stretch of the N36, Ronse and Kluisbergen's linking road, is one of the hardest and most televisual bits of the race. It's a kilometre long but it's dead straight; it descends very gently at first, but then rises up in a drag that adds 20 metres of elevation in 500 metres. What's more, the prevailing south-west wind is a cross-tailwind here.

Crosswinds are as effective as climbs at prising pelotons apart. In a headwind, riders slot in behind each other in order to take advantage of the shelter, which contributes to a significant energy saving. In a cross-headwind, riders must ride behind but also to one side of the rider in front. In a 90-degree crosswind, riders must move up slightly so their handlebars are not far from level with the hips of the rider in front (these are approximations – wind rarely behaves rationally or goes in perfect straight lines, and even if it does, roads do not). As riders seek shelter to the side of the rider in front they take up lateral space, and there is only so much room on a road before the edge prevents any more riders fitting in. A rider who is squeezed out and can't get the lateral shelter is therefore using a lot more energy and, sooner or later, a gap will form. In hard, flat races with persistent crosswinds (they don't have to be that strong, although it helps), there will be successive waves of riders spread across the road, with gaps between each one, and these gaps have a tendency to expand. Cross-tailwinds have a reputation for being the hardest of all because the speed is higher, which magnifies mistakes.

This particular stretch of cross-tailwind is one of the worst in cycling because it comes at the top of the longest climb of the Tour of Flanders. The Kwaremont doesn't always break the peloton; it just strings it out into a line. It's on the main road afterwards that things split up. The motorcycle-mounted television cameras can also get long zooms on shots here, in which the foreshortening makes it look like groups are actually quite close together, before the helicopter panning shot shows how big the gap actually is.

There's the briefest of lulls. The strongest riders have forced their way towards the front on the Kwaremont, but with 85 kilometres still to go it's too early for team leaders to attack or ride right on the front. But Sky seem to like the look of the fact that there is a small gap behind the first 35 riders or so. Three of their riders, Hayman, Ian Stannard and Geraint Thomas, surge to the front, with the team leader Juan Antonio Flecha just behind. Garmin are well represented, with four riders. There are three BMCs. They pass Jeremy Hunt, whose race will soon be over, but the pace is slowing slightly at the front, and as they turn left at the top at an isolated house with white and red walls, opposite the other end of Ronde van Vlaanderenstraat, the peloton has not quite been broken by Sky's effort. There is a ball of 40 riders at the front, then a long tail of another 50 or so in a single line, a small fissure and then another group of about 30.

The descent to the foot of the Paterberg is two kilometres long and fast. It is a swooping, narrow road with one left bend through which, depending on the weather and circumstances, riders might need to brake. It's made dangerous by the fact that the Paterberg starts immediately at the bottom and the riders are desperate to move as far up the peloton as they can. The race is showing signs of possibly coming back together – Hammond, Docker and Turgot still lead, then Clarke, Chavanel, Veelers and Van Dijk are descending in a group of four just 100 metres in front of the peloton.

What the television cameras don't show is the crash, further back, which cleaves the bunch into two parts. Nuyens should have known it was coming – he'd moved up on the Kwaremont but he is still towards the back of the field, behind the crash. The road is full of bikes and bodies but it's every man for himself. Nuyens walks over bikes, pushing riders out of the way. *Survival of the fittest*, he thinks, though he's barely surviving.

The Paterberg is a different kind of effort from the Kwaremont. The longer climb favours riders who can sustain high power outputs for long periods of time, but you can punch your way up the Paterberg. It's nasty, brutish and short.

It begins with a sharp, steep right-hander that kills momentum, and to brake here is fatal. There is still the feeling that the race is changing, in flux. The three leaders' time at the front looks like it will be short – they have lost their fluency, and struggle up the climb. Sixty seconds later, the fresher Clarke and Chavanel drop Van Dijk and Veelers almost immediately, the latter pair's parts in the race now played out. And not far behind, Philippe Gilbert leads the peloton, with Boonen, Geraint Thomas and Tyler Farrar just behind. Gilbert is pushing hard – it's not an attack, but he is testing himself and his rivals. It's possible to deduce how hard it is not just by Gilbert's speed and the fact that the peloton is being pulled into a line again and that he's closing fast on Clarke and Chavanel, but also by Boonen's riding style. The Belgian has a 'tell' that makes it obvious when he's riding at or close to his limit: a nodding which starts with his head, then infects his whole body so that his back is literally bending with the effort.

Clarke and Chavanel are coming back to the peloton. The Paterberg is steepest in the middle, and the top gets shallower again before a sharp left turn, and at the turn Gilbert is just one bike length off Chavanel's back wheel; the peloton is in single file behind him.

The order at the top: Hammond, Turgot and Docker, 30 seconds clear. Then Clarke and Chavanel, whose escape looks done. Gilbert leads a line of riders, first of whom is Boonen. Then Lars Boom, Greg Van Avermaet, who looks like he is struggling, and Fabian Cancellara, who is strong but already has no team-mates anywhere near. They're followed by Filippo Pozzato, an Italian rider and perennial fifth-to-15th-finisher in the Ronde, and then Hincapie, which means there are already two BMCs in the top seven of the peloton. Fifty riders pass through. Then there is a gap to the next group of 80. This group is more bunched up, which means it's not moving as fast. These riders look like they are essentially falling out of the race, which is bad news for Stijn Devolder and Nick Nuyens, still picking their way through the back markers as they reach the top.

CHAPTER 7

Koppenberg

The Australian rider Allan Peiper tells a story about Eric Vanderaerden, the mercurial Limburger who won the Tour of Flanders in 1985. In *A Peiper's Tale,* he wrote of the aftermath of a crash which his then Panasonic team-mate Vanderaerden suffered in the 1988 Tirreno–Adriatico race: 'Afterwards, in the showers, his soigneur Ruud Bakker got a brush and scrubbed all the gravel and dirt out of his wounds. We were staying in this pissy little town and the only medical thing there was a vet, so Ruud got the vet to sew up Eric's arm. He was a tough guy, a hard bastard. Nobody gave Eric any shit.'

The 1985 race that Vanderaerden won was probably the hardest edition of the Tour of Flanders in the last 50 years or more. The rain began just as the 173 starters left the Grote Markt in Sint-Niklaas on the morning of 7 April, Easter Sunday, and it didn't stop all day as a persistent area of low pressure pulled a characteristically north-European blanket of thick grey cloud over the region. In his social history of cycling, *One More Kilometre and We're in the Showers,* Tim Hilton described Belgium's spring as 'a specialised form of winter, often cold and raining'.

The temperature for the 1985 Ronde hovered at between two

and five degrees Celsius, which led one journalist to describe the conditions as 'Siberian'. By the first *helling* of the day – the Molenberg, which came at just after halfway – the peloton was already down to 60 riders. Only 24 riders finished, their faces and jerseys painted with a dirty wash of grey watercolour. Sean Kelly, an Irish rider renowned for being able to withstand cold and wet conditions and who shares Leif Hoste's joint record for second-places finishes in the Ronde with three, wrote in his autobiography *Hunger* that if he hadn't deliberately pissed himself at the bottom of the Muur van Geraardsbergen in order to warm his legs, he wouldn't have got over the climb. Allan Peiper told me that he remembered getting to the top of the Parikeberg with 20 kilometres to go, where the landscape opens up and becomes very exposed. 'I've still got the picture in my mind of the wind and the rain. I had never been so cold,' he said. That edition left such an impression on Flemish cycling fans that it was voted the greatest in the hundred years of the race in the poll run by *Het Nieuwsblad* in 2013.

The funny thing is that Vanderaerden was considered a bit soft, or at least flawed, compared with the stereotypical *Flandrien*. He was from Limburg, which is the easternmost province of Flanders, at the opposite end of the region from the provinces of West and East Flanders in which the Ronde takes place. Flemish cycling journalist Michel Wuyts described him as a 'loafer'. There was never any doubting Vanderaerden's talent – he won over 200 races before he even turned professional and is the only rider ever to have won a full set of the junior, amateur and professional versions of the Tour of Flanders. When he was 15, he already had a 500-strong supporters' club and he brought a lot of fans to races, which meant organisers were already starting to pay him start money as a young amateur. And winning the Ronde in the way he did – along with Paris–Roubaix two years afterwards – meant that nobody doubted his hardness, yet opinion was tempered by the suspicion that he lacked resilience and focus. He also had a reputation for liking a party and for falling out with his team managers sooner or later. He was on the receiving end of a spectacular series of allegations from his team manager Jan Raas when he was sacked by the WordPerfect team at the end of 1993. These included calling another directeur sportif (the former Tour de France winner Joop Zoetemelk) a 'bloody old bastard', and being accused of 'reading porn mags'.

I wasn't a huge fan of Vanderaerden when I was a teenage follower of the sport back in the 1980s. I liked Sean Kelly, and Vanderaerden and Kelly were enemies. There was also something about the way Vanderaerden rode – he was kind of chippy and a bit arrogant, a clogger with a blond bubble perm and a belligerent face who looked as if he might be as at home in a scrap in a pub as he plainly was in physical bunch sprints. But since watching a bit of grainy YouTube footage of his 1985 win, and reading back through the old race reports in *Winning* magazine, I've come round to something close to resembling the opinion shared by a large portion of *Het Nieuwsblad*'s readership: that if you want to understand the Tour of Flanders, the 1985 race will tell you a lot.

When I spoke to Vanderaerden, he told me he didn't like the cold and wet conditions any more than anybody else, but that a combination of youth (he was only 23 when he won the Ronde) and an ability to compartmentalise enabled him to shut out the weather. 'When I was young I could turn on a button and just race,' he said. 'When we had to do 250 kilometres in the rain, my rivals already had bad morale. Nobody likes to ride in the rain, especially in March or April because it's also very cold. But I could say to myself, *keep on going, you are not afraid of the water*. In 1985 the weather was so bad and cold, we were busy with just one thing – to keep on moving. It was only survival, even on the flat.'

Though the 1985 race was televisual and compelling for its appalling conditions, the rain did wash out a lot of the tactical nuance. The 60-strong peloton was halved again on the second climb of the race, the Oude Kwaremont, leaving a group of 30, six of whom were from Vanderaerden's team, Panasonic, with 100 kilometres still to race.

The Dutch team Panasonic were exceptionally strong, especially in the Classics. Their manager Peter Post was organised, autocratic and a little humourless, and described by journalist Geoffrey Nicholson as 'a QC among dressing-room lawyers'. Post consciously developed a philosophy for Panasonic, and its forerunner TI-Raleigh, which paralleled the national football team's concept of 'total football'. By running a well-drilled and talented team of riders, many of whom were capable of winning races, he went against the orthodoxy of teams being based around single leaders with the rest of the riders operating as domestiques according to a preset plan. The idea was that if several different riders from the team were capable of winning a race, the team could ride for whoever was in the best position, so the leadership effectively rotated according to circumstances. (This system wasn't perfect, and Post had his favourites and biases. Allan Peiper told me about being in a group just behind the winning break, which consisted of Italian rider Moreno Argentin and Belgian Rudy Dhaenens in the 1990 Ronde. He wanted to chase and had the legs to do so, but Post told him not to work as his team-mate Eddy Planckaert was in the next chasing group. 'Post came up to me in the car and screamed out of the window at me, "Don't ride one metre on the front; they are coming from behind with Planckaert,"' recalled Peiper. 'They caught us at the bottom of the Muur, and Dhaenens and Argentin were long gone. I came up next to Eddy and asked him how he was, and he told me he was cooked.')

In the context of the 1985 Ronde, Panasonic's strength – six riders in the 30-strong lead group – meant that one of them would probably win, especially as three of those six were Vanderaerden, who'd been second in Dwars door Vlaanderen that season, Australian rider Phil Anderson, who'd won E3 Prijs, and Eddy Planckaert, who'd won Omloop Het Volk.

Vanderaerden's chances were almost scuppered between the Oude Kwaremont and the third *helling*, the Koppenberg, which the Belgian rider used to call 'the witch's wall'. He suffered a flat, had to wait for a wheel change from Panasonic domestique Ludo De Keulenaer, and was forced to chase.

The Koppenberg is the worst climb in the Tour of Flanders. It's not got the steepest average gradient: it's nine per cent, while the Paterberg averages 13 per cent. Nor is it the longest: it's only 682 metres long. And it tops out at 78 metres, which makes it one of the lowest climbs of the Ronde. It does, however, have the steepest pitch – a section at 22 per cent, though this alone is not what makes it hard. (After all, the Paterberg has a stretch at 20 per cent.) It's the combination of gradient, narrowness between two steep banks and one of the worst stretches of cobblestones in the entire race that make the Koppenberg such a formidable obstacle. Modern bike technology has tamed it a little, but in the mid-1980s riders had fewer gears and, with larger bottom gears, had to muscle their bikes up the steepest pitches. This meant they were more prone to stalling, and this was made even worse in wet weather. In 1987 a Danish rider, Jesper Skibby, was knocked off his bike by a race car on the climb when he was just ahead of the peloton. The driver of the car – panicking, revving and seeing the bunch bearing down on him in the rear-view mirror – took the handbrake off, hit a policeman and ran straight over the Dane's bike; also over the spot where his foot would have been had he not managed to just pull it out of the way. After that, the organisers withdrew the climb from the race, and it remained dormant until it was resurfaced (better than before but still bad), marginally widened at its tightest pinch, and reintroduced in 2002.

Vanderaerden's ascent of the Koppenberg in 1985 was what put him back in the race. He started the climb well behind what was left of the peloton, but up ahead it was chaos. Fans, policemen and photographers stood in the gutter on the edge of the road, blocking the way, and only three riders at the front got up without putting their feet down: Anderson, Planckaert and the Skala team's Nico Verhoeven. Greg LeMond, a future Tour de France winner, stalled on the steepest section and brought the rest of the group to a standstill. While the riders shouldered their bikes and clacked and slipped their way up, Vanderaerden had had a clear run at the hill and then somehow also managed to stay upright as he picked a weaving path through the walking riders even as bikes swung into him. He emerged near the front in the manner of Foinavon in the 1967 Grand National. 'My luck was that the bunch was only 30 or 35 riders when I punctured,' Vanderaerden told me. 'That meant I didn't have to start the Koppenberg in 120th position. I was already catching the leaders by the foot of the climb.'

He'd moved from last position at the bottom to 12th position at the top, and of the 12 riders who subsequently came together at the front of the race, four were Panasonics – Vanderaerden, Planckaert, Anderson and De Keulenaer. Good news for Peter Post, but Vanderaerden knew his biggest rivals now were his own team-mates. Dutch rider Hennie Kuiper attacked on the Berendries climb; Vanderaerden set off in pursuit on the next ascent, Tenbossestraat. But before he reached Kuiper, Anderson counter-attacked, caught Vanderaerden and then the Panasonic pair reached the Dutchman on the approach to Geraardsbergen. 'I knew I had to attack on the Muur,' Vanderaerden said. 'I could win in a sprint against Anderson but I knew that if I didn't attack [he] would try something, so I went up the Muur at 100 per cent.'

Anderson's memory of the attack is somewhat different. He said in a recent interview, 'Vanderaerden was yelling at me to ease up, so I eased up a little bit, and as I did Vanderaerden attacked. I just had to sit with Kuiper as Vanderaerden rode away.'

Kuiper was wasted from having attacked earlier, and Anderson was trapped. All Vanderaerden had to do was maintain his trajectory over the Bosberg and the Flierendries, a nasty sting-in-the-tail climb in Ninove which made its only ever appearance in the Ronde that year. Anderson was, in his own words, 'pissed off'. As was Sean Kelly, who trailed in six minutes down. 'The race was grim, but not as grim as reaching the finish to discover that Vanderaerden had won,' he wrote in *Hunger*.

It was only seven years since Merckx had retired, and the Belgian public thought they'd found his successor. But Vanderaerden never won Flanders again, though he rode it another eight times, and finished third in 1987 a week before winning Paris–Roubaix. He won over a hundred races as a professional, but the second half of his career never lived up to the early promise. 'Everybody was waiting for a new champion who could win every race,' Vanderaerden told me. 'I could win a lot, but not every race. They were expecting [too much] of me, and I couldn't handle the pressure. If I rode two weeks without winning, the press already started asking how it was possible I wasn't winning any more.'

Vanderaerden also denied being a *Flandrien*. 'I don't think so,' he said. 'Everybody called me a *Flandrien*,' he continued. 'But I'm just a good Belgian cyclist, I think.'

Steengat is an almost-straight cobbled track out of the village of Melden, which sits on the south bank of the Schelde about four kilometres south-west of Oudenaarde. From the village, Steengat starts with a shallow rise then steepens past the last

houses, a vague S-bend halfway up obscuring the top and forming a false summit, though the shape of the hill means it's easy
to infer where the actual summit is. Steengat translates as the
'stone hole' and is the name of the road that the Ronde calls the
Koppenberg. The Koppenberg is really the name of the eastern
end of a ridge-cum-hill with a flat top (the western end is the
Rotelenberg), and then, just to confuse things, over the top of
the climb Steengat turns into a road called Koppenberg. This
road continues down the western side of the hill, then splits into
three branches, all called Koppenberg, which peter out towards
the edge of Oudenaarde.

I parked at the bottom and walked past the houses up the
drag and past the sign indicating the edge of Melden village.
Another sign warns of a 2.5-tonne weight limit and advises that
only local traffic should use the road. The cobbles were fine, the
gradient was shallow and the open fields on either side gave this
part of the climb a sense of space. But up ahead, a line of tall
trees with overhanging branches and a similar line of smaller
trees opposite them turned Steengat into a tunnel, whose sense
of claustrophobia was made worse as the road sunk between
two steep banks.

The state of the cobbles deteriorated here as the gradient
steepened and soil, leaves and organic detritus blurred the
line between countryside and road. Ivy covered the ground
and wound itself around the beeches and silver birches, while
bare roots poked through the banks where the earth had been
washed away. It was chilly, dark and dank through these few
dozen metres of road, with moss growing on the cobbles and
grass poking up between some of the gaps. (The road faces
north-west so it is sheltered from direct sunlight almost all year
round and the road surface can be damp even when there has
been no rain for a while.)

Over the crux, and through the sunken part of the road, the

countryside opened out again and Steengat's gradient eased for a final curve to the plateau at the top, where a small cluster of houses and a building site with the shell of another large new building stood surrounded by muddy fields.

The Koppenberg is one of the Ronde's great set pieces. The television company who cover the race installs fixed cameras at four different points on the climb, in addition to the motorbike-mounted and helicopter cameras, and the producers tend to linger on the shots as riders go past, before showing a final panning shot and then switching to the next position. The Koppenberg, however, is rarely the pivotal climb in the race as it's too early. The riders don't love it (Bernard Hinault rode the race once and never came back, citing the Koppenberg as one of his reasons for staying away: 'I told the organisers that it wasn't a race but a kind of war game.') but there's a rubber-necker's thrill in watching the peloton negotiating a piece of road that so clearly isn't designed for cyclists, especially large groups of them. The organisers now at least keep the spectators away from the banked section, where a few used to spill onto the road and interfere with the race.

There's a house on the corner of the entrance to the Koppenberg in Melden, with a bright red door and a faded old sign across the front on which you can just make out the word 'bieren'. It's different from the other houses in this part of the village – taller and with steps leading up to the door. I got talking to the current owners, Ellen and Piet, who explained the link between themselves and the building's past and also its very small role in the Tour of Flanders.

When the Ronde is described as a day that transcends everyday life and brings the nation together, buildings like this are the evidence that it's more than a cliché. It dates from the 1800s and it used to be a barbershop and a brewery. After that it was a café known as the Golden Scissors and then the Café Meurez, which closed in 1985. For 28 years it was used as a storage facility and was rotting into a ruin with trees growing inside and out before Ellen and Piet, a social worker and graphic designer, took it on as a doer-upper a few years ago. Ellen's grandparents had run the café, so there was a family connection.

Ellen told me that the first television in Melden was installed here in 1959 and so, even before Steengat became part of the Ronde's folklore, the people would congregate at the café to watch the race. Then, when the race started passing regularly, its high upper floor gave everybody a good view of the riders. The building was a focal point for the community for the rest of the year as well: marriages were celebrated here; rumour has it there were boxing fights held here many years ago; and when the Schelde flooded, people brought their furniture here, to store on higher ground. Ellen and Piet tried to ignore the Ronde, but now they have an open house on the day of the race for 80 or more people to come and watch the race on a big screen, with a sweepstake and a kitty for the drinks. 'The Ronde van Vlaanderen is folklore,' Ellen said. 'Everyone comes, and there is tension in the air. I don't follow sports but I do get nervous for the race.'

She laughed, and added: 'When the race comes, it takes 30 seconds and the riders have all passed.'

Walter Godefroot, the winner of the Tour of Flanders in 1968 and 1978, originally brought the Koppenberg to the attention of the organisers. There's an apocryphal story that he had been aware of the climb for years but wanted to keep it a secret until he retired in order to avoid having to race over it. Yet the Koppenberg first appeared in the 1976 Ronde, three years before he stopped his career, shoehorned in between the New Kruisberg and the Taaienberg. It gained instant notoriety when Eddy Merckx, the double Ronde winner and defending champion, bounced off Italian champion Francesco Moser on the climb and toppled to the side, putting his right foot down. He tried to use his left to get the bike going again but the gradient was too much, so the greatest cyclist in history was forced to hobble alongside his bike, pushing it up before remounting. This turned out to be important. The only five riders to crest the climb on their bikes – Walter Planckaert, Moser, Marc Demeyer, Roger De Vlaeminck and Freddy Maertens – were never caught and finished first to fifth.

A year later, Merckx had put himself ahead of the race before the Koppenberg by attacking on the first climb, the Oude Kwaremont. He was pursued by two Flemish riders, Maertens and De Vlaeminck. This was an act of intergenerational warfare as well as an expression of Belgian geopolitics. Maertens, the reigning world champion, was an up-and-coming rival to Merckx, seven years younger and coming into his prime just as Merckx was leaving his behind. Maertens was a less complete rider than Merckx, and Geoffrey Nicholson wrote of him that he climbed 'as though he were pushing a barrel', but he was a prolific sprinter, Classics rider and short-distance time-triallist, who had won over 30 races the previous year and equalled Merckx and the pre-war rider Charles Pélissier in winning eight stages in a single Tour de France. De Vlaeminck was part of the same generation as Merckx, but he actively played his Flemish identity against that of the Brussels-born rider, and a chippy, hyperactive personality against the diffident superiority complex projected by his rival. (After retirement, De Vlaeminck never stopped sniping, providing a running commentary on the careers of subsequent Belgian cyclists, like Tom Boonen.)

Maertens – sandy-haired and with a torso straight out of a chest-expander advert, and born right up in the corner of West Flanders in Nieuwpoort on the coast between De Panne and Ostend – was an oddball. He had a friendly face, a boxer's nose, an addictive personality and the ability to wind up Merckx. Specifically, they fell out because Merckx alleged that Maertens hadn't helped him at the 1973 world championships road race, in an incident described in great detail in Maertens's autobiography *Fall from Grace*. The book is full of italics conveying outrage or sarcasm or allowing the reader to feel that the fourth wall has been broken and that they are party to the *true* meaning behind the surface meaning of the words.

Maertens states that the 1973 Worlds, which took place in Barcelona, were '*the most sordid machination ever practised on me*' (his italics). Merckx asked Maertens to lead him out when the two were away close to the finish with Felice Gimondi and Luis Ocaña, then proceeded not to sprint as Felice Gimondi sat in and burst past to win. Maertens was bitter at having passed up his own chance of victory, feeling that Merckx preferred Gimondi to win than his own team-mate, though publicly Merckx blamed Maertens. However, if it hadn't been this particular incident, it would have been something else – Maertens was a threat to Merckx and Belgium was too small to accommodate them both without friction.

Maertens won ten races in 1978, including Omloop Het Volk and E3, then his career stalled. There were allegations of doping, rumours of alcohol problems and a tax bill that he finally paid off in 2011.

De Vlaeminck was a native of East Flanders, born in Eeklo, in the sandy and infertile land of the Meetjesland between Ghent and Bruges. His parents owned a merry-go-round and travelled from one *kermis*, or town fair, to the next, and his nickname was 'The Gypsy'. It's ironic that his family had travelling and rootlessness in their blood, while he has lived within ten kilometres of Eeklo his whole life, training on flat roads running by hop fields on broad plains.

He had the rare distinction of winning his first ever race as a professional, the 1969 Omloop Het Volk, and was one of three riders who won all five of cycling's Monuments – the biggest one-day races in the world: Milan–San Remo, Flanders, Paris–Roubaix, Liège–Bastogne–Liège and the Tour of Lombardy. The other two were Rik Van Looy, his boyhood hero, and Merckx, but De Vlaeminck lacked the all-round ability of the latter – he wasn't much interested in Grand Tours or stage races, save for a six-year winning streak in Tirreno–Adriatico. Though De Vlaeminck was proudly Flandrian, defined himself against Merckx and said that his first memory of cycling was seeing pictures of Briek Schotte fighting in races against another hero of Flemish cycling, Rik Van Steenbergen, he didn't see himself in the same tradition of *Flandriens*.

So as Merckx threw down the gauntlet in the 1977 Tour of Flanders, De Vlaeminck and Maertens chased. Maertens had been confident of winning – he'd even told his wife to bring his best suit to the finish so he could wear it to his victory celebration. De Vlaeminck had suffered bad luck with a puncture but had chased back on.

Maertens had planned to have a bike change on the Koppenberg so he could have a lower gear for the steep climb. However, at a meeting of the teams' managers the day before, the race jury had specifically banned changing bikes at the bottom of the climb because of the potential for chaos.

Unfortunately for Maertens, his manager was Lomme Driessens, a mendacious blowhard whose lack of self-awareness was in diametric opposition to his capacity for self-promotion and whose nickname was 'Lomme the liar'. Driessens hadn't bothered with the meeting, and the bike change went ahead as planned, though they concocted some cock-and-bull story about a mechanical problem, which nobody believed.

The Flemish pair caught then dropped Merckx. But during the race Jos Fabri – a UCI commissaire and the chairman of the national sport committee of the Belgian Cycling Federation, who had often clashed with Maertens – was driven up to the rider and he informed him that he was out of the race. But curiously, he wasn't forced to stop riding.

The damage had been done as far as winning the race was concerned, but Driessens and Maertens came up with a way to influence the outcome and at least come away with something. Maertens would ride on the front, pacing De Vlaeminck to the finish, and the latter has never denied that money changed hands, though if you ask Maertens about it, he'll tell you that the East Flandrian welshed on the deal by underpaying the allegedly agreed 300,000 francs by half. At the finish, Maertens was too exhausted to sprint and crossed the line second before being almost immediately disqualified, while De Vlaeminck was roundly booed. Shortly afterwards, it was revealed that Maertens had supplied a positive doping test, along with third-placed Walter Planckaert, and Maertens was disqualified for the second time.

In the Centrum Ronde Van Vlaanderen there's a row of cobblestones, each engraved with the name of a winner of the race along with the year they won it. Sitting on Roger De Vlaeminck's 1977 cobblestone, there's a smaller one, with 'Freddy Maertens, moral victor' engraved on it.

Chavanel and Clarke have got their gap back. Gilbert's surge on the Paterberg was neither an effort to chase them down, nor did he have any intention of forcing the issue after the top. The crash on the descent beforehand had left the peloton in two pieces, with all the strongest, save for Devolder and Nuyens, at the front. The strongest riders duly rode hard up the Paterberg, so the first group of 50 was strung out, but it's too early to be riding hard on the front on the flat. So now Gilbert – and therefore every other one of the riders who followed him – sit up over the top of the Paterberg, lose their momentum, and Chavanel and Clarke have a stay of execution.

The descent of the Paterberg is a narrow and fast one back down to the Schelde valley, on to Driesstraat, a flat road which runs parallel to the portion of the N8 that links Kluisbergen and Oudenaarde. There's a house on the left on Driesstraat which the television cameras try to pick out most years, where the owners have had the images of several famous cyclists, including Boonen, Van Petegem, Merckx and Lance Armstrong painted on one wall of their building.

The peloton is still in three pieces behind the three leaders and their two pursuers. Most of the favourites are in a line of 38 riders about 150 metres behind Chavanel and Clarke. Then there's another 300 metres to a larger group of 90 or so, including Devolder and Nuyens. After that, a group of 15 are chasing close behind.

The group of favourites is moving fast. There are little attacks keeping the momentum going – Hincapie, Thomas, Farrar, Cooke and Rabobank's Tom Leezer ride off the front but they are chased, and it's Quick Step's Steegmans who again brings them to heel, defending Chavanel's escape. Behind, Devolder has his head down and is single-handedly working to reduce the gap, chasing at the front of the second main group, though this is effectively going to ensure he cannot win. If he rides hard, he'll catch the leaders, be too tired to follow the real moves when they happen and definitely lose the race. If he doesn't ride hard, then there are two possibilities: either somebody else rides and he will be back at the front with fresh legs and therefore a chance, however small, of winning the race, or nobody rides and he definitely loses the race. The only tactically sound decision is to not ride and to hope somebody else chases. This is the only course of action that doesn't lead to assured defeat. However, as Devolder's former and future manager Dirk Demol says of him, 'When Stijn has something in mind he doesn't look back.'

Nuyens, on the other hand, has faced exactly the same choice and is in the happy situation that somebody else – Devolder – *is* chasing the leaders down. His race is still hanging by a thread but he can see a possible escape route, even though Devolder thinks that Nuyens has given up. Inch by inch, Devolder pulls his passengers back into the race.

Just before the Koppenberg, Chavanel and Clarke catch the three leaders, to make a group of five, barely 100 metres ahead of the next group. When the leaders turn a corner and look back diagonally across the field by the road they can see the next group still breathing down their necks. Andreas Klier from Garmin attacks the favourites' group and jumps into the space behind the leading five riders to give himself the smallest of head starts – about 50 metres – on the Koppenberg.

Chavanel and Clarke drop their companions almost immediately on the climb. Behind, with the favourites' group smaller than expected, there is less of a fight to be at the front but Gilbert leads them up, followed by Boonen, just as happened on the Paterberg. Behind, Devolder has closed the gap to about 100 metres.

Gilbert is riding so strongly that as he passes Klier, towards the top of the steepest section, he's created a ten-metre gap to Boonen. It's not a race-winning advantage but the Walloon rider is looking formidably strong. Eleven more riders follow – Boonen, Flecha, Cooke, Cancellara, Van Avermaet, Hushovd, Voeckler, Pozzato, Leukemans, Steegmans and Ballan – before a more significant gap to Hincapie and Langeveld, who are at the front of the remnants of the lead group.

These aren't necessarily the 12 strongest riders, but they are the 12 riders who have combined a good position at the bottom of the Koppenberg with being extremely strong. Geraint Thomas, for instance, is not among them – he started the Koppenberg towards the back of the group and got trapped in the traffic on the narrowest part of the climb then overtook rider after rider once the blockage had eased, but it's not been enough to put him right at the front, even though he looks like he has the physical capacity to be there. Meanwhile, Klier is probably not – according to his own estimate and that of his manager Jonathan Vaughters – in the top 40 or 50 strongest riders in the race, yet with one well-timed move a few minutes before the Koppenberg, he has put himself in the favourites' group.

Gilbert, however, currently does look like he's the strongest rider. On both the Paterberg and Koppenberg, he's ridden at the front and put a couple of bike lengths into Boonen, who has invariably been second. What the cycling world does not yet know is that he's about to emerge as the most powerful uphill sprinter in the world – he'll win all three of the Ardennes Classics, Amstel Gold, La Flèche Wallonne and Liège–Bastogne–Liège later in the month.

It's relatively uncommon for Walloon riders to prosper in the cobbled Classics, although this is partly a function of cycling being a lot less popular in the French-speaking part of Belgium. There are fewer riders, so the statistically logical consequence is fewer riders doing well on the cobbles – Criquielion's 1987 Ronde victory was a rare one by a Walloon, and even he lived right on the language border. Gilbert, however, is a two-time winner of Omloop Het Volk, the Tour of Lombardy and Paris–Tours, and he's already won Amstel Gold once as well. Het Volk is a cobbled race, Lombardy a mountainous Classic, Paris–Tours a flat Classic and Amstel Gold a hilly Classic, so he has the ability to shine on almost any terrain. He's even twice been voted 'Flandrian of the year', an award presented to the best Belgian cyclist of the season, by *Het Nieuwsblad* before 2011.

Gilbert started his career with the French Française des Jeux team, whose manager Marc Madiot – an irascible and cantankerous traditionalist with a reputation for spotting young talent – saw him at the amateur Côte Picarde race and signed him as a 20-year-old for the 2003 season. Gilbert had wanted to be a Classics rider but he went to France to avoid the pressure of the Belgian media.

He spent six years with Française des Jeux then moved to Silence–Lotto in 2009. His manager at Lotto is Marc Sergeant, a sad-eyed Flamand who'd also done some work with the Belgian national junior squad and had been watching Gilbert for some years before he turned professional. Sergeant had also had a front-row seat in Criquielion's 1987 victory.

Coming to the Bosberg that year, a ten-rider lead group was three minutes clear. The good and bad news was that there were three extremely fast finishers in the group: Sean Kelly, Eric Vanderaerden and Adri van der Poel. Sergeant, riding in the colours of the Belgian national champion, knew he couldn't beat these three riders in a sprint, but he also knew that an attacker might have a chance because none of the three would want to do the chasing. He grew up in Affligem, not far north of Geraardsbergen, and trained almost every day on the roads used by the race. He resolved to attack at the left-hand turn with five kilometres to go. Too late: Criquielion had decided to make his own attack at the top of the Bosberg. 'After the cobbles it goes a little bit up, and then there is a slight downhill,' Sergeant says of that race. 'The downhill is not much, but Criquielion came from behind and passed us. He was smart – he had fitted a 12-tooth gear for the first time and I had a 13. He lived maybe three kilometres from the Bosberg, and he knew there was a three-quarters tailwind to the finish. Nobody reacted. Then I reacted, and Allan Peiper was on my wheel. I swung off, the momentum stopped, and I knew it was finished.'

None of the sprinters chased. Vanderaerden refused to lead

Kelly to the finish. Kelly was good friends with Criquielion and preferred him to win than anybody else, if he couldn't. Sergeant was left with fifth place, which would be one of eight career top tens in the race.

Sergeant doesn't exactly know what it takes to win Flanders, but he knows he didn't have it. He also thinks Gilbert does have it but is compromised every year by his focus on the Ardennes Classics three weeks down the line. 'There was always someone better than me. I said I wasn't good enough, and people said, "But maybe you can win," but I always replied no, there's something missing. I don't know what it was, but there was always one guy stronger than me.'

In 1995, the year after he retired (and achieved his final top ten in the Ronde – eighth), Sergeant took an offer to follow the race on a motorcycle. 'Johan Museeuw went solo for the last 30 kilometres, from Tenbosse. I was behind him on the motorcycle. I saw something in him which I was not able to do. Sometimes you have to admit you are not good enough.'

Sergeant thinks Gilbert had been extremely smart in leaving Belgium behind – he would see his results occasionally in the press but the stories were always low-key, keeping the pressure off him. One day in 2008, Gilbert approached Sergeant and said, 'Okay, Marc, I am ready. I don't think I have the support to win a Classic, so if you want me I'm ready to come.'

A story had floated around that Gilbert had had to persuade the Lotto management to select him for the Tour of Flanders in his first season there, but Sergeant always laughs at stories like this. Gilbert came third, runner-up in the bunch sprint to Heinrich Haussler, and a minute behind winner Devolder. As a rider, Gilbert is aggressive and punchy, which are both assets in the Ronde. He's also hot-headed in a race, which is an asset or a drawback depending on how lucky he is or how well he can time his efforts.

The 21-minute phase of the race from the bottom of the Oude Kwaremont to the top of the Koppenberg has broken the peloton up, and there are still 75 kilometres to go. At the summit, Chavanel and Clarke are clear. They are followed by Turgot, Hammond, Docker and Klier, who are mixed in with the front runners to make a group of 15. Then another 18, including Thomas and Hincapie. Another nine. And then, 30 seconds behind Gilbert, Devolder leads Nuyens and a couple of Ag2r riders.

The route after the descent of the Koppenberg follows narrow twisting roads through extremely open, cultivated farmland, so most of the groups at or near the front can see each other across the fields. They have a couple of kilometres of this terrain before joining the N60, which joins Oudenaarde and Ronse. (If they carried on south they'd reach the top of the New Kruisberg, where the race passed three-quarters of an hour ago.)

Behind Chavanel and Clarke, the group has swelled to 18, which consists of 13 of the strongest individuals, plus four (Turgot, Hammond, Docker and Klier) who got themselves off the front before the Koppenberg. More importantly, there are three Garmin riders, two Quick Step riders, two BMC riders and two Sky riders. If these teams were willing to work, they could keep this group clear of the rest of the field, especially as Quick Step also have a rider off the front in Chavanel. But they have to balance that against pulling Gilbert and Cancellara to a position from which they could attack, so the group dithers. Realistically, only a handful of them would be riding on the front, and that probably wouldn't be enough to keep them away.

As this group turns on to the N60, there's a long, wide straight section of dual carriageway. The next two groups have merged, forming a 40-rider group who are bearing down on the group of 18, and behind them another group of 20, and then another. These groups can't possibly stay apart – the gravity pulling them together is too strong. And finally back in the safety of the re-established peloton, which is not much smaller than it was before, is Nick Nuyens.

Nuyens has his first moment of calm for well over an hour. He checks the damage, and it's not too significant. Bad luck, followed by good luck, and his race has evened itself out. Though it's been stressful, he hasn't had to make much of the effort of chasing himself, though he's used up a couple of team-mates. He's still in the race.

CHAPTER 8

Steenbeekdries

I parked on a narrow band of cobbles in front of a small cottage in Aarsele on the outskirts of Tielt. Tielt is right in the centre of the triangle formed by the towns of Bruges, Ghent and Kortrijk, north of the Flemish Ardennes; it's also just next door to Kanegem, birthplace of Briek Schotte. The cottage had a steep roof with orange tiles – and it sat between two larger houses on a quite busy main road, on which lorries rattled past. The front garden was neatly kept, with a circular pond and a lawn, and shrubs and bushes along the borders. It looked homely.

I'd come to the house to find the oldest living winner of the Ronde. 'You've got to talk to Roger Decock,' Guy Fransen, *Het Nieuwsblad*'s sports editor, had told me. I got his number, and we worked out that we'd be communicating in French, which Decock speaks fluently with a thick Flemish accent and occasional Belgian quirks in vocabulary such as saying 'septante' for 'seventy' instead of 'soixante-dix'.

Decock greeted me with a firm handshake as I remarked that he seemed in good form. 'I think so,' he said. 'I look okay on the outside.'

There must have been something in the water in 1952,

because of the five men who won the Monuments that year, two are still alive, in their late eighties: Giuseppe Minardi, born in 1928 and winner of the Tour of Lombardy, and Decock, who was born in 1927. Ferdi Kübler, born in 1919 and winner of Liège–Bastogne–Liège that year, passed away while I was writing this book, so Decock and Minardi are the two oldest Monuments winners left. Flanders was Decock's biggest win, although he also won Paris–Nice in 1951 and the Championship of Flanders the same year.

We were going to talk about his career, but first he wanted to show me a couple of things. 'There's the trophy for the Ronde van Vlaanderen,' he said.

Sitting on the kitchen worktop – among stacks of family photographs, a loudly-ticking carriage clock of the kind that your grandparents had, and an empty beer glass with the Kwaremont logo – was a large gold-coloured cup with two ornate handles and, sitting atop the lid, a racing cyclist cast in the same metal as the cup. The words, 'Roger Decock, Winnaar, Ronde van Vlaanderen 1952, Beroeps renners [professional riders]' were engraved on a metal plate joined to the marble base.

He pointed to a photograph. 'That's me in a race in Wetteren. The rider behind is Briek Schotte,' he said. The clock pinged the quarter-hour. He added, 'Do you want to see my other trophies?'

Decock was a promising youth footballer who helped make ends meet during the Second World War by smuggling black-market goods, primarily cigarettes, between his home in Izegem and Menin on the French border. He also worked as a delivery boy, cycling 50 kilometres to pick up consignments of wheat, 50 kilos at a time, then cycling another 50 kilometres back to deliver them to the bakery. 'I got 700 or 800 francs a delivery,' he said.

He started to race in 1943, though there weren't many events on during the war – he rode only 15 in his first year. He became an Independent in the late 1940s, turned professional for the Arliguie–Hutchinson team in September 1949, then signed for Alcyon–Dunlop in 1950. The following season he signed for Bertin–Wolber, where he had his greatest success: as well as his Paris–Nice and Championships of Flanders wins, he was fourth in Ghent–Wevelgem and 17th overall in the Tour de France, with two second places on stages. He would have finished higher up in the Tour, but when the Dutch rider Wim van Est crashed in a mountain stage, flew off the road and tumbled into a ravine, Decock was the only rider who had seen him. He stopped and waited before Van Est was rescued, using inner tubes that had been tied together, and slipped down the GC. He thinks that without that time loss, he could have finished on the final podium. In the year of his Flanders win, 1952, he also got top 12s in Liège–Bastogne–Liège, La Flèche Wallonne and Paris–Roubaix. He was a good time-triallist and a good sprinter, though his best asset was his racing brain. A book was written about him a few years ago, called *Sluw en Slim*, which means 'cunning and clever'.

After we'd looked at his Championship of Flanders trophy and the plaque he was presented for winning Paris–Nice (known as Paris–Côte d'Azur in those days), Decock showed me through picture albums of his racing days. They contained pages and pages of black and white photographs under tissue-thin protective films, not just the official race shots, but snaps of him and his contemporaries at work and play. There were shots of the Tour of Morocco, where the stages started at 5 a.m. in order to avoid the heat of the day, and one of a cyclists' football match. He points out himself, Schotte again, André Declerck, who was fourth in Paris–Roubaix in 1951 and Marcel Kint, who won the World Championships in 1938 and Paris–Roubaix in 1943.

Decock's Flanders win came in poor weather – much like the previous year's race, which was the last of the three won by Fiorenzo Magni. With the Italian not coming to defend his crown in 1952, the race was open. 'It was 275 kilometres, and 275 riders,' Decock said. 'We passed Maldegem, Ostend, Torhout, Berchem and the Kwaremont, and I was second over the top. Then Ronse, the Kruisberg, Edelareberg and the Muur in Grammont [Geraardsbergen].'

The future triple Tour de France champion Louison Bobet, who would also go on to win the Tour of Flanders in 1955, attacked on the Muur and went away alone. 'It was still raining and windy and we were catching Bobet, then overtook him,' said Decock. 'With five kilometres to the finish in Wetteren, there were five of us. Loretto Petrucci, who won Milan–San Remo two times, including that year – he was riding in the same team as Coppi. There was Briek Schotte, Wim van Est and Attilio Redolfi. I stayed in Petrucci's wheel into Wetteren. There was very hard pavé there, it climbed up to the station and we dropped Van Est and Redolfi. They had put the finish 200 metres further on than previous years. As we climbed, Briek attacked and took one or two lengths. I attacked immediately on the left and I won by ten or 15 metres.'

Before meeting Decock, I'd found a photograph of him on the internet, the original of which was hanging on the wall in his front room, a sepia image of a young man with Brylcreemed hair and a gap-toothed smile. Pinkish flesh tones had been added by a retoucher, along with red for his lips and blue for his eyes, with the champion's jersey, reading 'Kampioen van Vlaanderen 1951' painted up in bright yellow. He looked young and fresh-faced.

As we sat in his kitchen, I looked from the 1950s images of a young man of obvious physical strength and then at the 88-year-old man whose gnarled hands were turning the pages of his photograph albums. Then I looked at the Tour of Flanders winner's trophy, which was as shiny and gleaming as the day it was presented. I'd been wondering to what extent new and old Flanders were separate things, but the old man who stood before me in a small house in Aarsele, showing me the winner's trophy from over 60 years ago and sharing his memories of bygone races, old friends and colourful memories, was evidence that they are one and the same, even if most things, sooner or later, change.

In 2010 I rode the Tour of Flanders sportive, which takes place the day before the race, for the third or fourth time. It's one of the most democratic and inclusive events I've ever experienced, with all humanity represented on two wheels on the roads of Flanders: normal people can ride a 30-kilometre route, head-bangers, overachievers and A-type personalities can ride the full 270 kilometres, and people who are somewhere in between can ride 70 kilometres or 140 kilometres, all based on the route of the race. I'd gone for the 140 – all the interesting bits, basically.

I'd started out with some colleagues but we'd temporarily lost each other along the way, so I was on my own for a while, albeit with 30,000 others sharing the road. I'd just come off the Koppenberg (like Merckx, I'd had to put my foot down on the climb; unlike Merckx, I'd been toppled into by a portly gentleman wearing mismatched kit), and had turned south on to the N60, into the teeth of a very strong cross-headwind coming from the south-west. A rider dressed in full Quick Step kit, with a team replica bike came past me. Though the term is borrowed from football, cycling snobs call people like this FKWs. Full-kit wankers.

The rider had a suspiciously smooth pedal stroke for an FKW, and seemed to be making absolutely no effort whatsoever despite going quite fast into the headwind. Then I saw the small

sticker on the top tube of his bike: Maes. This was no wanker –
it was Nikolas Maes, a fourth-year professional who'd signed for
Quick Step at the start of the year.

I sat behind him, taking full advantage of the draft he was
offering. It wasn't hard to keep up – the wind was blowing in
his face, plus he wasn't trying.

Then we turned left onto Mariaborrestraat, which starts with
about 50 metres of tarmac, followed by a stretch of cobbles sloping slightly downhill for two or three hundred metres before
it flattens out. I stayed behind Maes and we accelerated on the
tarmac, then clattered onto the cobbles. Or rather, I clattered
onto the cobbles; he floated over them ahead of me, still looking
like he wasn't trying. There was a facility to his progress over
the cobbles that was mesmerising. Within a couple of hundred
metres, he'd completely disappeared. I didn't catch up with him
again until a Quick Step team training camp in Calp, Spain,
in early 2016.

Baden Cooke told me that during Classics season every year,
he moved to Belgium for several weeks. When he was starting
out as a pro, he'd got talking to an older rider, Tristan Hoffman,
who would later end up being his directeur sportif at Saxo
Bank. Hoffman told him the biggest mistake he'd made was not
learning the roads of the Classics properly. So for two months
every year Cooke lived in Belgium, and in between races, he
rode around training, learning the roads. 'I wouldn't just learn
about the climbs, I'd learn the run-ins as well, and at night I
would watch videos of past races,' he said. 'It was like study for
me – homework. I watched them over and over and over again.'

Even so, he feels like he never cracked it, but at least learned
enough to handle the important parts of the Ronde. 'Ninety
per cent of the time I still didn't know where I was,' he said.
'But then we would pass a certain pub or house or picket fence,
and I'd pick up where I was. For an Aussie, I had a pretty good

understanding. It's almost impossible to know where you are in those races unless you're Peter Van Petegem. I tried and it gave me an advantage. Not over the Belgians, but over the others.' (Cooke was being modest – the second time he ever raced on the cobbles, in the 2002 Dwars door Vlaanderen, he won. Then again, having been on the same Mercury team as Van Petegem, who grew up in the region, he knew what to do: 'I'd never been up the Kwaremont in my life. I didn't know much, but I knew to follow Peter. I followed him for the entire day, until I nobbed off with a [kilometre] to go.')

Nikolas Maes, on the other hand, is *Vlaamse Ardennen* born and bred. He grew up just south of Kluisbergen, at the foot of the Kluisberg, and about two kilometres from the bottom of the Oude Kwaremont. He still trains three or four times a week on roads used in the Ronde and says that he knows the roads by heart. His parents now live in a house at the bottom of the Koppenberg and before he left the Quick Step team for Lotto Soudal in 2017, every year they hosted a get-together for Maes and his team-mates, including Tom Boonen and Stijn Vandenbergh (also local – he grew up in Volkegem, just outside Oudenaarde, and rode up and down the Volkegemberg on his way to and from school every day), for Maes to guide them on a long ride around the hills. 'Small roads, up, down, five hours, 150 [kilometres] with 2,150 metres of climbing. That's a lot for the *Vlaamse Ardennen* – if each hill is 100 metres, that's 21 hills,' Maes told me.

In Calp, I told Maes how easily he'd dropped me on the cobbles. There's a technique to riding them which involves relaxing the grip on the handlebars enough to allow the bike to find its own way forward, but holding them tight enough that the wheel doesn't get knocked sideways. There's a delicate balance involving maintaining a level of tension and being in complete control, though most of the cobbles come on uphills, which requires a different technique again. Lotto's directeur sportif Marc Sergeant told me, 'Cobbles on hills make you slip a bit so you lose energy more than on normal roads. Riders like Cancellara, Boonen and Peter Sagan handle that very well.' But good climbing technique on cobbles is only part of the story. 'The race is not about the hills,' said Maes. 'The hills are not the toughest places in the race. The toughest places are going into the hill, with everybody fighting for their lives to get in the front. And if you count the 15 or 16 hills, and all the cobbles in between, and the places you have to go *à bloc*, it's 30 times. So you have to fight for the hill, then do the effort of riding the hill, then if you lose any distance you have to do another effort afterwards. That's three efforts for each hill – multiply that by 30 and you have about 100 efforts. So you have to know every corner and every stone. You have to know when, and more importantly how, you have to be on the front. You have to do it economically.'

Maes's job in the Ronde so far has generally been to police the breaks for the first 200 kilometres. Anything he can do after that is helpful, but going into the last two hours he's generally finished. 'The last two years I was responsible for the escapees, and that means my race starts from kilometre zero. The leaders are in the back, chatting with each other, but I'm already on the max. We have to watch who goes away, and if they can stay away we have to chase them. If I go *à bloc* from kilometre zero, normally my boiling point is around 220 or 230 kilometres. Four of the eight guys in a team have to be sacrificed in the first and middle part of the race. You can't win a race with eight leaders. You need guys like me to win a race like the Ronde van Vlaanderen.'

Mariaborrestraat, where the expanding gap between Nikolas Maes's back wheel and my front one was a visual metaphor for the gulf between ordinary cyclists and professionals in terms of riding skills, came after the ninth of 18 *hellingen* in the 2011 race. It was a kind of halfway point for 2011, though for that edition it came at almost three-quarters of the actual distance.

The hills of the Ronde are traditionally stacked into the last 100 kilometres of the race, although as with all the Ronde's traditions, this is a relatively recent development. First of all the climbs weren't included at all, then they were situated far from the finish, which until the 1970s was in or around Ghent. It's only since the finish was moved to Meerbeke, and subsequently Oudenaarde, that they've become the focal point of the race.

The 18 *hellingen* of 2011 were not quite a record. In 2003 and 2015, there were 19 climbs; the organisers have not quite dared to make it a round 20 yet.

The number of climbs has crept up steadily over the years. The first two editions didn't feature the *Vlaamse Ardennen* at all, then the third edition, after the First World War, included the Tiegemberg – which is north of the Schelde between Oudenaarde and Kortrijk and therefore not technically in the Flemish Ardennes – and the (New) Kwaremont. For nine editions this was enough, then in 1928 they added the Kruisberg, in Ronse, and two years later the Edelareberg – now the main road climb out of Oudenaarde on the way to Brakel – to make four. For the 18 races after 1932 the Tiegemberg was taken out, so the race included three climbs: Kwaremont, Kruisberg and Edelareberg.

Things started getting more complicated after 1950, when five climbs were featured, for the first time: the Tiegemberg, Kwaremont, Kruisberg and Edelareberg, and then the new climb of the Muur in Geraardsbergen. Through the 1950s, many more climbs were introduced – the Kluisberg, Eikenberg and Valkenberg, for example – but the number tackled in the race stayed between four and five. In 1961 the route featured six climbs, and through the 1960s the total fluctuated between four and six. The *Vlaamse Ardennen* were beginning to become the most important aspect of the race.

The Bosberg appeared for the first time in 1970, as the number of climbs jumped to a record eight, and in 1976 the total nudged up to nine as the Koppenberg made its first appearance in the Ronde. Then, as the race bedded into its new finish in Meerbeke, the rate of increase accelerated: ten climbs in 1980, 11 climbs in 1981, 12 climbs in 1983 and 13 climbs in 1986.

By 1993 there were 16 climbs in the race, and the next increase was the record 19 in 2003, since when the total has hit a plateau and ranged between 15 and 19.

None of the climbs is that difficult taken on its own. Most are short – the Kwaremont and the Muur van Geraardsbergen (including the climb through the town below the Muur) are comparatively long, but a fresh rider can punch their way over any of the others. It's the repetition which wears the peloton down, and whichever climbs come 15th, 16th and 17th will be decisive. There are certain combinations which the organisers have relied on for years at a time – the Oude Kwaremont–Paterberg–Koppenberg trio was used in 1986 and 1987, the first years the Paterberg was used, then after the Koppenberg's reintroduction in 2002, that trio has appeared in that order every year except 2007, when the Koppenberg was withdrawn. They also like to follow that trio with the Mariaborrestraat cobbles, which lead directly on to the Steenbeekdries climb and – a rare thing in the race – the cobbled descent of the Stationsberg, and then just a couple of kilometres later, the Taaienberg. And it just so happens the Eikenberg is another few kilometres to the north of the Taaienberg.

There are two big concentrations of Ronde climbs in the Flemish Ardennes. The first is in the south-west corner between Ronse and Oudenaarde – the Kruisberg, Kwaremont,

Paterberg and Koppenberg, for example. Then to the south-east of Oudenaarde there's another dense concentration including the Eikenberg, Varent and Wolvenberg. On the Meerbeke route, the race tackled the south-west climbs first, then the ones near Oudenaarde, then went to Geraardsbergen via a set of ascents including the Leberg, Valkenberg or Berendries, and Tenbossestraat in Brakel. (The Molenberg, another fixture, is a little out on a limb directly east of Oudenaarde.) Now that the finish is in Oudenaarde, the climbs in the south-west corner are integral parts of the circuits that make up the second half of the race.

The Ronde favours all these climbs partly out of necessity – there aren't that many cobbled climbs to choose from – and partly out of tradition. But there are dozens of unexplored alternatives which may never appear in the race but offer tantalising possibilities. For instance, there's a parallel climb to the Molenberg, the Konkelstraat, that curves up on an extremely narrow road through a steep forest. Or there's a cut-through I found when looking at the route between the Oude Kwaremont and Paterberg. On the descent from the ridge to the bottom of the Paterberg, there's a left turn with a steep cobbled descent called Watermolenstraat, which is followed by an extended set of flat cobbles. If you continue on this road, you'll end up back in Kwaremont village. Watermolenstraat is also known as the Kalkhoveberg, which has never appeared in the Tour of Flanders but has been on the route of Dwars door Vlaanderen. According to my official *Vlaamse Ardennen* map from the Centrum Ronde van Vlaanderen, the Kalkhoveberg has the steepest average gradient of any of the listed climbs. At 13.5 per cent, it's even steeper than the Paterberg, though it's short at only 250 metres.

The race is still finding new climbs, though at a slower rate than during the 1970s and 1980s, when new ascents were introduced almost every year. Since 2004, only three new climbs have been used: the Eikenmolen, which popped up in 2007 as the last climb before the Muur; Kaperij, which made its debut in 2011; and the Kanarieberg which leads up from the main road east of Ronse in the direction of Oudenaarde and first appeared on the route in 2014.

However, even if the race runs out of new climbs, which would take years, it finds new ways to tackle the existing ones. Maes told me that the Paterberg was his favourite climb until they stuck it at the end of the race. 'I like the Côte de Trieu. I used to like the Paterberg. It fits my strengths – it's short, it's aggressive, steep, a little bit technical, you come down the hill before at a relaxing speed, so no power, and then, bang, you turn into it and you have to go immediately at your maximum,' he said. 'But the last few years I've been suffering on it like hell because it's late in the final, so I'm fucked up.'

Chavanel and Clarke ride through the feed zone, at the top of a long drag on the N60; their lead is 15 seconds. Clarke attacked 20 kilometres ago, and Chavanel 15, so they've gained approximately a second per kilometre, which is a poor return. They can squeeze out a small advantage here in that the bunch has just been consolidated from a collection of small groups into a big group of around 80, and the extra weight and uncertainty slows them down. The bunch is also slower through the feed zone. Chavanel and Clarke turn left on to Mariaborrestraat. With one hand, Clarke peels a banana and stuffs it into his mouth in one go, a reminder that professional cyclists are primarily well above average at three things: pedalling, sleeping and eating.

At the end of Mariaborrestraat, the riders will turn on to Steenbeekdries, which is *helling* nine. It's an open climb, starting in the shadow of a few houses on the junction with Mariaborrestraat, then dragging up at a not-too-steep angle across wide fields. The other side of Steenbeekdries is the

Stationsberg, a cobbled descent that rattles down to a 180-degree bend with a railway track bisecting its apex. Steenbeekdries is not steep or long, but it's not easy. It's open, there are no tents or buildings to shelter behind, and the prevailing wind comes from 90 degrees to the right.

The peloton is indecisive. The riders are bunching up, which means they've decelerated. Andreas Klier is always wary of this section of the race. The three previous climbs are so hard that somebody important will be off the back, either a leader or a strong domestique, and though the bunch often comes back together again here, it is nervous and fragile – it is down to almost a third of its original size so teams are already running out of domestiques.

Roger Hammond, still at the front, chases after Chavanel and Clarke but he's the only one, and he looks perplexed when he turns around and there is nobody on his wheel and a 20-metre gap back to the peloton. The gap to the front pair increases to 20 seconds. They've gained five seconds in a couple of hundred metres. This could be it.

Lars Bak, a Dane who rides for HTC, drifts off the front and rides past Hammond, who has lost interest. Then Geraint Thomas goes to the front as the climb bites, and the increase in pace immediately elongates the bunch into a line. Thomas has been at the front a lot – his job is to bring Flecha into position for the climbs, although Flecha doesn't need looking after. 'He goes where he wants,' says Thomas. 'He'll chop you up, sometimes even when you're on the same team.'

Quick Step's Steegmans, who has been at the front of the bunch a lot, follows Thomas. Steegmans is his team's policeman. He joined the Tjallingii break after the Paddestraat, he sat on the front of the bunch before the Kwaremont and then on the climb after Chavanel attacked, he chased an abortive break by Hincapie, Thomas and a few others on the flat road between the Paterberg and Koppenberg, and now he's sitting on Thomas's back wheel again. There is a well-known saying about there being two types of football player: there are those who are good at playing football and then there are those who are good at stopping others playing football. Steegmans is the cycling equivalent of the second category, in this race at least. His role is to be a fun-sucker, chasing down attacks, sitting on attacks and discouraging others from making attacks.

The race is poised, however. Behind Thomas and Steegmans are lurking Boonen, Flecha and Hushovd. The bunch rides in a long line down the Stationsberg, round the hairpin at the bottom, and through the streets of Etikhove. BMC's Greg Van Avermaet attacks, and this time it's Boonen himself who follows; while Steegmans lets them get on with it – it's not his job to chase down a move containing a team-mate. Flecha follows, then Rabobank's Langeveld, and there is a gap.

Who chases? Not Quick Step, BMC, Sky or Rabobank, because they are the four teams represented in this break. Leopard are severely depleted – having taken such responsibility for chasing Tjallingii's attack, the passage of the Kwaremont, Paterberg and Koppenberg, only two more of their riders apart from Cancellara have made it back into the peloton of 80 riders. Cancellara is already concerned at the lack of potential support. It's too dangerous a move not to chase, however, and it is the world champion himself, Thor Hushovd, who leads the bunch. The gap stabilises, and by the time Chavanel and Clarke are on the Taaienberg, just ahead, it starts to come back in.

Flanders is on first-name terms with its most famous cyclists. Mention 'Briek', or 'Eddy' in the context of cycling and everybody will automatically know to whom you are referring. It's also the case with Tom Boonen, although he's known by the affectionate 'Tommeke'. There was also Rik. And then another

Rik. Which meant that a differentiation had to be made. Rik Van Steenbergen, the double winner of the Tour of Flanders and three-time world road race champion in the late 1940s and 1950s achieved first-name recognition in Belgium. But when his namesake Rik Van Looy dominated the Classics in the late 1950s and 1960s, Van Steenbergen became 'Rik I' and Van Looy 'Rik II'.

They were the best Classics riders in the world during their careers. Van Steenbergen still holds the joint record for World Championship wins and while he professed not to love the poor weather and gritty racing of the Tour of Flanders, still won it at the age of 19 in 1944, then again two years later. Van Looy won all five Monuments. Van Looy's two Ronde wins came in 1959 and 1962 – as well as the Monuments, he won two World Championships and 37 stages across the three Grand Tours.

They both also maintained a complicated relationship with their sport and the public and with their own talent. So did Eddy Merckx, Roger De Vlacminck, Johan Museeuw and Tom Boonen – perhaps it comes with the territory.

The French cyclist Raphaël Géminiani described Van Steenbergen as a 'cold Fleming', only happy when he was cycling. It might be more accurately said that Van Steenbergen was only happy when he was paid. He'd gained the habit of grifting, ducking and diving to make ends meet during the war, and through his life put the acquisition of money first, anything else second. That included taking part in the Ronde – according to cycling historian Les Woodland, Van Steenbergen skipped his country's biggest race on occasions when he could make more money racing on the track.

Van Steenbergen had a long and successful career. Having won the Ronde at 19, he didn't retire until he was 43. Yet he still managed to muck it all up. The friends he made turned out to be more interested in his money than in him, and he filled his life with bad business deals, drinking and gambling, before marrying a woman called Doreen, from Wigan, who helped him stabilise his life. Woodland crushingly described what might have been rock bottom for Rik I, his participation in a 1969 soft porn movie called *Pandore*: 'He convincingly acted the role of a fat naked sailor in a Belgian sex film.'

Rik II was almost the best rider who ever lived, and it was his misfortune to have his career overlap with that of the best – Merckx. As a young rider he matched and then eclipsed Van Steenbergen, which led to uneasy relations between the two, though it could be said that Van Looy rarely needed an excuse to fall out with somebody. As Jan Janssen, the 1968 Tour de France winner, said of Van Looy, 'As a rider: none better. As a person: nothing.' Van Looy retired at the end of the summer of 1970, by which time Eddy Merckx had won his second Tour de France, unable to stand having Merckx do to him what he had done to Van Steenbergen. In retirement he made no secret of his glee that Merckx may have won a broader set of races, but that his younger rival never matched him in winning every race then designated as a Classic. Paris–Tours always eluded Merckx, while Van Looy won it twice. His Flanders wins, in 1959 and 1962, sandwiched the sole win by a British rider, Tom Simpson, who won a controversial two-man sprint against Nino Defilippis. The Italian cyclist stopped riding early, not realising that the finishing barrier had blown away, and Simpson over-took him on the line.

Van Looy should have won the Ronde more often. He was a deadly sprinter and a Classics specialist in an era when the race was flatter and favourable to his talents. The Ronde has a habit of preventing even its best-suited riders from dominating it.

CHAPTER 9

Taaienberg

The Taaienberg is the archetypal Flemish *helling*: a side road off a side road between villages, in the middle of nowhere south of Oudenaarde. There's a draggy run-in on a narrow strip of *betonweg*, then the climb steepens to around 15 per cent when the cobbles start, with trees either side which make it seem almost like a tunnel. There's a straight, a corner, then another straight, and at the top there is a very long false flat, which in the context of a race is harder than the uphill. It's Tom Boonen's favourite climb. 'Everybody is fighting and it's a big sprint to get there. I can do 900 watts over it, and everybody at the back is in the shit,' he says.

The Taaienberg pops up in a few races – a bit of local knowledge helps with these, as there's a smooth shallow concrete drain on the right-hand side, just wide enough for a single file of riders, and it goes up the climb and a long way along the drag at the top, but not in the Ronde, when the organisers fence off the one smooth line it offers. Boonen often uses it as a leg-stretcher in the first race of the Belgian season, Omloop Het Nieuwsblad, though never as a springboard for victory – some fans call this climb the Boonenberg, in his honour.

Chavanel and Clarke are approaching the top of the steepest section when the Flecha, Boonen, Van Avermaet and Langeveld group hits the cobbles at the bottom. Boonen's tactics are questionable – by covering Van Avermaet's attack, he was doing the job of defending Chavanel's position, but now Boonen is rolling through, helping the group chase. The idea must be to join Chavanel at the front, but the pursuit from the peloton is inevitable. If he does join Chavanel and they are chased and caught, Quick Step will have moved from a position of strength to a neutral one. If he doesn't join Chavanel, he has wasted energy. Better to let Chavanel get on with it.

Flecha leads the quartet of escapees up the climb. Van Avermaet looks pained, Boonen's head is nodding again and Langeveld drops back a little, just as Hushovd leads the peloton up to them when they reach the drag. Now would be the perfect moment to counter-attack – with Chavanel and Clarke pulled back again to no more than a 75-metre lead and the peloton weakened on the climb – but the opportunity is missed, deliberately or otherwise. Boonen and Flecha have already made their attempt, Hushovd has made his effort to close the gap and Gilbert and Cancellara sit tight; nobody wants to go. If any of the first 16 riders were to look over their shoulder, they might also see that there is a ten-metre gap back to another four riders, then ten metres to the rest of the peloton. The bonds that are holding the bunch together are still very weak.

Langeveld goes to the front again and forces the issue. If the Dutch rider is going to win, he'll break a hex that stretches back to 1945. Earlier in 2011, Langeveld won Omloop Het Nieuwsblad. Nobody has ever won the Omloop and then gone on to win Flanders in the same season, though the parcours is very similar. (It starts and finishes in Ghent, and a lot of the local riders call it 'Ghent–Ghent', rather than by its official name.) There's something about the peaking process which means that holding top form from the last weekend of February, for the Omloop, right through to the first weekend of April is difficult. It shouldn't be impossible – Nick Nuyens came second in both just three years previously, in 2008, and at some point somebody will win both in the same season, probably Peter Sagan, but the 65-year hex has gained its own momentum and some Flanders contenders miss the Omloop out completely.

These days the Ronde and Omloop are owned by the same company, Flanders Classics, although the Omloop was originally set up in competition with the Ronde at the end of the Second World War. *Sportwereld* – the paper for which the race's founder Karel Van Wijnendaele wrote – had been bought by the publishing company Corelio who owned the national newspapers *De Standaard*, a conservative paper which had first printed in 1918, and *Het Nieuwsblad*, which had been set up as a more populist, mainstream organ in 1929. *Het Nieuwsblad* took over the running of the Ronde until a large-scale restructuring led to Flanders Classics being hived off in 2010 and set up as an independent race organiser owned by an umbrella company called 'De Vijver' ('The Pond'), which also controls a television production house called Woestijnvis ('Desert fish', an industry in-joke around a famous incorrect answer in a television quiz), and two television channels. The race had become too large and unwieldy for the newspaper through the 1990s and 2000s and they'd been trying to sell it for some time, with the Amaury Sport Organisation, owners of the Tour de France, among the interested parties.

Het Volk had existed since 1891. They started the Omloop as a direct rival to the Ronde van Vlaanderen in 1945 and for a year – until they were warned off for the 1940s equivalent of trademark infringement – they called their race the Omloop van Vlaanderen (*omloop* is the Flemish word for 'circuit'). During the Second World War, *De Standaard* and *Het Nieuwsblad* ceased publication but their journalists created a paper called *Het Algemeen Nieuws*, whose stories were vetted by the occupying forces. When the war finished, the journalists, including Van Wijnendaele, were accused of collaborating, though they were eventually allowed to reinstate their original two titles. (Van Wijnendaele was let off the hook after Field Marshal Montgomery apparently wrote a letter stating that Van Wijnendaele had hidden a British pilot in his house during the war.)

It was in opposition to *Het Nieuwsblad* that *Het Volk* set up the Omloop. For many years, *Het Volk* and *Het Nieuwsblad* were rival newspapers and organised their rival races. By the 1990s, *Het Volk*'s circulation was dwindling and the paper was bought out by Corelio in 1994, which meant that the races were also now owned by the same company. By 2001, *Het Volk* was just *Het Nieuwsblad* with a different front page, and in 2008 it closed entirely. The final surviving asset, the race, had its name changed to Omloop Het Nieuwsblad in 2009.

Now that both races are owned by the same company – along with the Dwars door Vlaanderen, Ghent–Wevelgem, Scheldeprijs and Brabantse Pijl events – there's less sense of rivalry between them. The last unresolved issue is that of finding the right rider to win both in the same year. Sebastian Langeveld, the 2011 Omloop winner, thinks it's possible, but not probable, that it will be him.

After an average season in 2010, Langeveld has gone back to basics for 2011. He remembered going well in his early years off the back of hard, unstructured training camps with Rabobank where the senior riders ripped the legs off each other on long, long rides, so he ditched the measured efforts over winter and just rode. He rode a lot and he rode hard, and he was flying as the season started. He beat Juan Antonio Flecha in a two-up sprint for the Omloop in cold and wet conditions. He crashed in Tirreno–Adriatico but was still feeling good.

Robbie McEwen had advised him to take it easy in Tirreno if he wanted to be good in the Classics. Spend little energy, ride round to finish and don't touch the wind. He suffered a setback when he crashed in Milan–San Remo and took a knock to the leg that took some time to recover from. He rested up, then rode in E3 and Ghent–Wevelgem, which then took place on the Saturday and Sunday the week before the Ronde, just to get the rhythm of racing back into his legs. Then a few extra kilometres after the second race. He didn't feel good, but that was normal.

The Friday before the 2011 Ronde Langeveld did his final training session, behind a motorbike as normal, and felt he might be up there. Maybe he wouldn't be able to follow the top three guys, or Cancellara, but if the selection were ten riders, he thought he might be competitive. In 2008 he'd been the first to pursue Devolder after the Muur and he had got within 15 seconds of the Belgian champion before faltering.

Langeveld's acceleration atop the Taaienberg is covered by Cancellara and Sky's Edvald Boasson Hagen. Then he goes again, followed this time by Boasson Hagen, Van Avermaet and Voeckler, but the elastic does not snap – the peloton remains in touch, albeit in an impossibly thin line that is breaking in places. The gap to Chavanel and Clarke, who have now been away for 20 and 25 kilometres respectively, is 13 seconds.

The race has come almost in a loop from the Stationsberg descent, which spat the riders out at the southern tip of the small town of Etikhove. The route went a few kilometres south then turned east up the Taaienberg then north at the top, so the riders are now passing through the centre of Etikhove itself. The peloton have contained Langeveld and, just as the inevitable slowing makes the riders bunch up into the twisting roads through the town centre, Boasson Hagen attacks and nobody follows.

*

De Kempen is 4,000 square miles of heathland, sandy soil and hardy trees spread over the provinces of Antwerp and Limburg in the north-eastern part of Flanders and over the border into the southern part of the Netherlands. It is bound on the west by the Schelde and on the east by the Meuse. It's a largely infertile, flat and wind-blown region whose forests were destroyed in the first thousand years AD by overgrazing, and the rest of Belgium refers to the locals as 'zandboeren' ('sand farmers'). Coalmining and the car industry brought jobs to the city of Genk during the 20th century, but that's mostly gone now.

Bleak the region may be – and a long way from the *Vlaamse Ardennen* both physically and culturally – but this is home to Tom Boonen, a triple winner of the Ronde. Boonen is not the only renowned Flanders winner from this part of Belgium – Rik Van Steenbergen, Rik Van Looy and Eric Vanderaerden are also Kempenaers. They can't grow much in De Kempen but they can grow champions.

Balen, Boonen's home, is a quiet town of 20,000 inhabitants in the centre of De Kempen. After having seem Boonen at a juvenile race, it's where Dirk Demol – his future directeur sportif at Quick Step – went to find him and his parents to see if he would like to sign for the Kortrijk Groeninge Spurters youth team. 'I wasn't only impressed because he won,' said Demol. 'It was his *coup de pédale*, how he turned his legs and pedalled. He was tall, like a giant already, but he didn't win with power; he won by pedalling.'

Demol's case was helped by the fact that he'd raced with Boonen's father, André, during the late 1970s and early 1980s. 'I didn't know that Tom was his son,' said Demol. 'I made an appointment on the phone and went with the manager of the team to see Tom. I rang the bell and André opened the door. I said, "André! Is Tom your son?" And he said, "I hope so!"'

The ice broken, Demol signed Boonen. 'He won 20, 25 races

that year, easy,' remembered Demol. The older man guided Boonen through his junior and under-23 years, then brought him on to US Postal in 2002. After one year on the American team, the rider left for Quick Step, where he stayed to the end of his career. As well as holding the joint record for Flanders wins, at three, he holds the joint record for Paris–Roubaix wins (four), Ghent–Wevelgem wins (three) and the outright record for E3 wins (five). He may be the greatest cobbled Classics rider of all time. He's certainly the most successful, and though he spent the first few years of his career vowing to be retired by age 30 (and living as if he was aiming to be burned out well before then), he mellowed and finally retired in 2017, at 37.

I met Boonen at the start of the 2016 season, at the same Etixx–Quick Step team training camp in Calp, at which I'd met Nikolas Maes. The hotel was crawling with journalists, photographers, sponsors and hangers-on, and most of the time Boonen was nowhere to be seen. This is common – I once spent the best part of five days hanging around in a hotel lobby in Qatar waiting to catch him for an interview and he'd perfected the art of getting from his room to the dining hall and back again without crossing the lobby, which should have been impossible. I saw him moving around the hotel a couple of times in Calp – he wasn't exactly scuttling, but I noticed he hugged the walls a bit and had a long stride and the world-weary round-shouldered slouch of somebody used to pre-empting the fact that everybody wants a piece of them. He's spent the entirety of his adult life – more, really, as he was just a boy when he came third in Paris–Roubaix after having been a professional cyclist for three months – in the public eye, and he doesn't go out of his way to court the attention that he's going to get whether he looks for it or not.

However, Boonen's ex-team-mate Kevin Hulsmans said of him, 'Tom is a social animal. He cannot be alone.' Boonen is actually a people person, very sociable, very balanced and popular with a lot of the press for being an engaging interviewee. There's a theory about this, put to me by a Belgian journalist, that the combination of his Kempen background, a strong family and especially a strong partner, have kept his feet on the ground. Linked to this is the fact that Boonen's long-time girlfriend Lore works in a youth offenders' institute with what my contact described as 'difficult young guys' – the inference being that Lore doesn't take any crap, least of all from Tom.

Boonen is one of a handful of riders to have won the Ronde three times. But there's a difference between him and other home winners of the race: he's the first Belgian cyclist since Eddy Merckx to transcend the sport and become a national figure. Guy Fransen, *Het Nieuwsblad*'s sports editor, pointed out to me that the only press asking questions of previous home winners Peter Van Petegem and Johan Museeuw, for example, were cycling journalists, whereas Boonen regularly appears on talk shows and on the covers of magazines. 'He's a good-looking young guy in a suit and can talk about other things than just cycling. Tom was put in a talk show with Natalia, a Flemish pop star, and it worked. The moderator could put questions to Tom about music; you wouldn't ask Stijn Devolder to be on a show with other guests,' he said.

Maybe it's an accident of timing; that he just happened to be the first big Belgian cycling star of the celebrity era. Or perhaps the very photogenic good looks, fast cars, tattoos and sharp suits made him a natural star, and a mid-career phase of bad and erratic behaviour made him a natural subject of the gossip columns. Either way, Boonen has negotiated his rise, fall and subsequent rise with surprisingly little collateral damage, notwithstanding the morning he woke up and found a complete stranger sitting in his living room. ('He'd been passing on his bike, saw that my window was open and thought, *Ah, it's Tom*

Boonen's house. I'll walk in. He wanted my autograph, but I just threw him out,' he said later.)

Now Boonen has ended up where he started – in Balen, surrounded by family. There were a few years in Monaco, the three cocaine positives, a tax case and speeding tickets, but he's been forgiven. As the Quick Step manager Patrick Lefevere once said, 'Tom has a face you cannot be mad at.'

Boonen didn't spend his childhood dreaming of winning the Ronde, as his junior and future team-mate Stijn Devolder did. 'I'm not a typical Belgian guy who grew up with the Tour of Flanders,' he told me. 'In 1996 I did a race a few kilometres away, and afterwards my dad and I went to the finish. That was my first experience of it.'

For Boonen, the battle in the Tour of Flanders is as much against the race as against his rivals. There's something about the route, the roads and the geography, and the way the peloton interacts with them, that puts everybody on edge. 'It's the hardest race to read,' Boonen told me. 'The race challenges you. It wants you to start racing, and it gives you everything to start racing. So you have this fight, to go into the climb. *Boom.* Then everybody sits up, and you go up the climb easy to try to save energy, then you do that all over again. But every time you do this, you reach the bottom of the climb full of adrenalin. You get to the bottom and you have a fight with the guy on your left and the guy to the right. You have to stay calm and keep thinking, but the race wants you to race. If you have a plan, it lasts about five minutes. I can't recall one year where we've made a plan and it has succeeded.' As Mike Tyson is said to have observed: 'Everyone has a plan until they get punched in the mouth.'

I used to think Boonen had it pretty easy. Obviously you don't become a professional cyclist – least of all a world champion and Classics winner – without hard work, but the gifts he had were extraordinary: the physiology to respond to a massive workload, which gave him huge endurance, and a very fast sprint (he won Tour de France stages in bunch finishes earlier in his career, though the last came in 2007). Races must be easy to win when you're the strongest rider and the best sprinter, but Boonen feels his first Tour of Flanders win, in 2005, was as much won by his head as by his legs.

Boonen had made it into the six-strong front group that went clear over the Valkenberg, the 14th of 17 climbs. His fellow escapees: Erik Zabel, an experienced and prolific sprinter; Zabel's then team-mate Andreas Klier; Alessandro Ballan, a future winner; Roberto Petito, an experienced rider who had previously won Tirreno–Adriatico; and Peter Van Petegem, the two-time winner.

Objectively, you'd have had to say that Telekom were in a strong position – Zabel was a good enough sprinter to have won the Tour de France's green jersey six times and Klier had come sixth in the Tour of Flanders the previous year. With two riders working together, especially a sprinter and a stayer like Zabel and Klier, they could either send Klier up the road and assume that nobody would want to lead Zabel back up to the front, or Klier could ride to keep things together for Zabel to win the sprint. Alternatively, Van Petegem was hugely dangerous: a fast finisher at the end of a long race and one of the best riders in the world on the cobbles. But there was more than that to the dynamic of the front group, and Boonen well knew it. 'Being able to oversee the combines that were being made and knowing the history between the riders helped me,' he said. 'We passed the Muur, and after that I was already feeling that they were staying in the back a little bit more. Some worked, but there was always somebody talking in the back. At that point I didn't speak Italian that well, and Petito and Ballan were talking. And Zabel and Klier were talking. And

Klier was talking to Van Petegem,' he continued. 'Everybody was talking except me.'

Boonen knew that Klier and Van Petegem were good friends. He surmised that they might not work against each other: if Van Petegem attacked, the chasing would be left to Boonen; alternatively they would keep it together for Zabel to win the sprint. Boonen almost broke their resolve on the Bosberg, surging up the climb, but Van Petegem was just able to stay with him. With eight kilometres to go, Boonen went again. 'I knew I had to go. If I stayed with them they'd all attack and nobody would ride. Peter went really hard and I was able to get back to him, and I knew that was the moment. I knew I had to get away, otherwise they'd destroy me.'

Klier had spent the race as a protected rider, and had tried to escape before Geraardsbergen. He said, 'I didn't work the whole race for Zabel. I attacked somewhere in Brakel but it just didn't happen. Tom went away with eight kilometres to go, and our directeur sportif said, "Look, we have to change the plan." It was crystal clear I had to ride for Zabel. So I rolled from eight to go to three to go, in the hope that we would catch Tom and Zabel could sprint, but it wasn't the case.'

At three kilometres to go Boonen had been cramping, but he saw his parents and brother by the side of the road, coincidentally very close to where Klier lived in Denderwinke. This gave him the final impetus he needed and he was able to ride solo to the finish. Klier's efforts weren't wasted – when it became clear that they weren't going to catch Boonen, the others lost interest a little and he attacked the group to finish second, with Zabel heading up the sprint to take the third spot on the podium.

A year later, it looked more straightforward. Boonen was world champion by then and he was the hot favourite for the Ronde. One of his strongest rivals was expected to be Discovery Channel's George Hincapie, so when Hincapie's team-mate Leif

Hoste attacked on the Valkenberg climb and took Boonen with him, it looked tactically suspect. Hoste and Boonen co-operated well in front and – with Hincapie trapped in the eight-strong group behind, and Boonen's team-mate Bettini also present to dissuade chasers – the pair stayed away, before Boonen predictably thrashed Hoste in the sprint.

Years later, Hincapie's friend and then team-mate Michael Barry alleged in his book *Shadows on the Road* that Hoste and Boonen had come to a financial arrangement, though both denied it and there was no evidence to suggest that they had. It is true that on one hand, Hoste's move guaranteed Discovery wouldn't win; on the other, it guaranteed second place (and Hincapie won the sprint for third). I wonder what Dirk Demol was thinking, driving the Discovery Channel team car behind the break with his rider Hoste, who he'd known from them both being from Bavikhove, and his old protégé Boonen. Immediately after the race, Demol explained that he'd told Hincapie that if he could drop the others, Hoste would not work with Boonen. 'When Leif attacked, it was not supposed to have been a race-deciding effort,' he said. 'We were trying to break up the Quick Step grip on the front of the race and figured a big effort could get the numbers down to maybe two of them and two of us and then we'd see how it went.'

Unfortunately for Discovery, the initial attack killed everybody except Boonen, and then Hincapie couldn't drop the others, though he tried on the Muur, by which time it was too late anyway. I emailed Hincapie to ask him about it. The intervening decade since the race has made him equanimous. 'I think it was more us just being upset that Hoste worked with Boonen, since I was his team-mate just behind,' he replied. 'Looking back, I don't really blame him; those guys had a much better relationship than we had as team-mates. I should have reacted when they went, but didn't, and missed out on a chance.'

Then he added: 'Boonen was so good that it would have been nearly impossible to beat him anyhow.'

Like most of the riders who won the Ronde three times, Boonen should have won it more often. The first win for his team-mate Stijn Devolder, in 2008, was contentious – though Boonen was trapped behind Devolder's attack anyway, Demol said that his form was questionable. Boonen told me that in 2009 he had one of his best years ever in the Tour of Flanders, but that he had to defend Devolder's attack.

But there's something about the race that has prevented anybody from winning it more than three times so far. Compared to the other cycling Monuments, the record number of wins is low. Eddy Merckx won Milan–San Remo seven times and Liège–Bastogne–Liège five times, Fausto Coppi won the Tour of Lombardy five times and Boonen and Roger De Vlaeminck won Paris–Roubaix four times. It's a similar story in the Grand Tours – the record number of wins in the Tour de France and Giro d'Italia by a single rider is five. But riders seem to get stuck on three in the Ronde. Six riders have done this: Achiel Buysse, Fiorenzo Magni, Eric Leman, Johan Museeuw, Boonen and Fabian Cancellara, but nobody has ever won a fourth. Often, bad luck got in the way, as with Boonen in 2009 or Johan Museeuw being injured after 1998; Magni, however, won the race three times and didn't return to try for a fourth victory.

The biggest reason for nobody going beyond three, so far, is that it's a more open and unpredictable race than the others. Having the best endurance used to be a good foundation for success in Milan–San Remo, and these days it's having the best sprint; the best climber tends to win Liège and Lombardy. But Flanders has more variables and tactics, which prevents it being as simple as the strongest rider winning. 'You have basically to be a good rider to win Flanders,' Boonen told me. 'You have to be able to do anything – to ride alone for ten kilometres at the end or be the fastest if you go to the finish line in a group. Sometimes, in the years I had bad results I had better legs than when I won the race. Sometimes you wake up, you do everything right and you win the race. Other years you are just two places too far behind into a corner where something happens or you are at the car at a bad moment. You don't know why, but nothing goes the way you want. It's not for no reason that the record stands on three. Everybody stops on three. If you have 15 years in a career, and even the biggest riders in the world were only able to win three – even in eras with fewer guys at the start – that means something. It's not an easy race to win.'

CHAPTER 10

Eikenberg

In the 20th century Sint-Martens-Latem, which lies between Deinze and Ghent, was an artists' colony where overlapping groups of post-impressionists, symbolists, luminists and expressionists worked under a loose and stylistically diverse association known as the Latem School, attracted by the landscape and the scenic meanders of the Leie. Latterly, low local taxes have attracted a more wealthy population, albeit one with less soul than before; a transition best symbolised by the concreting of the river banks, which reduced flooding along with the picturesque aesthetic. Sint-Martens-Latem was also where Karel Van Wijnendaele lived in the later part of his life; the creator of the Ronde is buried in the municipal cemetery in the town alongside his second wife, Elvira Huybrechts.

Fietsen Godefroot is a cavernous bike shop on the main road past the town. It's part of a row of low, wide industrial buildings and units including a BMW showroom, a bathroom shop and, next door to Fietsen Godefroot, a clothes shop called Katastrof. This is almost the edge of Sint-Martens-Latem – on the other side of the road there is an empty ploughed field, then one more street of houses before the countryside begins.

Inside Fietsen Godefroot there is a large showroom, full of every kind of bike, and a steep staircase leading up to a wide balcony which runs all the way round the shop, with more bikes on display. Double Tour of Flanders winner Walter Godefroot owns the bike shop that bears his name, though he has more or less retired and it's his two sons who deal with the day-to-day running these days. Godefroot comes in every now and again to help out for a couple of hours, which I suspect is as much for the benefit of Godefroot himself as for the shop.

The day I visited was in the run-up to Christmas so the staff were busy. Five mechanics were on duty, as well as Godefroot's son Christophe. I met Godefroot out on the shop floor and he showed me to the office, where we sat and talked in French, with his son poking his head round the door to help with translations every now and again. When he was a professional, Godefroot's nickname was 'De Vlaamse Bulldog', but he was genial company. He still looked wiry and tough, in a grandfather-chic claret cardigan and striped shirt, his complexion ruddied by broken capillaries, There was still something of the bulldog in him too – his default expression was quite stern and he smiled mainly with his eyes rather than with his mouth. He told me that a bike crash a couple of years ago, in which he broke his nose, had slowed him down. 'I'm not the same as before. I get tired more quickly,' he said.

Godefroot is an authentic *Flandrien*. His two wins in the Ronde, separated by ten years between 1968 and 1978, were accompanied by a second place, a third (subsequently stripped after a positive test), a fourth, and six more top-15 placings. I told him that he was one of the most successful and consistent riders in the history of the race. 'Merci,' he replied, in an unsurprised tone of voice.

Godefroot was born in 1943 and grew up in Drongen, a western suburb of Ghent. His mother worked in a textile factory;

his father drove a lorry that delivered textiles. 'We were happy. We had enough to eat, but there wasn't much more left over,' he said. 'My parents built a house. We say of Flemish people that they have a "brick in the stomach". It means that the dream of every Flemish person is to build a little house.'

Drongen happened to be the location of one of the best gymnastics clubs in Belgium, and it's where the sporty kids gravitated. Godefroot joined and found he was good at it: he was the junior champion of East Flanders on the parallel bars, and his coach thought he had the potential to be national champion. 'He was right,' Godefroot said. 'But he got the wrong sport.'

Godefroot's father Urbain had been a cyclist, an Independent, and the online cycling archives list him as having raced in 1939, although no results exist. But the Second World War, followed by a bout of bronchitis and the responsibilities of fatherhood, finished his cycling career. 'I had an uncle who told me I should cycle,' said Godefroot. 'One Sunday, he said there was a race in Zwevegem. My dad had an old bike; he said I could use it. I got some shorts from one guy, a jersey from another, and my uncle took me in the car.'

He was seventh in his first race, then second in his next. He was near the front in all seven of the races he did that year. He left school at 16, and trained as a carpenter, working from 7 in the morning until 6:30 at night, stopping at 5 p.m. twice a week to do some training. 'I worked more than 50 hours each week; cycling was on top of that. Sometimes I was so cooked. But that was life at the time,' he said. He soon noticed he was earning more from cycling than from his job. 'I understood immediately that when I sprinted, I won money. It was one hour of work, and I won more money on Saturday and Sunday at races than I earned the rest of the week as a carpenter. I quickly understood, eh?'

Godefroot won a lot of races as an amateur, and trained but didn't race through his military service in Germany, then managed to get late selection for the Tokyo Olympics in 1964 by winning three stages and coming third overall at the Tour of Tunisia, behind Gösta Pettersson, a future Giro d'Italia champion, and Lucien Aimar, who would win the Tour de France two years later. In Tokyo he took the bronze medal, which was enough to get him a professional contract for 1965 with the Wiel's–Groene Leeuw team. 'I was up and running,' he said.

The spread of ten years between Godefroot's two Flanders wins, in 1968 and 1978, is the longest in the race's history. Those ten years were also a period of transition for the race. In 1968 the Ronde was quite faithful to the model established in the third edition in 1919 – long, with a brief foray into the *Vlaamse Ardennen*, and the finish a long way from the hills, in Ghent. By 1978, the number of climbs had increased significantly, to eight, with the now-traditional Oude Kwaremont, Taaienberg and Koppenberg all getting incorporated into the route between 1974 and 1976. When the finish moved from Ghent to Meerbeke in 1973, the nature of the race changed significantly – the climbs became the most important factor, rather than an individual element. The Muur and Bosberg had both appeared in the race before the finish was moved to Meerbeke, but from 1975 they appeared as a pair just before the final run-in. This had the effect of reducing the size of the group contesting the win (in the ten years leading up to the change of route in 1973, the average size of the group contesting the win was over six; between 1973 and 2012, when the route changed again, the average size was just over two, with 22 solo wins).

Godefroot had already been successful before 1968. He'd won the Belgian championships in his first season and Liège–Bastogne–Liège in 1967, plus a Tour de France stage that would be the first of ten in his career.

Paul Deman, who won the first ever Ronde in 1913 over a 324 km course that only 16 of 37 competitors (all of them Belgian) completed. (Offside)

The archetypal *Flandrien* Briek Schotte and Rik Van Steenbergen escape the pile-up in the background during the 1944 Ronde. The latter would emerge victorious, aged just 19. (Offside)

Fiorenzo Magni, the 'Lion of Flanders', wraps up his third consecutive victory in the 1951 race, winning by a massive five minutes and 35 seconds. (Offside)

In the rain, Roger Decock celebrates victory in the 1952 Ronde after outsprinting Loretto Petrucci to the finish line. (Offside)

In 1969, having been marked out of the Ronde the year before, Eddy Merckx decided to take on the race on his own, breaking away with 73 km in the wind and rain still to go. (Offside)

Only 24 of 173 starters finished the 1985 Ronde, won by Eric Vanderaerden in
'Siberian' conditions. Here he makes his winning attack on the Muur
van Geraardsbergen (Offside)

Jesper Skibby is knocked off his bike on Koppenberg during the 1987 Ronde, after
which the climb was removed from the race until 2002. (Graham Watson)

Jacky Durand, the last French winner of the Ronde, climbs the Muur in 1992 on the way to his surprise victory. (Offside)

Johan Museeuw in 1993, on the way to the first of his three Ronde victories during the 1990s when he was the dominant cobbled Classics rider. (Graham Watson)

Tom Boonen attacks on the Koppenberg in 2006 on the way to retaining his title. For many, this is the worst climb in the Ronde, due its combination of steep gradient, narrowness and cobbles. (Graham Watson)

Stijn Devolder, who grew up in Bavikhove, celebrates winning the Ronde in 2008, helped by his team leader Tom Boonen ensuring that none of his rivals chased him down. (Graham Watson)

After humiliating Boonen on the Muur the year before, Fabian Cancellara leads his key rivals during the Ronde in 2011. (Graham Watson)

Geraint Thomas, who would finish the 2011 race in tenth place in only his second appearance in the Ronde.

(Graham Watson)

For some 40 km in 2011, Sylvain Chavanel and Simon Clarke led a break before the latter was dropped at the Molenberg. (Graham Watson)

Philippe Gilbert was aggressive in the 2011 race, but would have to wait until 2017 for his victory. (Graham Watson)

Cancellara leads from Chavanel and Nick Nuyens as they make the race-defining attack in the finale. (Graham Watson)

But it's Nuyens, the man whose family background perfectly illustrates the connection between the old and the new of Flanders, who wins through. (Graham Watson)

The 1968 Ronde was long, at 249km, but not especially hilly, with only four bergs: the Kwaremont (still, at that point, the climb up the main road), Kloosterstraat, which climbs through Geraardsbergen and takes riders to a point very close to the foot of the Muur, plus the Valkenberg and Kasteeldreef. I asked Godefroot about the race and mentioned that the group of 16 who'd contested the win contained some very big names: Rudi Altig, the 1964 Ronde winner and a former world champion and Vuelta a España winner; Jan Janssen, who would win the Tour de France that summer; Lucien Aimar, the 1966 Tour de France winner; Rik Van Looy, winner of all five of cycling's Monuments. And not forgetting Eddy Merckx. However, the strength of the men in the group was only the second most interesting thing about it. 'Merckx attacked. Van Looy took him back,' he said. 'Van Looy blocked Merckx, and when Guido Reybrouck attacked, I reacted. Reybrouck was Merckx's team-mate.' Godefroot and Van Looy were working Merckx and his team-mate over, even though they themselves were not team-mates. They'd found common cause in trying to defeat Merckx.

Godefroot was two years older than Merckx, though they had both turned professional in 1965. Merckx was a prodigious talent – world amateur champion at 19, winner of Milan–San Remo in 1966 and 1967, and a future winner of five yellow jerseys. Van Looy, nearing the end of his career by 1968, could see that Merckx was going to be the biggest threat to his position as the best Belgian Classics rider in history, and he didn't take it well. They were team-mates during the 1965 season and they didn't get on. Merckx told the Belgian television interviewer Johny Vansevenant about the Paris–Luxembourg race that season. Van Looy was the defending champion but Merckx was riding better and came 14th, while Van Looy was back in 44th. During the days, Merckx beat Van Looy; in the evenings at the team hotel, Van Looy paid him back. 'They made fun of me in the evenings, at the table,' said Merckx to Vansevenant. 'They called me Jack Palance. And I used to eat dessert rice with syrup after my meal. They laughed at me for that.' Van Looy dismissed the mockery as banter rather than bullying, but the pair never really made up.

Van Looy's approach to the finale of the 1968 Ronde was therefore an anybody-but-Merckx policy, and Godefroot was the beneficiary. Van Looy wasn't a hugely sociable individual but he liked Godefroot. Every time Merckx attacked, Van Looy chased him, even though it also harmed his own chances. On the other hand, when Ward Sels, the 1966 winner, attacked, nobody followed immediately. 'Everybody said, "Okay, Sels is going to win,"' said Godefroot. 'But there were more attacks. We could see Sels in front of us, and he was completely finished.'

The race eventually came down to a sprint between 16 riders. 'It was easy to win. They weren't as fast as me,' Godefroot said.

Godefroot was part of a golden generation of Belgian Classics riders, and his results in the late 1960s especially were formidable: as well as the 1968 Tour of Flanders and 1967 Liège–Bastogne–Liège, there were also two Paris–Roubaix wins. While Godefroot would disagree, it was unfortunate for him that his career more or less overlapped completely with that of Eddy Merckx. An entire cohort of Belgian cyclists' careers were overshadowed by Merckx, as were those of subsequent generations. But Godefroot was realistic about his talents and how they compared to Merckx's, even though the latter spoke very highly of him, saying once that Godefroot was the only rider he never beat in a direct fight for victory. 'If I was a footballer, I wouldn't be the centre-forward,' he said. 'Merckx and Van Looy were centre-forwards, scoring the goals. I'd be in the middle, organising the team, being the playmaker.'

This reminded me of something that riders and managers have often said to me and others, that cycling champions don't make great cycling managers – the best managers are either domestiques or road captains because they better understand the fallibility of the rank-and-file riders and are therefore better at managing resources and dealing with crises or unexpected events, whereas champions tend to expect perfection. Of course, this is a generalisation and there are exceptions – Bjarne Riis won the Tour de France, and while his doping history is well documented and taints his achievements significantly, I've spoken to many of the riders he managed at CSC and Saxo Bank, including Nick Nuyens, and almost universally they rate him as an excellent manager. But generalisation or not, Walter Godefroot also went on to be a very successful team manager and he was in the team car when Riis won his Tour.

Godefroot always rode well in the Tour of Flanders – he only missed one edition between 1966 and 1979, when ligament damage from a crash in an early-season race in 1972 kept him on the sidelines. After his first win, he was in the top 20 every time, save for the disqualification in 1974.

The final win, in 1978, bookended his career. Over the Muur van Geraardsbergen, Godefroot was away with compatriot Michel Pollentier and Germany's Gregor Braun. Pollentier told Godefroot that he couldn't help with the pacemaking because his team-mate Freddy Maertens was in the next group, though that didn't stop Pollentier from making several attacks. 'Braun was contributing, but Pollentier attacked several times, really hard. I got him back easily but then he stayed in my wheel. Braun kept on getting left behind when Pollentier attacked, but then he caught us,' said Godefroot. 'I told Braun to stay in my wheel. I spoke to him on a financial level. He continued to ride. He was third and got the prize money. If he'd been dropped, he wouldn't have earned anything.'

Godefroot thinks he could have won the race more often. A crash put him at the back of the peloton just when the race was being ripped to pieces in crosswinds in 1969 before Eddy Merckx attacked solo, and he was narrowly outsprinted by Eric Leman in 1970. But despite him being a Flemish rider, the Ronde wasn't his biggest priority. 'For me, Paris–Roubaix was a lot more important at the time. The Ronde was important in Flanders but when I won Paris–Roubaix and Bordeaux–Paris in the same year, it changed everything for me. The Ronde became more international recently.'

I thanked Godefroot for his time and he offered to show me around the shop. There were several large storage areas, functional and very well organised with equipment separated by manufacturer, and a games room complete with bar billiards table, a pinball machine and Babyfoot table. Fietsen Godefroot used to be based in smaller premises behind Ghent station, but the shop did well so they moved to the larger premises, which Godefroot much preferred. He reeled off the list of suppliers whose bikes he sold, and spoke more expansively about the shop than of his racing career. 'I'm prouder of the shop,' he said. 'When I won races, I'd done my job and I was happy. But I'm not in love with the bike. Jan Janssen once said to me, "Walter, you don't like cycling, do you?" What I liked was beating others.'

At 30 seconds, Chavanel and Clarke's lead is the biggest it has been since they escaped, though Boasson Hagen is between them and the peloton. The race is between the Taaienberg and Eikenberg, just a few kilometres south-east of Oudenaarde, and it's not that Chavanel and Clarke have sped up, but that the peloton is trying not to spend valuable resources by chasing.

Rabobank are the most active in this phase of the race. Langeveld's attacks – first with Boonen before the Taaienberg, then after the drag at the top – failed to stick, just as Tjallingii's 75 kilometres earlier had. But they are trying again: their rider

Tom Leezer takes up the pacemaking in the run-up to the Eikenberg, with Lars Boom just a couple of riders behind him.

The Eikenberg starts as a twisty-turny road through a ramshackle collection of houses, farm buildings and sheds, before crossing a low bridge over the Markebeek. The cobbles begin at the bridge and run almost all the way to the top, over a kilometre later, with a brief stretch of patchy tarmac about 100 metres long two-thirds of the way up. It's a forgiving climb, compared with many of the others – it's never more than ten per cent, and there are extended patches of concrete on either side and in places on the road itself.

Ahead, on the long left-hand bend just before the tarmac section, Boasson Hagen is only 20 metres behind Chavanel and Clarke; Leezer still leads the peloton, with Van Avermaet, Flecha and Boonen still riding very near the front, along with Boom. Leezer can't maintain the pace and drops back, while Van Avermaet and Boom sit side by side on the front. As the road straightens out, Boom attacks and the reaction from Boonen is immediate. But then Boonen sits up, which is curious. Boonen had covered the Van Avermaet attack before the Taaienberg, then carried on working. This time, he sits up and allows Boom – a former world cyclocross champion and world under-23 time-trial champion – to ride clear. Boom accelerates on the cobbles then hits the tarmac stretch with the impetus to create a gap.

The top of the Eikenberg is a right-hand dog-leg on to the N8. The attacks in the peloton have reduced the gaps again, and Chavanel and Clarke turn the corner six seconds clear of Boasson Hagen. There are another four seconds before Boom makes the turning, then another eight to the peloton. All the groups are within touching distance of each other, but the key thing is the momentum. Boom seems to be making the smoothest progress, and it's likely that he'll catch Boasson Hagen on the

N8, which is flat here. Two riders generally move faster than one, so it's also likely that Boom and Boasson Hagen will catch Chavanel and Clarke, while the leaders in the peloton – minus Boonen, Langeveld and Flecha, who all now have team-mates in front – will be trying to marshal enough team support to chase them down, which will take time. On the other hand, wide flat roads on open countryside make escapees very visible. The Chavanel group is still extremely vulnerable.

Boom catches Boasson Hagen and they are just behind Chavanel and Clarke as they turn left on to the flat cobbles of Holleweg. The peloton is not far behind but is showing signs of wanting to chase, with BMC and Leopard visible at the front. The leading quartet should find common cause in working together but they haven't quite worked that out yet – on the cobbles, Chavanel surges and goes away, with Boom and Boasson Hagen catching Clarke. When Boasson Hagen does finally lead the trio up to Chavanel, he shouts at the French rider and shakes his head. They'll be far stronger working together than against each other; no point in surging off the front, is the message.

Behind, Leopard have committed their rider Martin Mortensen to the chase. The Danish rider was fifth in the under-23 Paris–Roubaix in 2006 but has settled into a role as a domestique. At the start of Holleweg, with 62 kilometres to the finish, the gap is 25 seconds.

Holleweg is the start of an open triangle of cobbled roads, which is followed by another stretch just afterwards. The peloton ride 1,500 metres on Holleweg before turning right on to the 800-metre Ruitersstraat, which is also cobbled. At the end of Ruitersstraat, they turn north for a couple of kilometres of *betonweg*, before coming back south again on Kerkgate. If they followed Kerkgate all the way to its end, they would come out back near the start of Holleweg, but in the race, as the Kerkgate cobbles pass through the village of Mater, the route turns east again and then turns towards the fourth set of cobbles, Jagerij. In the space of six kilometres, there are 4.6 kilometres of pavé, a middle eight of flat cobbles among the bergs and hills.

At the junction of Holleweg and Ruitersstraat, Mortensen has brought the gap down to 20 seconds. On the twisting roads before Kerkgate, the Chavanel quartet's lead is evaporating, going down to 15 then inside ten seconds, as the peloton is strung out again into single file. Chavanel and Clarke have been away for 30 kilometres now and they're still not even out of sight of the bunch.

The back roads of Flanders are full of 90-degree turns, as they zigzag around farms, fields, towns and woods. The lanes are narrow and there is no camber on these bends, which means the racing line is extremely narrow and any deviation off it forces riders to decelerate. It is on one of these, as Kleistraat turns left on to Bronstraat – two innocuous roads to and from nowhere in particular – that Mortensen misjudges where that racing line is. He has closed the gap to nine seconds, when he shoots wide (in fact, this bend is more like 120 degrees) and straight into the driveway of a house on the corner, coming to an almost complete halt. The riders immediately behind him brake and swerve wide, which means that the riders behind *them* are travelling faster than the riders ahead and there's a traffic jam. While nobody crashes, the momentum is completely killed; Mortensen doesn't have the physical or psychological energy to renew his effort and drifts to the back with tired legs, while nobody else is interested in chasing. On Kerkgate, there is a truce and the bunch visibly sits up through Mater, save for a foray off the front from FDJ's veteran French rider Frédéric Guesdon, who won Paris–Roubaix in 1997 and came sixth in the Ronde in 2003. If the bunch lets him go, perhaps he can join the front four.

Guesdon is dangerous, even at 39 years old. As he dangles

around 75 metres off the front, a small chase group forms and BMC's Van Avermaet bridges up with Sky's Mat Hayman and Rabobank's Tom Leezer.

Hayman and Leezer won't work, or at least not too hard; they are defending the positions of Boasson Hagen and Boom, their team-mates in the front quartet. But Guesdon and Van Avermaet are putting themselves in a stronger position. Guesdon's the team leader in FDJ, so he's in it for himself, but Van Avermaet has suddenly taken the pressure off BMC to have to do any chasing. Quick Step, Rabobank, Sky and BMC all have riders off the front; of the big teams, that only leaves Leopard and Lotto unrepresented, and Lotto have so far looked uninterested in doing the work of chasing. Quick Step manager Wilfried Peeters has seen that Mortensen, now exhausted, is the last of Cancellara's team-mates left in the front group. The Swiss rider is almost completely isolated.

As the race leaves Jagerij with 53 kilometres to go, the first quartet is 22 seconds clear of the second quartet, who are another ten in front of the peloton. Peeters sends a message over the radio to his riders: 'Perfect. Perfect.'

CHAPTER 11

Flanders II

In some parts of the 'traditional' cycling countries – Belgium, France, Spain and Italy – cycling seems to be an expression of regional pride as much as national pride. Though the internationalisation of the sport in the 21st century is diluting this tendency, by reputation the most passionate fans come from Flanders, Brittany, the Basque Country and Tuscany. These regions have also produced a surfeit of professional riders, lots of local racing and a large following for the sport, and they remain hotbeds of cycling talent. Bike races held in these regions have special atmospheres, and their fans are extremely knowledgable about the sport.

It could be coincidental but the first three regions especially have strong separatist movements. (Also, the Liga Nord political party – which advocates policies ranging between greater autonomy for the northern regions of Italy and outright secession from the south – came second in Tuscany in the last elections in 2015.) One of the defining aspects of bike races in Flanders, Brittany and the Basque Country is the omnipresence of the local flags – the black lion rampant with red claws on a yellow background (black claws for the Flemish nationalists) of the *Vlaamse Leeuw* for Flanders, the black and white stripes of the Breton *Gwenn-ha-du* and the red, white and green *ikurrina* of the Basque Country.

There are similarities between the bike racing in Brittany and Flanders. An almost autonomous circuit of local races evolved in both regions that were linked to local religious festivals. In Brittany, each village held festivals of penitence, known as Pardons, and through the 20th century bike races, usually based on laps of a shortish circuit, became part of the entertainment. The Flemish equivalent is the *kermis*, a celebration of the local patron saint, where bike races, similarly based on circuits, are often the highlight. In the second half of the 20th century it became possible for riders to make a good career out of participating only in this kind of race in their local regions, with no need to turn professional and participate internationally.

The Ronde is an expression of Flemish culture, and regional identity is at the centre of its importance in Flanders. There's a lot more to this than it being a big bike race that happens to take place in the region. The race was consciously developed as part of a movement known as *wielerflamingantisme* – literally: cycling Flemish nationalism (the French term 'flamingantisme', which described the Flemish movement, is more often used than the Flemish *Vlaamsgezind* – the French term was initially derogatory but was adopted as a badge of honour). The Ronde's founder Karel Van Wijnendaele used the success of Flemish riders between the wars to further promote the cause of Flemish regional pride and emancipation. This was necessary because the Flemish majority had been economically, culturally and institutionally suppressed by the French–speaking minority through the 1800s. But paradoxically it also highlights one of the quirks of the region, that historically Flanders has been an ill–defined entity, as has Belgium, which only came into being in 1830 (though this is earlier than modern Italy or Germany, for example). Traditionally, the race has mainly taken place in the provinces of East and West Flanders, yet these are only two of five provinces that make up the modern region of Flanders. Since 2017 the race has started in Antwerp, which is in the province of the same name, and barely touches West Flanders, which is the most cycling-mad province of all. And all this doesn't take into account that in the past, 'true' Flanders consisted only of the provinces of East and West Flanders – Limburg and Brabant were never historically part of the region. So when we say that the Tour of Flanders is the most important unifying event for its region, what do we mean? To understand the Ronde, you have to understand Flanders and Belgium and what they are and what they are not.

In his practical book on cycle touring, *Get Away by Bike*, Les Woodland included a short section on Belgium. 'Belgium is the oddest country in Europe and if it didn't already exist, nobody would find a need to invent it,' he wrote.

In *The Factory of Facts*, his memoir of growing up as a Belgian expat in the USA, Luc Sante wrote, 'It is an accidental country, a nation by default, a haphazard assemblage of dissonant and sometimes warring elements. Its hallmarks are ambivalence, invisibility, secretiveness, self-doubt, passivity, irony and derision.'

The television presenter John Oliver was more cutting: 'Belgium is the casual acquaintance France crops out of its Instagram photos.'

Belgium is a living experiment in compromise and coexistence. In the last quarter of the 20th century it became a federal state, which means its three regions of Flanders, Wallonia and Brussels are partially self-governing. From independence in 1830 to 1970, Belgium was a unitary state with a single government and national parliament. The Flemish and Walloon regions were officially created in 1980, and it was in 1993 that the country became a federal state, giving each region its own parliament (while keeping the national parliament).

There are some intractable complications built into the system that are uniquely Belgian. The Flemish parliament governs Flanders and the Flemish community (which are almost, but not quite, the same thing). The Walloon parliament covers Wallonia. Yet while the Flemish parliament absorbed the Flemish community, the Walloon parliament did not, so there is also a government for the French-speaking community, which is separate from the Walloon parliament.

There is also a parliament of the Brussels-Capital region. To complicate matters further, though Brussels is predominantly francophone (yet officially bilingual) and not administratively part of Flanders, it is the capital of the Flemish region as Ghent was considered too small to hold the seat of government. It is also surrounded by the province of Flemish Brabant, a fact Flemish nationalists like to celebrate once a year on the first Sunday of September by cycling around the city in an event known as *De Gordel* (the belt). Furthermore, there is also a parliament of the German-speaking community, since there is a region of some 75,000 German-speaking Belgians in the far east of Wallonia.

To make matters even more complicated, politics and voting patterns in Belgium are not just regional but have traditionally also been sharply divided along lines of class, religion and language, and there are no significant parties participating in both Walloon and Flemish politics, leading to an eternal stalemate between Flemish and Walloon interests, albeit with a slight population advantage for the former.

There are a few consequences to this complex system. It means that elections invariably lead to coalitions (the last single-party government in Belgium was in 1954). That's if a compromise can be found – Belgium existed without a government for 541 days between June 2010 and the end of 2011 while the various political parties struggled to find a coalition that would hold. The previous election in 2007 had taken 194 days to form a government, though each of the four previous coalitions had served out their full four-year terms.

There is also an ongoing debate, exacerbated by that period of 541 days in 2010-11, about whether the separate communities should just split up and form independent states – or even be absorbed into the Netherlands and France – along linguistic lines. (This won't happen in the case of Flanders; it would be less difficult for Wallonia to become part of France, although there are historical reasons the two have almost always been separate, and while some opinion polls occasionally portray Walloons as potentially amenable to the idea, the Rassemblement Wallonie France political party – whose explicit aim is the secession of the region – achieved 0.5 per cent of the vote in the 2014 legislative elections. Furthermore, Brussels would form an intractable problem as it's geographically located in Flanders and is the capital city of that region, so the Flemish would not be keen on letting it go; nor would the Bruxellois be that keen on their home becoming a regional city in France.)

These chaotic compromises are rooted in a long history of arbitrary, fluid and occasionally violent border changes, with loose affiliations of tribes, then provinces bubbling up in a thick geopolitical soup. One of the defining features of Flanders is that there are few natural borders save for the coast, which suited the locals just fine during expansionary adventures but which various European powers have also taken as tacit permission to just walk in and take over.

After the region emerged from the sea during the last ice age, a mix of Celts and German tribes occupied the land, and were then supplanted by and incorporated into Gallo–Celtic warrior clans who showed up in the second century BC. There were five principal tribes: the Menapii lived in East Flanders and Antwerp; the Nervii in West Flanders, Brabant and Hainaut; the Aduatics in Namur; the Treviri in Luxembourg; and the Eburoni in Liège, Limburg and Brabant. Collectively, these tribes were known as the Belgae, a name given to them by the Romans who conquered their land between 57 and 52 BC. The territory occupied by Belgica, the lands of the Belgae, was seven times larger than modern Belgium, including a large area of modern France and a bit of Germany, with loosely defined borders. The Romans stopped not far from where the language line now sits, ignoring the marshy north in modern-day Flanders and the Netherlands. Julius Caesar himself admired the fighting prowess of the locals, saying, *'De Galli Belgae fortissimo sunt'* ('Of all the people of Gaul, the Belgae are the most brave').

As the Roman Empire declined over the next few hundred years, there were successive invasions of Germanic and Viking tribes from the north and east, and the legacies of this are the current language line and a very ethnically mixed population. Flanders, along with the Netherlands, developed a Germanic language, while Wallonia spoke Vulgar Latin, which evolved at different times into Walloon and French. The language line cuts through Belgium, but it's a more or less unbroken border that has been in place since about 300 AD and goes east from Dunkirk all the way to Maastricht in the Netherlands, then due south along the German border all the way through Switzerland.

There were other early signs of what was to become modern Belgium. In the seventh century, the name Flanders was given to a narrow strip of coastline between Bruges and the North Sea. Meanwhile, the territory of Belgium was absorbed into the vast Carolingian Empire, which expanded through the eighth century to cover a huge swathe of central Europe including what would now be northern Italy, most of France, Switzerland, large parts of Germany, plus Belgium and the Netherlands. The king of the Carolingian Empire was Charlemagne, who was also crowned Holy Roman Emperor by the Pope in 800.

Charlemagne died in 814 and his territories were split between his three grandchildren by the Treaty of Verdun in 843. The details were complex but essentially Charles the Bald got France, Louis the German got the territory east of the Rhine, which consisted of modern Germany and Switzerland, and Lothar got the middle slice which included Belgium and the Netherlands and stretched south all the way to the Mediterranean. At this point Belgium still consisted of semi-autonomous dukedoms and cities, but the division of territory meant that Flanders owed allegiance to France whereas Brabant and Limburg were part of Middle Francia, Lothar's portion of the empire.

The Holy Roman Empire enjoyed its own slow-motion dis-integration over the next several hundred years, and Belgium itself settled into feudal states and counties in a much more rec-ognisable form. Flanders, Namur, Brabant, Hainaut, Limburg and Luxembourg and Liège were the most prominent, and these have an echo in the provinces of modern Belgium. As cities like Bruges, Ghent and Antwerp developed into international trade and cultural centres, French and Burgundian dukes ruled the territory.

Through the 14th and 15th centuries Burgundy ruled over most of Belgium and the Netherlands but when Mary, the heir to the Duchy of Burgundy, married the Holy Roman Emperor Maximillian of the Habsburgs and subsequently died, the Low Countries were absorbed into the Habsburg empire, which was ruled alternately from Austria and Spain. The Spanish Habsburgs spread Catholicism throughout the territory.

By 1543, the Habsburg King Charles V, who was born in Ghent, had created a territory called the Union of 17 Provinces, which consisted almost entirely of the modern Benelux coun-tries (though one of the 17, the county of Artois, spilled over the modern border into France). Under Charles V, Antwerp became one of the richest and most important cities in the world, and the population in general in the Low Countries enjoyed high levels of education compared with most of the rest of Europe. An educated population is a sceptical population, however, and in the late 1500s there were mutinous uprisings against the Spanish taxation system, along with a wave of Protestantism combined with anti-Catholicism. In a 1572 revolt, the northern provinces freed themselves from Spanish rule, and within ten years the 17 Provinces had been split into two – the Dutch United Provinces declared their independence in 1581 and would eventually become the modern Netherlands. The southern provinces (modern Belgium and Luxembourg), at this point known as the Spanish Netherlands, were brought back under Habsburg rule and accepted the imposition of Catholicism. This religious schism between the Calvinist Netherlands and Belgium has endured and is the biggest reason that a united Flanders and Netherlands is an impossibility.

Under Spanish rule, Belgium was cut off from the world and withered as Protestants and skilled workers departed, leading to a long period of isolation. The port of Antwerp was closed and it declined as a trading centre. When the last Spanish Habsburg emperor, Carlos II, died without an heir, King Louis XIV of France had designs on expanding French territory into the Spanish Netherlands, but the British and Dutch – neither of whom wanted to see a stronger France – fought back. This forced Louis to cede the region to the Austrian Habsburgs in 1713, who ruled until 1792 – with the exception of one year, as the citizens of the Spanish Netherlands caught the Europe-wide revolutionary fervour of 1789 and for 13 months, for the first time ever, there was an independent United Belgian States, complete with a yellow, black and red flag and Brussels as its capital city. It was known in Flemish as *Verenigde Nederlandse*

Staten and in French as *Les États Belgiques Unis*. For the first time since the era of Julius Caesar, an official entity known as Belgium existed. However, this uprising – known as the Brabant Revolution – was crushed by the Austrians in 1790, then in 1792 the French moved in. They wouldn't last long, but their presence did contribute to the long-term decline of the Walloon language, which was gradually supplanted by French.

Napoleon came to power in 1799 and intended to use a rebuilt and renovated Antwerp port to take trade away from Great Britain and as his strategic base for a planned invasion. He described the port as a 'pistol pointed at the heart of England'.

Under the French, the territory was renamed yet again: for the next 19 years, it would be known as *Les Neuf Départements Réunis* (the Nine United Departments). The nine *départements* corresponded almost exactly with modern-day Belgium and Luxembourg: East and West Flanders, Antwerp, Brabant and Limburg (with a sliver of the Dutch part of Limburg, now north of the border), of modern-day Flanders; Liège, Hainaut, Namur and Luxembourg (plus the Grand Duchy), of modern-day Wallonia.

Napoleon's plans were thwarted by his having overextended himself near Moscow in 1812 and military defeat to the Duke of Wellington at Waterloo in 1815. The Congress of Vienna, held over 1814–1815, was intended to limit the powers of the major European countries, especially Napoleonic France, so that equilibrium between them would prevent more wars. The Napoleonic Empire was broken up, with the British pushing successfully for the creation of a United Kingdom of the Netherlands, which was nothing less than the reunification of modern-day Belgium, the Netherlands and Luxembourg.

Unfortunately, it was not a happy reunion. The head of state was William I, the recently crowned king of the Netherlands. The French-speakers of Wallonia would not accept rule by

Dutch speakers, while the Catholics of Flanders grated at the cohabitation with a Protestant country: through the entire history of this part of the world, the 15 years between 1815 and 1830 possibly saw greater unity between Flemish and Walloons than any other time, against the common enemy of the Dutch. The cultural differences between north and south were too great and in 1830, disgruntled patriots and nationalists plotted a revolution.

It's often reported that the touch-paper for the 1830 revolution in Belgium was lit when the audience at a performance of Daniel Auber's opera *La Muette de Portici* in Brussels got caught up with the singing of a patriotic aria, spilled out onto the streets and started the uprising then and there. However, it was more organised than this. King William had planned a festival to celebrate his 15 years in power: three days of fireworks, feasts and performances in late August, with the opera to be the closing act, one day after the king's birthday. The plans went down badly with the Bruxellois, and posters were put up around the city, reading, 'Monday 23rd: fireworks; Tuesday 24th: illuminations; Wednesday 25th: revolution.'

The crowd were indeed fired up by the opera. They started a demonstration, which turned into riots, and the rebellion spread quickly across the country. By October, William had lost control.

In order to acquire legitimacy, the revolutionaries of Belgium submitted their case for independence to the London Conference of 1830, which consisted of the major European powers: Austria, Britain, France, Prussia and Russia (and minus the Netherlands, who had been humiliated by Belgium's secession). One of the proposals made – by Charles Maurice de Talleyrand-Périgord, the French ambassador to Britain – was to split Belgium up. Antwerp province (but not Antwerp itself) and Limburg would be returned to the Netherlands; Liège, Namur and Luxembourg would go to Prussia; a small part of East Flanders, Brabant and Hainaut would go to France; and finally West Flanders, along with the city of Antwerp and the rest of East Flanders, would form the small Free State of Antwerp, which would be under British protection. It's interesting to consider how different the modern history of this region would have been had the Talleyrand Plan been accepted. Would cycling have become the tool of Flemish emancipation if there had been no subjugation at the hands of French-speakers through the 19th century? Talleyrand's agenda was anti-Belgium, however. He once said, prophetically, 'There are no Belgians, never have been any, never will be any.'

Ultimately, the English backed another French plan, which was to grant full independence and install a constitutional monarchy. The British foreign secretary, Lord Palmerston, vetoed the French choice of king – the Duke of Nemours, son of the French King Louis Philippe – and put forward his own favoured candidate, Leopold of Saxe-Coburg. Leopold was an ambitious Bavarian prince and high-altitude social climber. He had previously married Princess Charlotte, daughter of the English Prince Regent George (who would be crowned King George IV in 1820), the heir to the British throne, and was expecting to live out his days as prince consort to the Queen of England. However, Charlotte's untimely death left Leopold searching for a role and, having turned down the throne of Greece, he accepted the crown as the King of the Belgians. With a figure-head monarch, an optimistic, prophetic and instructive motto ('Unity makes strength') and a new republican constitution, built on forward-thinking 19th-century liberalism and, ironically, the Napoleonic Code, Belgium was independent. The question now was, how was this going to work?

The answer was: very well for French speakers and very badly for Flemish speakers, at least for the first 100 years. The history of modern Belgium often pits Walloons against Flemish, but it's more complicated than that. French was the language of the aristocracy, of the bourgeoisie and of international diplomacy, and it had prestige. Flemish was seen as the language of peasants. It had been a prestige language in the 13th century, but French took over as Burgundy established dominance over the region.

The tension after independence didn't exist just between the two geographical regions, but also between the working class and the ruling classes in Flanders itself, and though the new constitution dictated that Belgium was now a monarchy, the revolution had been based around bourgeois disaffection rather than a working-class uprising. The ruling classes therefore adopted the use of French, with Flemish speakers seen as second-class citizens, and there were shifts in population that reflected the economic realities of the time and which further entrenched French as the dominant language (even though in the census of 1846 only 42 per cent of 4.3 million Belgians spoke French, compared with 57 per cent who spoke Flemish).

Wallonia, with its coalfields, benefited hugely from the industrial revolution, and Flemish workers migrated there, having to communicate in French. There were also certain demographic and political realities that entrenched power with the francophones – only about ten per cent of the population had the vote, and they tended to be the middle and upper classes, who spoke French.

Belgium grew rich in the second half of the 19th century. It became industrialised, especially in Wallonia, and for a time was the fourth-biggest manufacturing power in the world. King Leopold II, Leopold I's son, also embarked on an infamous and disgraceful adventure in central Africa, taking the Congo as his personal property under the guise of altruistic benevolence and making a £3 million profit from the exploitation of its natural resources and slave labour. In doing so, he contributed directly to a number of deaths – commonly estimated between three and ten million people but possibly even more than that. Belgium eventually took over the Congo from Leopold, who had spent part of the loot on turning Brussels into a grand Art Nouveau city.

Crucially, and somewhat unusually given the history of the region, Belgium was not invaded between independence in 1830 and the First World War. This at least gave the nascent state some stability, even though unrest at the oppression of the Flemish was already starting to bubble up through the 19th century.

The first Belgian constitution decreed that use of language was 'free', which the French-speaking ruling classes used to empower themselves further at the expense of the Flemish-speakers. The legal system, education system, government and army all conducted business in French. The consequences of this could be dire – in 1873 a pair of Flemish speakers were wrongly found guilty and executed after a murder trial in which they could not understand proceedings. It was only at the end of the 19th century that Flemish was given equal status, but even then it took a long time for reality to reflect that.

In 1914, Belgium was overrun by German forces at the start of the First World War. The Flemish movement gained more sympathy when it emerged that Flemish troops had gone to their death having been given orders in French (still the language of the army) or, worse, had been executed for not following orders they didn't understand. But the Germans fomented disagreements between Flemish and francophone interests, favouring the former, and after the war there was a general rejection of Germanic culture which meant that the Flemish movement needed a different impetus. On one hand, the Flemish movement adopted a pacifist standpoint in the 1920s; on the other, the *IJzertoren*, a war memorial built in Diksmuide in West Flanders, was seen as a thinly veiled monument to Flemish nationalism. But universal suffrage for males in 1918 (for women it came in 1948) meant that the balance between Flemish and franco-phone Belgium could tilt back away from the French speakers, even though the class prejudices would take a lot longer to be eradicated.

The Second World War was another setback for Flemish interests. There were accusations of collaboration, and the sit-uation was best illustrated by the position of the king, Leopold III, who was suspected of not resisting the German invasion anywhere near strongly enough, in contrast to the conduct of his father Albert I during the First World War. Albert had fought the Germans, retreated to a corner of Flanders near De Panne, opened the dykes to create a flood between his forces and the invaders, and successfully held out to the end of the war. Leopold III, on the other hand, spent the war loosely under house arrest, and though a referendum on the matter after the war voted narrowly in favour of allowing him to return (with voting patterns following regional lines: the Flemish favoured his return, the more socialist and working-class Walloons rejected it), he abdicated in 1950.

But after the war, the ascendancy of Flanders and the decline of Wallonia began. Heavy industry started to shrink and mines closed in the southern provinces, while the Marshall Plan for post-war European reconstruction led to heavy investment in Flanders. As Flanders has gained the ascendancy, the political power has shifted, with an increasingly confident nationalist movement bemoaning the net outflow of money from Flanders to Wallonia. Today, Flanders is the economic and cultural powerhouse, and Wallonia is suffering from post-industrial stagnation.

The Tour of Flanders has changed to reflect these social changes. At first it was an expression of Flemish potential and then, as local riders dominated, it became proof – along with Flemish victories in the Tour de France from the 1910s onwards – that the Flemish could win. Now, there's less need for the Flemish to prove themselves by winning the Ronde, although they still often do so. The race is a huge international affair, one of the biggest bike races in the world, and attracts fans from all over the globe. Flanders – once a strip of chilly, salty, marshy coastline, and for centuries an inward-looking backwater – has become an international, ambitious, outward-looking region. The race also covers up, but doesn't negate, the background tension that constantly exists in Belgium, a reminder that the country is at once more than and less than the sum of its parts.

CHAPTER 12

Molenberg

The Moldergemmolen, the watermill which gives the Molenberg its name, was built in the 13th century as the property of the Benedictine Abbey at Ename near Oudenaarde. It's still there, just where the Molenberg turns off from the road between Sint-Denijs-Boekel and Sint-Blasius-Boekel, although the original building is long gone – it was burned down in 1451 during the Revolt of Ghent against the Burgundian duke Philip the Good. The mill has undergone various transformations since – it's been a sawmill, an oil press and a flour mill. Of course, it's nothing of the sort now. The Moldergembeek still rushes under the bridge by the mill, down a steep man-made waterfall, and a decaying wooden wheel of about 12 feet in diameter is still attached to the wall, though the bushes growing through the radial spokes suggest it hasn't turned in a while. The mill was closed in 1968 and it's now an upmarket restaurant, *De Mechelse Koekoek*, though one of the neighbours told me the millstone is still *in situ*. The wheel is the only external evidence that this used to be a mill, but a more modern aspect of local heritage is celebrated with a poem inscribed on a Perspex screen mounted on the wall: '*De Molenberg*' by Willie Verhegghe. '*De*

Molenberg' describes the 'frightening cracking and crunching of the chains' as the race goes up the climb, and the 'cobblestones putting their claws in the calves without mercy, making the thighs dance in an orgy of sweat and dust'.

When I visited, I took a photo of the poem. It was only later, when I was at the Muur van Geraardsbergen, that I saw more of Verhegghe's works and realised that the Tour of Flanders has its own poet laureate, who has spent almost half a century creating permanent memories of transient moments and impressions. The permanence is literal – one of the poems on the Muur is carved into a sheet of iron. The chroniclers of the Ronde have generally been the journalists of the written press but their stories are just that: stories, with a start, a middle and an ending. Verhegghe's poetry might be more akin to the work of the photographers: taking snapshots and images of specific moments. I tracked him down through the least poetic of means – his LinkedIn page.

Verhegghe's first memory of cycling was watching the 1951 Tour of Flanders, the third of Fiorenzo Magni's wins, as a four-year-old boy. The race passed his street in Denderleeuw, the town between Geraardsbergen and Aalst, where he was born and grew up. 'I was watching the race, holding my father's hand,' he said. 'I was scared because of the noise, and the policemen passing on their big motorbikes. I remember Magni was alone. He passed us in the direction of Wetteren, in Ghent, where the finish was. It's my favourite memory of the race. I didn't understand what was happening, but it left a big impression on me.'

Verhegghe writes poetry about anything and everything. One online writers' directory describes him as having a 'socially critical gaze', but cycling is a theme that has engaged him all his life. His first book of poetry, *Icarus on my Knee*, which was published in 1969, contained two poems about the sport, and though he hasn't counted, he estimates that he's written over

300 poems about cycling. 'If I may say,' he said, 'I am the champion in Flemish poetry about cycling.' I suggested he is the Tom Boonen of the art form and he laughed. 'Or the Merckx!' he said.

Verhegghe got hooked on cycling when he was a child. One of his friends at school was the younger brother of Edgard Sorgeloos, a Tour de France stage winner and one of Rik Van Looy's most favoured domestiques between 1959 and 1966. 'For me, cycling is the most poetic form of sport,' he said. 'You have the different and beautiful landscapes the riders pass through. You have tragedy. It's a very hard sport. It's also very pure and simple. You have the cyclist and you have the bike. The two together are so beautiful – the basic form of a human being and a very simple machine, the bike, working together. In cycling, there is human drama, tragedy and victory, and all the things that lie between these extremes.'

The commission for the Molenberg poem came from the mayor of Zwalm. '*De Molenberg*' is an impressionistic account of the climb, which compares the waiting crowds to the spectators in the Colosseum. 'It's about the berg itself, the landscape and cycling fans,' said Verhegghe. 'There is a link to the history of ancient Rome, a world of suffering and victory, things that you can find in the Ronde. I wrote the poem because I find this is one of the most difficult climbs of the Tour of Flanders. I suffered a lot on it during my own rides.'

The Molenberg happens to be my favourite climb in the Tour of Flanders. It's aesthetically pleasing – the narrow cobbled bridge over the Moldergembeek gives it a sense of separation from the bland flat tarmac of the road at the bottom. Then the road opens out into a triangular cobbled space which – house conversions and restaurant rebuilding aside – probably doesn't look hugely different from the way it did 100 years ago or more. The houses opposite the mill used to be one property where the mill owner lived, but when the mill closed it was split into two. The Molenberg itself, narrow and badly cambered, runs along one side of this triangle, then twists steeply up between tall bushes on either side of the road. The cobbles might be the worst on the Flanders route, comparable to those of the Koppenberg – they're rounded and quite large but so are the gaps between them, plus subsidence has collapsed their foundations, turning what might once have been something resembling straight lines into a snaggle-toothed grin of a farm track. The subsidence is so bad further up that when I sat on the grassy bank near the top to watch the 2015 race pass, feeling the first warmth of the spring sunshine on my back, the smell of burned clutches hanging in the air, I could hear the team cars struggling up in the wake of the riders and grounding loudly on the hump in the middle of the road, to ironic cheers from the spectators.

The road that leads to the Molenberg is called the Smarre. It's two lanes wide, flat, nondescript. The race has approached from both sides, although the northern approach is used more often. The entry to the Molenberg is horrible, even by Tour of Flanders standards: a 90-degree turn on to one of the narrowest bergs in the race, so single file only. The difference in width between the Smarre and the Molenberg is huge. Along both the Smarre and the first 20 metres of the climb, there's space for car parking. It is surfaced with gravel and the loose stones often kick up and spread over the entry point, which also has a shallow, semi-circular drain running across the divide between tarmac and cobbles. This is usually full of gravel as well. The peloton often stalls here; sometimes there are crashes.

The Molenberg is only 17 cobblestones wide at the bottom; as the road crosses the bridge 30 metres in, it's even narrower – 14 cobbles wide with mossy walls at about a cyclist's shin height with a long drop to the stream below. The Molenberg drags up from the bridge past the restaurants, then steepens into its S-bend of riotous cobbles at 14 per cent; well-maintained detached houses behind neat bushes on one side, a soggy-looking open field on the other. Like the Koppenberg, the cobbles are almost always damp, even on dry days, and overtaking on the first half of the climb is all but impossible: Peter Van Petegem told me, 'You have to stop at the bottom, then sprint. But when you are first at the bottom, you are first at the top.'

The gradient gets shallower in the second half, but not by much, and though after about 250 metres the rutted, mossy *kasseien* give way to tarmac, the road keeps dragging up for another 200 metres. The sharpness of the bend at the bottom, the narrowness of the entrance and then the bridge, the gravel, the terrible surface and the steepness all combine to make this one of the most interesting climbs of the race.

The Molenberg made its first appearance only in 1983 but it has been in the race most years since. Of the 31 times the race has ascended it, nine have been as the first climb in the race, which neutralises its effect a little, although there's no more dramatic or apt way to announce the beginning of the *Vlaamse Ardennen* than the 90-degree turn from wide road to cobbled track at the bottom.

There's one more noteworthy thing about the Molenberg: there's no descent, at least not for some kilometres. The riders turn right at the top, taking a similarly narrow road that crosses a dead-flat plateau of ploughed fields, and it is as open a landscape as it's possible to imagine – there's not a tree within 200 metres of the road for most of its length. Verhegghe told me this was one of his favourite landscapes on the Ronde route. There's a single windmill nearby, the Vinkemolen, a wooden structure whose body rotates on a pyramid of massive beams, fixed with huge chains, and whose sails catch the wind uninterrupted from the south-west. It's both ironic and a measure of how strong the wind can be in these parts, that the Vinkemolen actually blew over in 1983 and had to be rebuilt.

The fact that there's no immediate descent means it's not easy to close any gaps that have formed on the climb. Andreas Klier told me about the road at the top: 'If you have the right wind here, you can go very fast away from the others because even if there are 20 of them, they can't rotate because the road is so narrow. If you have two in the front and five chasing, it's already difficult for the five. Normally there's an 80 per cent chance of a west wind; here the wind is almost behind the riders, so it's fast. The climb is slow, you get to the top, change to the big ring, sprint to the T-junction, turn right and speed up. It's an important climb.'

Just like the Kwaremont, the climb of the Molenberg only does half the damage – it's the windblown flats afterwards which really widen the gaps.

Peter Van Petegem lived within a few hundred metres of the Molenberg for the latter part of his career, in Sint-Maria-Horebeke, and he reckons he climbed it two or three thousand times. 'I rode it every time after training. After a six-hour ride, I'd do the Molenberg ten times. Up, then a small road directly down to make a little circuit. I did that ten times every day,' he told me.

Living close by had its advantages on the day of the race. 'The day before the race I would call my wife and ask how it was on the climb, whether I should go left or right or up the middle.'

Van Petegem won the Ronde in 1999 and in 2003 (when he also won Paris–Roubaix, which remains a rare double), and was a popular rider at home. He fit the stereotype of the *Flandrien* quite well in some ways – he was stoic and unpretentious and mostly unconcerned with fripperies like races between mid-April and the end of the season. (He rode well in the World Championships from time to time, and made an abortive attempt at seeing if he could be competitive in stage races, coming third in Paris–Nice, but through his career he focused more and more on the cobbled Classics, and he actively avoided the Tour de France after 1998.) He was also, it was said, fond of a Belgian beer or two, and his local credentials were impeccable – he was born and grew up in Brakel, in the heart of the *Vlaamse Ardennen*. Yet, when we talked about *Flandriens*, he told me he always disliked the cold weather, even if he could bear it better than others during the race. 'I like more the sun,' he confessed.

I met Van Petegem at the offices of the insurance company where he now works, on the outskirts of Oudenaarde. My memory of him as a rider was that he looked like a tough bastard – massive Desperate Dan jaw, permanent five o'clock shadow, brooding brow and legs like a footballer. Not beautiful on a bike; kind of resolute. My opinion of him was also coloured by reading an interview Lionel Birnie did with him in *Cycle Sport* in 1999, where Van Petegem had not exactly stood the magazine up but had left them waiting for some time. 'I called him and he said to come to his house at 9:30 a.m.,' Lionel told me when I asked him about it.

'So we arrived at 9:30 and he was in his kit getting ready to go training. He said we could do the interview after he got back at 4:30, but that we could follow him out and take photos during the first part of his ride. So we followed him for about a kilometre out through town, then he darted onto a cycle path, turned right as we got stuck at the traffic lights and fucked off. That was the last we saw of him, so the photographer and I went for lunch, sat around for the afternoon and went to see him at his house at 4:30.' I concluded years ago that there was a kind of direct, unapologetic hardness about him, and I presumed the number of seconds he hesitated about going out riding instead of doing the interview was around zero. His old directeur sportif at Lotto, Allan Peiper, once said of him, 'Van Petegem is mentally very, very strong. He knows where he stands. He likes to drink a beer and doesn't give a shit what anybody says about it.'

But that was hard to square with the polite and affable middle-aged man who welcomed me to the modern, open-plan interior of the ProAssur insurance company's office. Around us: coloured Perspex screens and an airy atmosphere created by floor-to-ceiling glass walls around the outside of the building. Its straight lines and neatness couldn't be further from the Molenberg, with its stone buildings, tall bushes and higgledy-piggledy road. Or from bike racing in general. Van Petegem has kept well in touch with the sport, was in the Garmin team car at the 2011 Tour of Flanders where he was employed to call the tactical shots, and is a regular interviewee around the time of the Ronde, but he's moved on from the circus. 'When you stop cycling at 37, it's too young to do nothing for the rest of your life. Life is more than sitting at home and doing nothing,' he told me.

Van Petegem always knew the Ronde was the race for him. When he was young, one of his father's friends was Ferdi Van Den Haute, a professional rider who won Ghent–Wevelgem, a Tour de France stage, the points jersey in the Tour of Spain and the Belgian national championships. His bedroom was plastered with posters of the stars of the sport, and he collected stickers of them to put in albums. He played football until he was 15, then started racing in 1985. 'I didn't race so much in the first year. Maybe 20 races,' he said. 'I was one of the smallest guys in the peloton so I had to be smart.'

The young Van Petegem and his father also watched the Tour of Flanders every year: 'My dad was very clever and knew the race. We saw it 15 times in one day.'

I asked Van Petegem why he was good at the race and he cited his strength and his ability to sprint (more useful in terms of getting to the front of the bunch for the climbs than in a bunch finish, although he had to outsprint other riders to win both his Rondes). He also had a visible and visceral enjoyment of the physical contact: when I asked him what he'd learned from his first experience of the race in 1993, he held up both fists and simply said, 'Fighting!' with almost a little too much relish.

But there's one more thing, the most important of all. When I interviewed Sebastian Langeveld about the 2011 race, he said something that I heard often, from different riders: 'I try to ride like Peter Van Petegem, to ride at the back.' Then he added, ruefully: 'But you have to be really strong to ride always at the back.' The Belgian cycling journalist Noël Truyers wrote about Van Petegem in *Cycle Sport* in early 2003: 'Van Petegem is a clever rider. He reads races like nobody else. He has got a nose for it. Yes, he always is at the back of the bunch, but he seldom misses the final breaks. He feels when the racing starts. All at once he is up there.'

Van Petegem seems to have inherited his father's affinity for the route, demonstrated by the latter's ability to spectate the race in 15 different places, and I don't think I know of a rider who understands the Tour of Flanders as well as him. Andreas Klier, maybe, but I sensed a difference in the way each had learned about the roads of the Ronde. Klier analysed the roads from the point of view of a scientist; with Van Petegem the knowledge was ingrained, less consciously learned. 'You have to know the parcours very well,' he said. 'Very important.'

Jonathan Vaughters, the Garmin manager who brought Van Petegem into the team car for the cobbled Classics season in 2011, confirmed this. 'He is unbelievably knowledgeable about every corner, every field and hill and cobbled section,'

Vaughters told me. 'I don't need a map,' Van Petegem said. 'I know every corner, every bad road. I know how to get to the front and where the wind was coming from. In the Ronde van Vlaanderen it's not like we ride east or south. It changes, so you have to always be thinking where it will be hard and where the wind is. Every year I rode twenty or thirty thousand kilometres here. I went to school in Ninove, and every day after school I came back, rode round and did the Muur and the Bosberg, then more riding and back to Brakel.'

Van Petegem's career got off to a false start. He turned professional in 1992 and rode for the big Dutch team PDM–Concorde that year, and the Belgian squad Lotto–Caloi in 1993. But his results were average, PDM folded at the end of the first year, and he fell out with the management at Lotto, which left him casting around for a ride in a smaller team. He got a contract for 1994 with Trident–Schick, a short-lived Belgian team who left little impression on the sport save for a memorably literal representation of the sponsor's product on the bright orange team jersey: a large picture of a Schick razor blade. Trident was not a long-term option for an ambitious rider, and Van Petegem gave himself a year to sort his career out. He won the Scheldeprijs, a flatter coda to the cobbled Classics season which takes place the Wednesday after Paris–Roubaix, and got a contract with the Dutch TVM team through Jesper Skibby, the Danish rider who had almost been run down by a race car on the Koppenberg in 1987. It was with TVM that Van Petegem first won the Tour of Flanders, in 1999.

The 1999 event was possibly the last great Flemish Ronde. There have been Flemish winners since – quite a few actually – but 1999 remains the last time Belgian riders enjoyed a clean sweep of the podium places. That year saw a three-way battle between three local greats: Van Petegem, Johan Museeuw and Frank Vandenbroucke. Museeuw was the dominant cobbled

Classics rider of the late 1990s and early 2000s, one of the few riders to win the Ronde three times and in 1999 the reigning champion. However, he was also on the comeback from a horrific injury to his knee sustained in the previous year's Paris–Roubaix, and he was in good but not great form. Vandenbroucke was born in Mouscron and grew up in Ploegsteert, just south of the language border in the far west of Wallonia, due south of Ypres and just over the French border from Armentières. He was a mercurial, talented, beautiful and troubled individual, and the yin of his prodigious, recklessly extravagant victories was inevitably balanced by the yang of drug addiction and psychological trouble; he died in October 2009.

In Geraardsbergen, Van Petegem and Museeuw rode up through the town at the head of a 20-strong group. Van Petegem was the strongest physically, Museeuw perhaps psychologically stronger, having won the race three times already. Vandenbroucke also looked okay, but as he took his position behind his two compatriots around the sharp corner towards the top of Geraardsbergen that announces the start of the Muur, he tangled with the Swiss rider Markus Zberg. Both came down and the rest of the group washed over them like a breaking wave. As stalled and fallen riders disentangled themselves from each other and from their bikes, Van Petegem and Museeuw simply rode away and over the Muur 15 seconds clear of the rest, with Van Petegem distancing Museeuw slightly over the top. This gave Van Petegem a crucial advantage – he knew he was the stronger of the two.

Vandenbroucke tore himself clear of the second group after the descent, chasing hard on the Bosberg and finally joining Museeuw and Van Petegem about a kilometre after the top. Save for a couple of attacks by Vandenbroucke, the three worked together to Meerbeke, partly because there were four Rabobank riders rotating at the front of the second group and the gap was starting to shrink. Better to guarantee a podium place in this context than risk being significantly outnumbered in a larger group.

The conclusion in the Belgian media about the 1999 Ronde was that Vandenbroucke was worked over a little by the two more experienced riders. Guy Fransen, sports editor of *Het Nieuwsblad*, said, 'For me, Van Petegem was the anti-hero, and the last one I wanted to win. I think everybody wanted Frank to win and the two older riders had a kind of coalition. I can't prove it, but I suspect they would be happy for each other to win, but not Frank.'

Van Petegem denied this to me: 'I think it's the opposite. Museeuw and Vandenbroucke were good friends ...'

What's certain is that the sprint was played out in a spirit of remarkable fair play. Van Petegem made one last attack, with just under a kilometre to go, and was chased down by Vandenbroucke. (This is where it looked as if Museeuw and Van Petegem might have had an understanding, unspoken or otherwise. When Van Petegem attacked, Museeuw didn't even try to follow, waiting for Vandenbroucke to take up the chase – textbook working-over tactics.) But then all three riders fanned out across the road and rode three abreast from about 450 metres to go. They had improvised an agreement to sprint it out man against man against man, without resorting to drafting or tactics. As they started to sprint, Van Petegem pulled ahead. 'After the crash, I could have gone solo but I wasn't ready to do it, so I waited for Museeuw, and Vandenbroucke came up to us on the Bosberg,' said Van Petegem. 'It was good that he was there, because there were three of us against four Rabobank riders. In the sprint, Vandenbroucke wanted to win; I wanted to win; I think it was me or him, and Museeuw was sitting there. But sometimes, when two dogs are fighting over their food, it's the third who takes it. It was a friendly sprint, but the winner would be who was strongest. The last 20 metres, it was, like, yes ... yes ... yes ... yes!'

It took Van Petegem some time to win the Ronde again. In 2000 he came third in Paris–Nice, but he believes the effort made him ill in the run-up to the Ronde, and things were already starting to fall apart with his new team, Mercury–Viatel. 'Everything was a bit shit with that team,' he told me. He was eighth in Flanders, but by summer Mercury – whose organisational structure was riddled with unrealistic ambition, impossible promises and dreams – had collapsed like weak concrete. Van Petegem crashed and didn't finish in 2001, and a year later he watched while Italy's Andrea Tafi rode away to a solo victory when he felt strong enough to win. He described Tafi as 'a lucky dog' in an interview with *Procycling* magazine a few years later.

Then came 2003, and another perfect confluence of form and circumstances. This time, Van Petegem attacked on the climb of Tenbossestraat, in Brakel. 'The most important thing is knowing the moment to go,' he said. 'Attacking with 80 kilometres to go is easy – everybody feels good then. But after 200 kilometres, it's hard and everybody's legs are feeling like shit. Sometimes the race is waiting for you to attack, so on Tenbosse, I went. My house was one kilometre away, and it felt like the whole of Brakel was standing there on the road.'

The attack wasn't the winning one. Van Petegem joined a couple of earlier escapees, France's Frédéric Guesdon and Belgium's Nico Mattan, and was caught in turn by Vandenbroucke and another Belgian, Dave Bruylandts, but this quintet was caught before Geraardsbergen. Van Petegem went away again on the Muur, with Vandenbroucke, and this time the gap held. Vandenbroucke had had a fraught few years since 1999, with crashes, episodes of depression, speeding tickets and a stash of drugs that he maintained belonged to his dog; 2003 was one last bright flaring of his brilliance, although he'd already won his last race at the top level. He tried in vain to drop his companion over the Bosberg, but the implacable Van Petegem resisted. The sprint was an anti-climax, no contest. 'Winning the Ronde was like a dream,' Van Petegem told me. 'All the races you've won before seem like nothing. For a Belgian guy, it's like you are the king.'

The race is in four bits: a front quartet of Chavanel, Clarke, Boasson Hagen and Boom; a second quartet of Guesdon, Van Avermaet, Hayman and Leezer; the peloton of 60 or so; then the rest – who knows how many – already out of it. They turn north from Jagerij, with the wind temporarily behind them. The route will take the Tour of Flanders through a tiny hamlet called Duisbeke, then turn east before the junction with the Smarre road. A right turn here, then south for a kilometre and a half to the Molenberg. There are 50 kilometres to go.

At the right turn the Guesdon quartet is stuck, 15 seconds in arrears, while the peloton sits back, another 20 seconds behind. Guesdon and his companions are vulnerable because they're not getting any closer to the leaders, and the bunch will halve their deficit by the bottom of the climb in the inevitable acceleration. This in turn could yet put pressure back on the front group. Chavanel and Clarke are now almost 40 kilometres into their break and the gap still hasn't been above a minute, though at least now they have reinforcements.

Geraint Thomas leads the bunch, Flecha is on his wheel. Philippe Gilbert sits near the front. So does Tom Boonen. Thor Hushovd too. It's not just a case of the favourites massing at the front before a climb, however. They're all there because of what happened on the Molenberg the year before.

The Molenberg came marginally closer to the finish in 2010 than in 2011, 44 kilometres out. A quartet of riders led by Bernhard Eisel had started the climb a few metres in front of the peloton – less a conscious attack than simply getting the approach right and reaching the sharp turn in first place. Halfway up, Eisel still led. But on the right-hand side of the road, just before the gradient eased for the final stretch of cobbles, Fabian Cancellara was moving up; no, attacking. It looked smooth but the speed was clear from the reaction of Tom Boonen, who visibly strained to match the acceleration.

By the right-hand turn at the top, the pair's lead was 20 metres over a group of eight, who were themselves a similar distance ahead of a broken line of riders. Thirty seconds later, it was clear Cancellara and Boonen were riding away from the field – the gap expanded, rapidly on the plateau at first, then more slowly, but inexorably. Boonen had team-mates in the next group and they made a nuisance of themselves by hindering the chase, putting themselves near the front then not rolling through, disrupting the speed and rhythm of the group. By the top of the Leberg, Boonen and Cancellara's lead was 25 seconds; at Tenbosse, with 25 kilometres to go, it was just under a minute ahead of a chasing trio, and another 20 seconds to the first also-rans.

The Boonen–Cancellara tandem was one of the great escapes of the Ronde's history, as meaningful and defining of its era as Magni's in 1951, which led to his third win, or Merckx's in 1969, Vanderaerden's in 1985 or Edwig Van Hooydonck's in 1989. Boonen and Cancellara were the greatest cobbled Classics riders of the 2000s (each would retire with three wins in the Ronde). In 2010 they were the national champions of their respective countries, their jerseys bright Fauvist dabs of primary colour against the muted background of a Flemish landscape painting. Their escape over the Molenberg that year also offered the tantalising promise of a clash of differing strengths and specialities. Boonen was the superior sprinter; Cancellara the best time-triallist in the world: if they came to the finish together, the Belgian would win. But if Cancellara could drop Boonen, there was little chance of him coming back.

Boonen was confident, even cocky: he'd had it in his head that he would attack on the Muur. Instead, it was the Swiss rider who surged away on that climb. A persistent and stubborn gap of a few metres opened up on the steepest part of the Muur; by the top, Boonen was humiliated: already 13 seconds behind. By the finish, Cancellara was one minute 15 seconds clear – the largest gap between first and second for 15 years. Now, a year later, his rivals are wary of a repeat performance.

Chavanel turns the corner into the Molenberg first. On the short stretch of flatter cobbles just after the bridge, he shifts up a gear and accelerates. Boasson Hagen and Boom follow at a distance; Clarke is dropped.

Half a minute later, Geraint Thomas leads the peloton into the climb, before Flecha takes over. Hushovd, Cancellara, Boonen, then Leukemans and Ballan accelerate, look at each other, and then relent. The increase in speed is enough to have caught Guesdon but history will not repeat itself. Cancellara sits tight.

At the top, Cancellara still leads but he starts to freewheel. The group starts to bunch up, in a process which often repeats itself at this point in a Classic. It's deep enough into the race that nobody has many team-mates to rely on, but still too far – efforts like Cancellara's 2010 win notwithstanding – to the finish to be too aggressive. The terrain forces the riders to race, then relent, in an irregular and unpredictable rhythm. But the lulls are getting shorter: something big is going to happen soon.

While the biggest favourites refuse to commit, others still see opportunity. Björn Leukemans, Devolder's team-mate on the Vacansoleil team, feels the deceleration that has spread among the big riders like a contagion and senses this is a good moment.

He attacks on the plateau road, past the Vinkemolen, and is countered by Baden Cooke.

Leukemans, fourth the previous year, is a strong Classics rider with a very consistent series of results: fourth in Flanders and Roubaix, seventh in the Amstel Gold Race and ninth in Liège–Bastogne–Liège – you don't get many riders finishing in the top ten of the cobbled races *and* Amstel and Liège, whose longer ascents suit the diesel climbers of the Grand Tours rather than the punchy, powerful specialists of the Ronde. His career has been non-linear – he's spent the majority of it riding for smaller teams in Belgium, and there was also the interregnum of a positive test and subsequent ban for artificial testosterone in 2008. (His excuse: he claimed he'd been having sex when the testers arrived and therefore had elevated levels of the hormone, an explanation that didn't wash with the authorities.) It's no surprise he's ended up at Vacansoleil, an eclectic collective of misfits, lone wolves, occasional reformed dopers and oddballs who don't seem to fit in elsewhere.

The peloton lets Leukemans and Cooke go. Cooke's instructions are to get himself ahead of the race so that he is available to help Nuyens in the final 30 minutes. Leukemans considers himself one of the strongest riders in the race, but he's never listed in the top tier of favourites. While the favourites watch Cancellara, and even Leukemans' team-mate Devolder to an extent, he has a bit more leeway to move.

Ahead, Chavanel is alone and riding hard. He's better alone in these races – he doesn't enjoy being in the bunch on the small roads of Flanders. He leads Boom and Boasson Hagen by 150 metres or so. Leukemans and Cooke catch what is left of the two original quartets – Hayman, Van Avermaet, Leezer and Clarke – to make a sextet, and then comes the bunch. The gap between Chavanel and the bunch is now almost a minute. There are 45 kilometres left. One hour.

CHAPTER 13

Leberg

I would contend that Fabian Cancellara is the best road cyclist of the 21st century so far. There's no quantifiable measure that fully supports this assertion, but I just *know*. Other candidates might include Paolo Bettini (too one-dimensional), Alejandro Valverde (hasn't won enough), Mark Cavendish (see Bettini), Chris Froome (also one-dimensional) and Alberto Contador (ditto). All of these cyclists are or were the best at what they did. Valverde was the closest of them to being a multi-tasker on the road – he won Classics and one Grand Tour, though his most impressive attributes were sheer longevity and a practised evasiveness whenever the issue of doping came up. But to compare the best sprinter in the world with the best Classics rider – or the best Grand Tour rider or the best time-triallist – and assert one specialist's superiority over another is to tacitly reveal one's own prejudices. Cancellara was the best time-triallist in the world for many years and the best Classics rider, but there's more to it than that.

In his 2006 essay 'Federer, Both Flesh and Not', David Foster Wallace described what he called 'Roger Federer Moments': 'Almost anyone who loves tennis and follows the men's tour on television has, over the last few years, had what might be termed Federer Moments. These are times, watching the young Swiss at play, when the jaw drops and eyes protrude and sounds are made that bring spouses in from other rooms to see if you're OK.'

Cycling doesn't offer the same immediacy of experience as tennis, but when I think back over the last 15 years in bike racing, there have been more Cancellara Moments than any other, and it's this – more than any straightforward athletic comparison with his peers – that makes me think he's the best. The 2010 Tour of Flanders was a Cancellara Moment. So was his win in Paris–Roubaix that year, along with a 2007 Tour de France stage win where he attacked the sprinters' teams in the final kilometre of the Compiègne stage and held them off, which should be impossible. Fabian being Fabian, he did this while wearing the yellow jersey (won by a hefty distance in the London prologue of the race, which was another Cancellara Moment). Although he didn't win, the 2008 Olympic road race was a Cancellara Moment – he managed to close a 30-second gap from the peloton to a five-rider front group in the final ten kilometres (though as is often the case with cycling, the surprise and impact of his appearance, as if from nowhere, came as much from patchy television coverage as from the exploit itself). A few riders get one or two Moments in their careers, and most get none; Cancellara was in double figures.

I've always found Cancellara intimidating, though that's not to say he's not good company. The two things I always notice about him – apart from his legs, which are like sides of beef – are his loud, deep voice and his perfect posture, which is a physical manifestation of his confidence. Then again, conversations with him can be quite goofy and random, and he has a quirky grip on the English language that is idiosyncratic enough to have been given its own name by cycling fans: Fabianese. The effect, deliberate or otherwise, is that it distracts or works as a defence mechanism. I once asked him about cycling tactics and was drawn into an enjoyable and unusable monologue of *non sequiturs* about belief and non-belief in God, and karma.

I'm in two minds about whether he's much fun to be around. He's egotistical, vain and unironic and he sulks a bit when he loses. The goofiness is endearing and I once spent a day with him in his hometown of Bern in Switzerland, during which he was an exuberant and helpful guide, taking me and a photographer out on his favourite recovery spin, a 35-kilometre loop through green hills and meadows coloured bright yellow with spring flowers. On the descents, he wove left and right like a downhill skier, bunny-hopping potholes and accelerating into the corners so that, even though we were in a car, there was no question of keeping up. At a *Cycle Sport* photo shoot a few years back, he'd found a tennis ball and started doing keepy-uppies, along with some impromptu gymnastics on the ladder into a swimming pool. He's irrepressible.

At the same time I think the competitive streak that has made him the best cyclist of the century is probably by necessity quite hard-edged. He's possibly aware of this, and differentiates between when he is 'on', which is to say focused on a certain target (and driving himself and those around him extremely hard) and 'off', when things are a lot more relaxed. My interpretation of things from watching him and his team at training camps and races is that there's a lot of unspoken tension and low-level stress when Cancellara is 'on'. He gorges on this tension, digests it and converts it into forward motion, but it strikes me that there's no room for fuck-ups. He once told me about shouting at his team-mate Volodymir Gustov from second or third wheel to keep pulling, in one race or another, even though the Ukrainian was spent. 'I was yelling, saying, "Come on! More! More!",' he said.

The Australian cyclist Brad McGee – who rode with

Cancellara at the Saxo Bank team in 2008, then was his directeur sportif at the same outfit in 2009 and 2010 – once said to me, 'Fabian is a very profound bike rider. He appears untouchable from the outside, but inside he is very different. He actually stresses more compared to other riders, but Fabian is unique because he takes it all inside him. He can be heavy-handed – he's got a big presence and a full voice. It's clear he's in charge but he suffers internal stress. He deals with it then uses it.'

To maintain authority like this requires a certain distance, and it might create victims. Baden Cooke, who rode on Saxo Bank with Cancellara in 2010, told me: 'When I won the Tour's green jersey I gave everybody a bonus out of my own money and made my team-mates feel like I couldn't have done it without them. Fabian didn't do that at all. It's bad business. When I won big races I was very generous, and I know that guys like Mark Cavendish are very generous when they win. And you know what? People keep working for them. It's not about the money; it's about respect.'

The Ronde held Cancellara at arm's length for a long time. He turned professional in 2001; an acquaintance who'd seen him winning the world junior time-trial championships in 1999 said he just looked like a fat kid on a bike but also gave the impression he could ride through a brick wall. He spent a few seasons picking up mainly time-trial wins – ten in his first three years – then announced himself to the wider cycling public by taking the yellow jersey in the prologue of the 2004 Tour de France. Though he'd also come fourth in Paris–Roubaix that year, he was pigeon-holed as a time-triallist.

At the Tour of Qatar in 2006, my colleague Lionel Birnie at *Cycle Sport* magazine interviewed him. Boonenmania was at its height – the Belgian had won the Tour of Flanders and Paris–Roubaix the previous year and looked unbeatable in both events. After a long chat with the Swiss, Lionel walked back over and said, 'He says he's going to win Paris–Roubaix. He's going to isolate Boonen from his team-mates and then attack.' I was sceptical, but two months later that's exactly what happened.

It took years longer for Cancellara to get a grip on the Tour of Flanders. He rode the Ronde seven times between 2003 and 2009 and his only top-20 finish was in 2006 when he came sixth behind Boonen, albeit at the back of the group that sprinted for third, one minute 17 seconds behind the Belgian. He managed a final-quarter attack in the 2007 event, during which he spent some time off the front, attacking before Tenbosse with Gert Steegmans and building a 30-second lead, which duly melted through the streets of Geraardsbergen. By the finish he was marooned in the group that contested 22nd place, 90 seconds behind the winner. His ongoing struggle with the Tour of Flanders was best illustrated with a photograph of him off his bike, near the top of the Koppenberg in 2009, his broken chain an apt metaphor for his relationship with the event. He shouldered his bike and traipsed back down the hill, in the opposite direction from the race.

I met Cancellara at his Trek team's winter training camp in L'Alfàs del Pi on the Costa Blanca in December 2015. I'd written down his results as a list – 73rd, 41st, 62nd, 6th, 53rd, 23rd, DNF – followed by ones, twos and threes for the wins and podium places, with a thick black line between the two sets of numbers. I showed him the list and asked what the difference was between before 2010 and after. 'Learning. Waiting,' he said. 'I broke my chain in 2009 and had to walk up the Koppenberg. Then after that, I won or I wasn't there. Even with the stupid crash in 2012, I think that would be a win as well. My relationship with the cobbles is . . . I don't say I love them; I like them because of the passion. There are so many things in those races; they are difficult, with drama and passion and history and emotions.'

I'd also drawn a Venn diagram of three circles, labelled 'team', 'physical strength' and 'tactics' and shown that to Cancellara as well. 'My wins were all of these things, and I think you can add mental strength to that. I sometimes have more of this or more of that but in the end, it's balance. The ideal plan always depends on [my] rivals, but we don't fix on them. We look at our strength, our goal and our mission. Our mission is to win and we adapt tactics and share and divide the jobs we need to do. What is the weather? How many rivals are there? How good is your shape?'

From the outside, Cancellara looked invincible. From the inside, things were less certain, and Baden Cooke explained the difference to me. 'We weren't going in there thinking we're going to blow everybody's doors off. We still thought he was the favourite and if we did everything right he would probably win, but from the outside looking in, I would assume, it would appear everyone knew we were going to win. But we were very aware of the risks and very aware of the competition. Every rider who had a chance – down to the 15th or 16th best rider – we discussed every single one and what to do if that guy went at 30 kilometres to go. We were very meticulous.'

Cancellara is not perfect. He may well have been the strongest bike rider in the world. Dirk Demol, who coached Tom Boonen as a young rider and managed him at Quick Step, was a directeur sportif at Trek for Cancellara's final few seasons and rated him as a better rider than the Belgian. 'Tom is talented. He's a hard worker. Together with the talent that makes him a champion. But when you talk about pure class, Fabian is still ahead of him,' he said. Physical strength won Cancellara a lot of races. It also lost him a lot. There was a suspicion that he was stronger in his legs than in his head and that his fearlessness in bike races was a substitute for a lack of imagination. He went through a mid-career phase of towing weaker but cleverer riders to the finish line and getting outsprinted. Sometimes, as in the 2010 Ronde, it made no difference. And when they changed the route in 2012, the biggest beneficiary of all was Cancellara. Though he crashed out that year, he won the next two, was injured in 2015 and didn't start, and still came second to Peter Sagan in his final attempt in 2016 at the age of 35. The new route favoured strong riders with strong teams, and offered less in the way of terrain for the more tactical riders to shine. Perfect for Cancellara, and if that change of route had been made in 2010, I have no doubt he'd have won the race more than three times.

Though the 2010 victory had the biggest impact in terms of his reputation – thanks to the narrative created by the 'Cancellara versus Boonen' battle – 2013 was more impressive: a cleaner, more decisive victory; even easy. He dispatched Peter Sagan on the Paterberg – he only reached the top with a handful of seconds' advantage, but the difference in body language was clear. While Cancellara turned left at the top, stood on his pedals and accelerated over the false flat into the descent, Sagan was already looking behind to work out if he should press on alone and come second, or wait for the next rider, Jürgen Roelandts, and win the sprint for second. In 14 kilometres from the top of the Paterberg to the finish in Oudenaarde, Cancellara put a minute and a half into Sagan and Roelandts. Michel Wuyts, the Flemish television commentator, described him as an 'orkaan' – a hurricane.

But Cancellara knew his shortcomings, even though he overcame them to an extent towards the end of his career. In the 2014 Ronde, his last win, he wasn't riding well enough to win solo, but found himself in a group with Greg Van Avermaet, Sep Vanmarcke and Stijn Vandenbergh. Three Belgians. Van Avermaet was strong (according to Demol, the strongest in the race), but he'd been more showy about it and had spent a lot of energy. Vanmarcke looked Cancellara's equal in terms of strength – when Cancellara attacked on the Oude Kwaremont, he was the only rider good enough to go with him, and he even led the Swiss rider up the Paterberg. (Van Avermaet and Vandenbergh had cleverly put themselves up the road 20 kilometres earlier, getting caught over the top of the Paterberg.) Vandenbergh was the least threatening – a physically imposing rider born and bred in the *Vlaamse Ardennen* with no semblance of a sprint and a reputation for tactical naïvety. Van Avermaet was a good sprinter and Vanmarcke was looking strong, but Cancellara played them off against each other.

When a gap opened between a Van Avermaet and Vandenbergh tandem and the other two on the run-in, Cancellara initially chased then sat up. If Vanmarcke had been smart or patient, he'd have called Cancellara's bluff. Yet he'd also been cornered into a situation where he knew he was very strong but was about to find himself sprinting for third place. The choice Cancellara had left him with was either definitely losing the race or possibly losing the race, and he chose the latter. Cancellara was in a similar position, but with his previous wins, he correctly gambled that Vanmarcke was more desperate than him not to miss out on the opportunity. 'I was almost dropped, but at the end you had three Belgians and me; I had won the race already and they hadn't. That's a tactic,' he said. I'd also asked if he was good, tactically. 'Good?' he replied. 'Um, I'm not bad.'

Cancellara's father moved from Italy to Switzerland and settled in Bern, but Cancellara absorbed more from his surroundings than from his heritage. He describes himself as Swiss and he grew up speaking German. But his former communications manager at Trek, Tim Vanderjeugd, theorised that Cancellara's personality was more fragmented and cosmopolitan, and that this came out according to what language he was speaking. 'He is uninhibited in Italian, somewhat lukewarm in French and Spanish, analytic and esoteric in English and superb in [Swiss] German,' he wrote in a long piece on the rider on his team's website. When I emailed Vanderjeugd to ask if these personality traits were always there or if it was the language that brought them out, he explained: 'The traits are certainly there to start, but they surface more easily in language A or B. The language is sort of a change in lighting, a mood. His proficiency or non-proficiency in each language sets the tone for the interview. He's always told Italian reporters more than anybody else. Just chatters away, loving how Italian sounds. French and Spanish media need to pull it out of him much, much more; he holds his cards closer. In English he freewheels the most and also gives the longest answers, whether he's making a point or not. And German is where he expresses himself the best, probably because he has the broadest vocabulary and the most nuance.'

Cancellara's hometown Bern contrasts sharply with Flanders. While the countryside of the *Vlaamse Ardennen* is muddy, rough, messy and smells of the chicken shit they use to fertilise the fields, around Bern it's all chocolate-box scenery, meadows of flowers, neat villages and manicured edges. Switzerland is the only place I've ever been, apart from Japan, where it looks like somebody has tidied up the countryside. Bern itself makes regular appearances in the top ten of the Mercer Quality of Living survey, while the only city in Belgium in the top 50 is Brussels. You couldn't imagine Cancellara living in Flanders, but he has an affinity with the region. Perhaps it's telling that Cancellara's biggest fan club is based in Belgium. He's not a *Flandrien* – though he's not Flemish, some international riders are considered honorary *Flandriens* by fans; however, he's not gritty or working-class enough to qualify. But he was nonetheless the dominant rider of the 2010s – even ahead of Boonen – whose best days were mainly before then.

How does Cancellara compare with previous winners of the Ronde? He won three times and spent a seven-year period (apart from the year he missed with injury) as the biggest favourite in the race. But he also had a mediocre run of seven attempts before that, and other three-time winners achieved more consistent high placings throughout their careers. Nevertheless, I think that if you put all the Tour of Flanders winners in a race together at their best, Cancellara would win.

Peter Van Petegem – who knew a thing or two about when it was appropriate to be at the back of the Ronde peloton and when it was appropriate to be at the front – once said, 'From Haaghoek on, you can't afford to be outside the first ten riders. From that moment on, you need to be aware that it can happen at any time. This is where the best of the race come forward.'

Therefore, it's bad news for Philippe Gilbert, who has punctured almost as Chavanel, 55 seconds ahead of the peloton, rattles onto the Haaghoek cobbles. It's bad timing but perhaps not fatal because the peloton is indecisive about whether to chase the Leukemans group, which is still not far ahead, 150 metres at most. Ag2r's Sébastien Minard has attacked in pursuit, marked by Geraint Thomas, who has been covering a lot of moves. Nine more riders drift up to them; too many, because the peloton itself is only around 50 riders in total and Thomas Voeckler pulls the group back. The race is not moving that fast. This gives Gilbert time for a wheel change, and a quick push from his team car gets him chasing; he'll hit the back of the bunch just at the junction with Haaghoek.

Haaghoek is a mile-long stretch of *kasseien* between the villages of Sint-Kornelis-Horebeke and Zegelsem; described as flat by the race organisers, it's arithmetically flat, rather than actually flat. There's an old statisticians' joke about a man who puts his head in an oven and his feet in a freezer and says, 'On average I feel fine.' The Haaghoek cobbles begin with a fast and gradual descent followed by a hard kick up through exposed fields, so although there is little net gain in altitude, the terrain is more complex than that. The road runs north-west to south-east, which means that there is a high likelihood of crosswinds, but the tunnel of fans through which the race proceeds gives the riders a little protection from this. The rise is significant enough that from the bottom the tents put up at what looks like the summit seem quite a long way up. For good measure, there's another drag up following the tents.

If the race followed Haaghoek all the way, they'd be spat out at the bottom onto the N8, which traverses the Flemish Ardennes, but about two-thirds of the way along there's a sharp left turn: the Leberg, *helling* 14. The Leberg is another lesson in the difference between averages and the real world: it's listed by the race organisation as being just over a kilometre long with an average gradient of three per cent. However, that average includes a long drag into the climb and a long drag out of it, and it disguises a 150-metre section of 13 per cent. There are no cobbles, so it's a pure test of power output.

Steegmans leads the peloton. He has been spoiling things ever since Maarten Tjallingii's attack 100 kilometres previously; now he is simultaneously defending Chavanel's attack and Tom Boonen's position in the peloton. As downhill turns to flat and then uphill, Thor Hushovd, the Norwegian world champion, surges. Attacking hard downhill just before an uphill is an effective tactic. Accelerating uphill is harder physically than accelerating downhill, and the aim is to achieve a five- or ten-kph advantage on rivals before they know what is happening, and to carry that differential into the climb, where it will be consequently much harder for anybody to match the speed. Hushovd hasn't hidden his intentions well enough, however, and while he turns the peloton back into a single line again (which might have happened on the narrow road, lined by fans, anyway), Steegmans has attached himself to the Norwegian's back wheel. Hushovd seems not to have confidence in his own attack – he looks back almost immediately, then a second time, to see what the damage is, even though he's been at the front for less than ten seconds and so must know that it is minimal. He sees Steegmans, riding just hard enough to dissuade Hushovd, but clearly communicating through his body language that there's no way he'll be pulling through to share the work.

There's a riding technique that is drummed into cyclists from an early age: don't ease off at the top of a hill in a race, because reaccelerating if somebody attacks is physically expensive (this also makes the false flat at the top of some climbs an excellent place to attack – because riders do ease up). Hushovd, either because his form is not brilliant or because he's forgotten this basic technique, slows down and drifts to the left side of the road.

As Hushovd slows, so does Steegmans. And on the right-hand side of the road, Boonen attacks. Not a gradual, ineffective surge like Hushovd's but a full sprint, out of the saddle, just as hill turns to flat. Cancellara follows; so does Filippo Pozzato. But nobody else is capable. Gilbert might have been able to, but he hasn't made it back to the front of the group after his chase back on.

It's different from Cancellara and Boonen's attack 12 months previously. In 2010, there were no riders up the road; this time, the trio are chasing nine escapees, including one of Boonen's team-mates. On one hand, Boonen's move is unnecessary – why chase Chavanel? On the other, if the front 12 come together there'll be two Quick Step riders, two Rabobanks and two Skys (albeit not necessarily the two most dangerous in each of these last two teams), which would suit Boonen just fine though Chavanel less so.

Thirty seconds after Boonen's attack, Cancellara pulls through. Pozzato sits at the back. Already it's clear that Cancellara and Boonen are committed to this move while Pozzato is happy to follow but not contribute. He is not as strong as the other two; this is his prerogative. It's also entirely characteristic – the Italian spent the 2009 Tour of Flanders following Tom Boonen almost all the way through the race, a tactic that backfired when Boonen's team-mate Stijn Devolder attacked to win the race a second time, while everybody watched Boonen. In the run-up to the race he'd got into a war of words with Gilbert in the press about this tendency. 'As he likes riding to make the favourites lose, he'll be focused on Cancellara,' said Gilbert. Pozzato's reply: 'If he keeps pissing me off, then yes, I won't leave him alone.'

In another 30 seconds, Cancellara leads Boonen and Pozzato straight past the six-rider group in front of them – Clarke, then Hayman, Leezer, Cooke, Van Avermaet and Leukemans. The acceleration by the Leukemans group to catch onto Cancellara's driving immediately drops Clarke and his part as a protagonist in the race is over. It takes Leukemans a big effort to bridge the very small gap between his front wheel and Pozzato's rear.

The riders in the peloton have been caught out. Langeveld is a little trapped – his Rabobank team-mates Leezer and Boom are both up the road. Boom had said in the team meeting that morning that he wanted to go early, so Langeveld's plan – as probably the strongest rider in the team and following his failed attempt to get away over the Taaienberg – is to wait, save energy and then follow the attacks by the big favourites at the end. But when Boonen went, he was sitting 20 riders back. One minute he could hear in his radio earpiece the team car reminding Boom to keep eating and drinking, the next, he realised Boonen and Cancellara were away. He might just have missed the most important attack of all. Now he has to gamble that somebody else – Garmin, he thinks, or BMC – will chase, and he has noticed two things in his favour: the weather is good, and there are still a few teams with numbers. If either of those things weren't true, the mood in the peloton could quickly turn pessimistic.

Thomas, also sitting further back in the group, hadn't been paying attention. In spite of 2010, he saw the move go and thought it had no chance; then he noticed it was Cancellara who'd gone. *Oh, crap*, he thinks to himself. *We're probably racing for second now. Or third.* To Thomas, Cancellara has always seemed like Muhammad Ali. But Thomas knows his boxing history: Ali didn't go through his career without taking a few beatings.

Nuyens is more confident. *A stupid attack by Boonen*, he thinks. Quick Step have Chavanel in front, and his suspicion is that Boonen and Chavanel might be trying to demonstrate their strength not only to the rest of the peloton but also, importantly, to each other. *Maybe it's not my day*, he thinks, but he looks around. He can see Flecha, Gilbert, Ballan and Hushovd, all with team-mates, and that is a good sign. The gap won't be closed immediately – the Leberg, Valkenberg and Tenbosse are relatively close together and the chase won't be fluent, but between Tenbosse and Geraardsbergen there are ten kilometres to work with.

Ahead, Cancellara turns the corner onto the Leberg. The Swiss cycling coach Paul Köchli – the former team manager of La Vie Claire, for whom Greg LeMond and Bernard Hinault both won the Tour de France and who was renowned for his analytical approach to the science of bike racing – described Cancellara's cornering technique as a 'power burst'. He studied the Swiss rider's pedalling technique during the Tour de Suisse in 2007 and noticed that going into corners, he stopped pedalling early but maintained the maximum possible speed to follow a perfect trajectory, then accelerated much more quickly than other riders. This acceleration only lasted around four seconds, but he both cornered faster than most other riders and could further out-accelerate them emerging from the bend.

The corner into the Leberg is cobbled, right-angled and narrow. Cancellara goes into it with Boonen on his wheel but, by the time the riders have straightened up again, the Swiss rider is four bike lengths clear, and Boonen, having slipped a little through the corner, is having to sprint to try to close the gap. Behind, it is worse: Cooke, sixth in line, skids and pulls his foot out; Leezer comes past him but he causes Hayman to stall as well. Cooke looks up and sees Cancellara far ahead; at that moment, seeing the power that the Swiss rider held coming out of the corner, Cooke's initial reaction is that the race is over.

The Leberg is a twisting climb. It initially curves to the right then immediately turns left, then right, then left, for the steep part. Then a double-S bend on the drag: left-right-left-right before the final left turn near the top and a few hundred more metres of false flat. Cancellara sprints into and out of each of the steep sections, and Boonen cannot close the gap. Behind the Belgian, Pozzato, Leukemans and Van Avermaet are chasing, with Cooke ten metres or so further back, and Leezer and Hayman unable to match the pace. Leukemans is regretting getting caught behind Pozzato. He is sure he has the legs to at least sit in behind Cancellara, but he needs to be in his wheel in order to do so, and he knows that to try to accelerate to chase him – which means riding *faster* than Cancellara – would be fatal. *Race over*, he thinks.

Two-thirds of the way up, Boonen finally makes contact with Cancellara's back wheel, but this coincides with the Swiss rider catching Boasson Hagen and Boom. Cancellara goes around them, but Boonen hesitates and suddenly Cancellara is riding away and Boonen can't get past the other two riders. The fans are closing in on the road around the final bend, and the Belgian would have to go the long way around to get to the front. Either way, after launching the attack in the first place, he's just been dropped. The Canadian cyclist Ryder Hesjedal once said, 'If you draw your sword and drop it, you die.' Boonen has just dropped his sword.

At the top, Cancellara is powering away, and in just a couple of kilometres of road, he has halved Chavanel's lead from a minute to 30 seconds. He's 30 metres clear of Boonen, Leukemans, Boasson Hagen and Boom, followed closely by Van Avermaet and Pozzato, then Hayman.

There are 40 kilometres to go. Fabian Cancellara has just detonated the Tour of Flanders.

CHAPTER 14

Valkenberg

I went to a cycling dinner a few years ago, an annual money-raiser for the Dave Rayner Fund, which supports young British riders who want to race abroad. The guest of honour was Eddy Merckx, who sat at table number one. There was a question-and-answer session on the stage, then food, followed by an interminable auction. At one point, my wife nudged me, pointed at the top table and said, 'Eddy Merckx looks very bored.'

It must be quite wearing being Eddy Merckx. The greatest cyclist of all time has made himself fully available to journalists, the bike industry and glommers-on in general for the 40 years of his retirement; the quid pro quo he has made in return for the lifelong adulation of grown men (and, to a lesser extent, women) is to relive the same questions, conversations and social situations again, again and again. As he sat there at the Rayner dinner – surrounded by starstruck well-wishers and people wearing the involuntary vacant smiles that proximity to celebrities sometimes causes – he stared into space, his arms folded, his face utterly neutral and unreadable. The world continued to revolve around him, and he looked indifferent to it.

There's little doubt that Merckx was the most successful cyclist in history. He won 525 races according to common consensus (the totals can be skewed by ambiguity over the inclusion of criteriums, which are not officially sanctioned events). Bearing in mind that the best and most durable sprinters in the world these days can get up to about 150, but that even breaking 100 victories is a rare feat, this is a phenomenal total. Boxing fans can argue over whether Muhammad Ali, Joe Louis, Rocky Marciano or Mike Tyson was the greatest heavyweight in history; tennis fans can compare and contrast Björn Borg, Rod Laver, Roger Federer and Pete Sampras. It's only contrary pedants like me who point out that Bernard Hinault had a more perfect record than Merckx in the Grand Tours (ten wins against Merckx's 11 but never finishing lower than second, whereas Merckx had some lower-top-ten placings at the beginning and end of his career).

So we stand back and look at the career and life of Eddy Merckx and agree he was the greatest. He also inspires misty-eyed nostalgia in a certain generation of cycling journalists, who lavished kitsch, hyperbolic and hammy nicknames upon him: the Tamburlaine of the Pedals, the Beethoven of the Big Ring, the Savage, the Executioner and the Cannibal. The headline in *L'Equipe* the morning after one of his greatest stage wins, at the 1969 Tour de France, was 'Merckxissimo'. But it was the 'Cannibal' which stuck; a gruesome reference less to his voracity than to his habit of devouring his opponents. What I rarely get from anybody I speak to about Merckx, however, is any sense of affection. There's admiration, but it's more elemental than empathetic, perhaps more akin to what people felt about the Old Testament God. This stems from his omnipotence – he crushed everybody, for many years, not giving the slightest impression that he was enjoying it. In fact the only humanity that comes out from his biographies is in defeat – his wife said he cried for two hours after he lost the 1966 World Championships. He also had a thin skin: he bitterly resented Rik Van Looy and his older team-mates for the piss-taking he suffered at their hands as a first-year professional, and Barry Hoban described him as 'the biggest cry-baby in the business when he didn't win'.

Perhaps the mistake is to apply the same standards to Merckx as other cyclists. Daniel Friebe, who wrote *Eddy Merckx: The Cannibal*, told me: 'Merckx's is a fairly difficult story to pigeon-hole or even fully understand because the usual tropes and stereotypes don't apply. He didn't have a difficult upbringing, there were no obvious chips on his shoulder, and yet he had this appetite for racing and winning that seemed almost pathological. I suppose my conclusion was that it became a kind of compulsion: fairly early in his career, he had reached the point where he wasn't craving elation or money or adulation – winning simply became a moral duty to himself. Without it, he couldn't get comfortable in his own skin.' Friebe also described Merckx's invincibility as a 'burden' – while other riders, by the nature of the sport and their fallibility, learn very early on that defeat is inevitable and even acceptable, for Merckx it took his own physical decline, from 1975 onwards, to learn this; not until he was 30, in other words. Once it happened, he loosened up, although his default expression – that blank stare in moments of self-absorption and escape – never went away.

I like the fact that while Merckx dominated just about every other major race, he never quite mastered the Tour of Flanders. He is the joint or outright record holder for wins at the Tour de France and Giro d'Italia, at Milan–San Remo and Liège–Bastogne–Liège and at the world road race championships, which is to say five out of the eight biggest races in the world (the five Monuments, Worlds and two most important Grand Tours). Yet he only won the Ronde twice, albeit both times in spectacular fashion. Ironically, given that it's now considered one of the hardest races on the calendar to win, one reason for him not being able to win it so often was that before the mid-1970s, the Ronde was not hard enough. The number of climbs featured in the race during his heyday, 1969 to 1975, was creeping up towards eight, but it was only in 1973 – following the move of the finish to Meerbeke and the climbs closer to the finish – that the race really started suiting him. Before then, there was a long stretch of flat roads to Ghent that neutralised Merckx's advantage or at least made him more vulnerable to the kind of ganging-up by his rivals that could level the playing field somewhat. If the parcours during the early 1970s had been anything like it has been since the 1980s, Merckx would have won more than two editions. Those two wins, also in 1969 and 1975 coincidentally, bookended his peak years – he won his first Tour de France in 1969, and rode his last as a genuine contender in 1975, when he was runner-up.

Perhaps it's apt that Merckx couldn't bend the Tour of Flanders to his will. He professed to be Belgian and nothing else – either because he was pathologically uncontroversial or because to express an identity one way or another, as one of the country's most famous and unifying figures, would have been unnecessarily divisive. When I asked Guy Fransen, the *Het Nieuwsblad* sports editor, about Merckx, he sighed and described him as the 'paterfamilias'. 'He is our ambassador. Our number one. Merckx, the king and the soccer team are the things that unify Belgium. When the Red Devils [the Belgian national team] play in the European Championship, they are Belgian,' he said. In 2005, the Flemish broadcasting organisation *VRT*, along with *De Standaard*, held a poll to determine 'De Grootste Belg' – the greatest Belgian of all time – and Merckx came third behind the humanitarian Father Damien and pioneering doctor Paul Janssen. The French-speaking

RTBF channel held a rival competition – 'Les Plus Grands Belges' – which saw Merckx one step further down. (Jacques Brel came first.)

Merckx was born in Flemish Brabant but grew up in Woluwe-Saint-Pierre in Brussels, so there was nothing Flandrian, in the purest sense of the word, about him. He spoke Flemish at home and French at school. The issue of his marriage ceremony, which was conducted in French, rankled with the Flandrian fans for years, and they never quite took him to their heart, their localist pride trumping the fact that he was clearly the greatest cyclist ever. He'd already reciprocated with his childhood ambition – while the Flemish cyclists dream of the Classics, Merckx was obsessed with the Tour de France. He failed to live up to the stereotype that cyclists, especially Flemish ones, hail from poor, working-class backgrounds – his family were shopkeepers and were relatively well off. Aesthetically, he didn't fit in either. He was six foot tall and lacked the compact, muscled body type of the stereotypical Flandrian. Yet he also looked comparatively inelegant in comparison with Grand Tour thoroughbreds like Fausto Coppi and Jacques Anquetil. And even the fact that his two Flanders wins were taken in stereotypically Flandrian conditions and style didn't make him a *Flandrien*.

The 1969 Tour of Flanders was Merckx's revenge against the race. The previous year, Walter Godefroot had sprinted to victory after Rik Van Looy had decided his own primary aim was for Merckx to lose, rather than for him to try to win himself, and marked Merckx out of it. In 1967, he'd been outnumbered by the Italian Salvarini team-mates Dino Zandegù and Felice Gimondi when the three of them had caught Barry Hoban and Noël Foré with 15 kilometres to go. Hoban said, 'They were doing the one-two on us, and every time Gimondi attacked, Merckx was countering, but Zandegù and Foré got away in the end and I wasn't crafty enough.'

In 1969, in howling wind and hammering rain, Merckx decided he would go it alone.

After 100 kilometres (with 160 still to go), the direction of the race changed and the wind was converted into a crosswind, which cut the race definitively into two pieces – a two-dozen-rider front group and everybody else. There were only four climbs that year: the (Nieuwe) Kwaremont; Kloosterstraat in Geraardsbergen; Valkenberg near Brakel; and Kasteeldreef, which runs parallel to the more well-known Berendries climb between Brakel and Zottegem. Merckx accelerated on the Kwaremont but couldn't shake his rivals, who sat on. On Kloosterstraat – which took the riders from the Dender river in Geraardsbergen up Abdijstraat and Oude Steenweg, behind the Muur – Merckx went again but he still couldn't get a gap.

The race turned again, and the wind became a headwind. Then Merckx just rode away. His team manager at the time was Lomme Driessens, who would later mismanage Freddy Maertens to a disqualification in the 1977 Ronde. There was one small piece of communication between them: Driessens wound down the window of his car after Merckx went away and asked him if he had taken leave of his senses, telling him he would have no chance in the headwind. There was method in Merckx's madness, however – his reasoning was that as everybody had been sitting on him anyway, he wouldn't give them the luxury of his back wheel any more. He told Driessens, '*Kust gij een beetje mijn kloten.*' 'Kiss my arse.'

By the Valkenberg climb, where he pressed home his advantage, his lead was a couple of minutes. At the finish, second-placed Felice Gimondi was five and a half minutes behind, and Marino Basso, who won an eight-man sprint for third, was eight minutes down.

The race was presented as a 'Goliath versus Davids', but it wasn't just a win of pure physical superiority; there was a tactical aspect as well, albeit built on Merckx's strength. Barry Hoban was in the chasing group and had a front-row seat when Merckx attacked through Geraardsbergen. 'Merckx really went on the Muur, from the bottom,' he told me. 'I was second over the top, three lengths behind. [Franco] Bitossi was three lengths off me. Nobody was on a wheel, so you could tell it was hard. I thought he would ease, because it was a long way to the finish. But he wasn't only the strongest; he had the strongest team. There were a dozen of us left, and three were Merckx's team-mates. We took a breather and started to organise a chase, but you had Jozef Spruyt, Julien Stevens and Bernard Van De Kerckhove – three great riders in their own right – who were Merckx's team-mates and were blocking for him.'

For the next five years, Merckx couldn't repeat his win. Three of the five next races, in 1970, 1972 and 1973, were won by Eric Leman (whose name was French but who was actually a West Flandrian). Leman was a good sprinter – he outkicked Godefroot and Merckx for his first win, took a seven-man sprint for his second and a four-man sprint for his third. In the context of the early 1970s, Leman was probably one of the best Flanders riders in history – durable enough to hang on over the climbs and cobbles, and the fastest sprinter to be able to do so. His retirement was spent contradicting the conclusion that many journalists and fans had reached: that because he was a sprinter, his three wins were soft, but his runners-up were Godefroot, André Dierickx (also a runner-up in Paris–Roubaix and Liège–Bastogne–Liège) and Freddy Maertens. There was nothing soft about his victories.

Barry Hoban, who beat Merckx in Ghent–Wevelgem in 1974, told me part of Leman's ability and motivation at the Tour of Flanders was that he was a West Flandrian. 'He was a hell of a strong rider and a good sprinter and he cost me a few wins,' Hoban said. 'The West Vlamings, like the Planckaerts, Freddy Maertens, Leman, Briek Schotte, Johan Museeuw, are hard men.

Leman wasn't tall but he had powerful thighs – when you grow up racing in West Flanders, you are racing all the time against the wind. He seemed to specialise in Flanders. Like an Italian rider most wants to win Milan–San Remo, a Flandrian most wants to win the Tour of Flanders.'

In 1975, Merckx possibly even surpassed his 1969 exploit. In four of the intervening five races, he'd come third twice, fourth and seventh, but the event was drifting towards a structure that really suited his talents as the strongest rider in the world. The finish moved to Meerbeke in 1973, and the route was tweaked to take the riders away from the Nieuwe Kwaremont to the Oude Kwaremont in 1974. It was on the Oude Kwaremont that Merckx attacked in 1975, with 100 kilometres to ride, and only Frans Verbeeck was able to follow. Merckx's memory of the escape is that he could hear Verbeeck's heavy breathing, interspersed with swearing, from behind him but that his compatriot wasn't contributing that much. It didn't matter – Merckx dropped Verbeeck with six kilometres to go, and Verbeeck had to be helped from his bike at the finish, albeit five minutes in front of the third-placed rider. 'There was nothing to be done,' said Verbeeck.

Merckx only won the Ronde twice. When he did so, it was in as impressive a way as anybody in the history of the race. Yet he finished in the top ten six more times and wasn't able to convert those strong positions into wins. His results in the race demonstrate both his lack of specific interest in his biggest local race – to Merckx, all races were equal and there to be won not prioritised – and his ability. He might have been the best Belgian winner ever, but he was never a Lion of Flanders.

It's a peculiar quirk of the dysfunctional way cycling works that the number one-ranked team at the start of the 2011 season had never raced together before. Teams come and go in cycling according to the availability of sponsors with enough money to pay for the naming rights, the salaries, the infrastructure, the travel and the other necessities. That team, Cancellara's Leopard–Trek outfit, had been born in conflict. Eight riders – Cancellara and the Schleck brothers were the pick of them – plus two team managers had left Bjarne Riis's Saxo Bank team to form a new outfit initially funded by Flavio Becca, a sugar daddy from Luxembourg with a fortune made in real estate and construction. They also poached Saxo's press officer, Brian Nygaard, to be the general manager, and got Trek on board as a secondary sponsor for the start of the season.

The riders they hired brought so many points with them that the team went straight in at number one, but they had trouble bedding in, and didn't win even a minor race until March, two months into the season. The iconography and marketing were slick, with black and white landscape photographs on the website and an ostentatiously confident motif displayed prominently everywhere: True Racing. That was all very well, but the disloyalty of the Schlecks to Riis and the perceived pillaging of Saxo Bank's resources had pissed a lot of people off and done what was previously considered impossible: making cycling fans feel sorry for Bjarne Riis.

So when Cancellara prised himself away from his rivals at the 2011 Ronde and started chasing down Sylvain Chavanel, it wasn't quite the same as the previous year. His 2010 Saxo Bank team had been a well-drilled support squad, with strong, experienced riders working for him right up until his attack with Boonen. By the Leberg in 2011, there were no other Leopard riders to be seen. Cancellara had already been isolated since Martin Mortensen overshot the corner on Bronstraat.

Leopard was not the only team with bonding issues. Garmin–Cervélo had been formed from a merger between the Garmin and Cervélo teams at the end of the previous season. However, the Cervélo riders had perceived it as more like a takeover. 'We went from punching above our level at Cervélo to punching below our level. It was not harmonious; it was a different mentality of team, and it upset the balance,' said one rider. On paper, the Classics team looked strong in terms of leaders – Hushovd and Haussler had come from Cervélo, while Tyler Farrar was a Garmin rider. But it also looked a little crowded. On the eve of the Ronde, however, the team's manager Jonathan Vaughters was more worried about the rest of the team, including himself. *The three leaders are strong*, he thought; *the rest of the team, not so much.* And he'd been left a directeur sportif short following an ethical rules infringement involving his rider Trent Lowe and a team manager, Matt White, which led to White being dismissed. (Lowe had been referred to an external doctor, which was against team rules.)

Vaughters didn't ride the cobbles in his own career as a rider, so he hadn't been confident in his ability to direct the race. His solution, on the advice of his rider Andreas Klier, was to draft in Peter Van Petegem. 'You've got to take Van Petegem – he knows everything,' Klier had told him. The problem was that Van Petegem had only met the riders two weeks previously at Milan–San Remo, which was not enough time to build rapport and trust. And then Vaughters' perception during the Ronde was that Van Petegem was not enjoying making the hard tactical decisions, so Vaughters ended up doing it anyway.

The route from the Leberg to *helling* 15, the Valkenberg, will take the riders in a spiral, initially with a gentle downhill, east through the villages of Elst and Michelbeke then south to the outskirts of Brakel before following the edge of the town west to the foot of the Valkenberg, which will take them back north again. At Elst they will cross over the road upon which, 90 kilometres earlier, the Leopard-led peloton was just catching the Tjallingii attack.

A kilometre after the top, Chavanel leads Cancellara by 26 seconds. The Boonen group – not working together that fluently and therefore losing ground – is another 20 seconds behind, with the peloton another 15 seconds in arrears. Boonen is in a difficult situation of his own making: he shouldn't chase his own team-mate; at the same time he has to chase Cancellara. In 2010 he had attacked with Cancellara and lasted 30 kilometres before getting dropped. This year, he lasted precisely one rotation.

It's a false flat down from the summit, making the Leberg another Flandrian climb with no real descent. This suits Cancellara – the more a race resembles a time trial, the better it is for him. The Boonen group is not working well together: Boom wants Pozzato to go through, but Pozzato won't. Leukemans notices Boasson Hagen loitering at the back and not contributing, and gesticulates at the Norwegian. Eventually, after a kilometre or so, the five riders start working together, although the momentum is still unconvincing and Boasson Hagen is still not pulling through, which is odd because if he did it would put more pressure on Sky's rival teams.

The teams who are on the back foot, however, are Lotto, Garmin and Saxo Bank. Nuyens thinks somebody will crack first and chase – if Cancellara had gone away with many riders, Nuyens' race would be over, but with the Swiss effectively on his own, he knows that there should be enough impetus in the chase that the race remains open. Lotto rider Gilbert was unlucky to have been caught at the back with a mechanical when Boonen launched his attack. But it's Garmin who take responsibility. Van Petegem tells the riders to work, saying over the radio, 'I think we have to work now because the gap is almost a minute. In Brakel, at Tenbosse, if it's more than 30 seconds, it's finished.'

Ahead, Cancellara is hunting Chavanel. At 37 kilometres

from the finish, the gap is 25 seconds. The Swiss rider covers the next kilometre five seconds faster than the Frenchman; the one after that four seconds faster; the next six seconds faster, so that when Chavanel is passing through the streets of Brakel just before the Valkenberg, he is sitting up, stretching and giving himself a chance to rest before Cancellara catches him. But the Boonen group is riding at the same speed as Chavanel, sitting 40 seconds behind the Frenchman, and while Cancellara is gaining five seconds a kilometre, they are making no inroads whatsoever. Behind, the peloton is also struggling to get back on terms with the Boonen group. Van Petegem and Vaughters decide that they need more manpower and that it's time to sacrifice Heinrich Haussler, instructing him to help with the chase. This partially answers the question of hierarchy within the Garmin team – as of this moment, Haussler will not win the Ronde but he may keep Hushovd and Farrar's chances alive.

The Valkenberg is half a kilometre long at an average of eight per cent, which makes it one of the steeper climbs overall on the route. However, it's extremely well surfaced with smooth, fast tarmac – when it first turned up in the Ronde in the 1950s it was cobbled, but in 1973 it was asphalted and it disappeared from the race route until 1996. It's an urban climb, with neat, well-kept houses on either side, the horizontal lines of the brickwork, windows and roofs offsetting the diagonal of the steeply rising road. It was here that Leif Hoste and Tom Boonen attacked in 2006 for their winning break, trapping Hoste's team-mate George Hincapie in the chasing group. A similar thing happened much further back, in 1964, when German rider Rudi Altig used the Valkenberg as the launchpad for a long solo break. In the group behind him, Flemish riders Rik Van Looy and the reigning world champion Benoni Beheyt – still feuding after the misunderstanding that led to Beheyt's Worlds win in Ronse – preferred to mark each other out of the race rather than chase Altig, and he won alone by four minutes.

Chavanel hits the climb ten seconds before Cancellara, but the Swiss rider is visibly gaining. Through the S-bend towards the top, Chavanel is standing up on his pedals to stretch out his legs and is looking back. Forty seconds further down the road, the Boonen group is only a matter of metres in front of the peloton.

Nick Nuyens has woken up. He has been hiding in the bunch and trying to avoid any more of the bad luck that blighted the second quarter of his race. He senses that it's time to move further to the front – he thinks Gilbert is going to try to attack. Or that another leader will. Between the climbs, it's the team riders doing the work but gaps are a lot smaller in terms of distance on climbs because of the lower speeds, and some riders can't help trying to bridge up to the next group. Sure enough, Gilbert goes, followed immediately by Voeckler, Ballan, Thomas and Nuyens himself.

Van Avermaet accelerates at the front, followed by Boonen, so no sooner has Gilbert caught the back of the group, than everything is stretched out in a line again. But Gilbert's move has drawn the peloton up and all the moves of the last ten kilometres, save for Cancellara's, have come to nothing. Nuyens is happy though. He saw that Gilbert was going extremely hard on the steep climb, and was able to follow him with relative ease. He thinks, *I'm in the race. I'm strong.*

Nuyens is in an interesting position in 2011. He was brought in at the start of the year by the Saxo Bank manager Bjarne Riis to be the leader in the Classics, which meant he had big shoes to fill. Cancellara had won the 2010 Ronde with the team and then left to help form the Leopard team, and Nuyens is no Cancellara. But Nuyens knows it. He thinks that when he is in good shape he is one of the best, and he sees big wins as a jigsaw puzzle. When he puts the pieces together – his strength, tactics, circumstances, training – he can win. He spent four seasons at Quick Step, learning from Johan Museeuw and then riding for Tom Boonen, but picking up big wins himself including the 2005 Omloop Het Volk. This gave him the confidence to move to Cofidis as a team leader in 2007, where he was seventh and then second the following year in the Ronde.

They said he couldn't win it, that he was good in races of 200 to 220 kilometres, but that the Classics were beyond him – an opinion that was reinforced when he had two unproductive years at Rabobank in 2009 and 2010, exacerbated by injury and illness. Fans lost belief, but two people didn't: Nuyens and Riis. Riis was renowned as a man-manager who built strong relationships with his riders; he told Nuyens to be less critical of himself, to take it easy and to focus only on the Tour of Flanders. So from November 2010, from his first training ride for the next season, he had only one goal. 'Don't stress about what the press is saying,' Riis told him. 'If it's not good, I will tell you. And I know you are good.' This was a new experience for Nuyens.

The winter in Belgium that year was a bad one with lots of snow. Classics riders have to ride for hours and hours through November and December to build endurance, but Riis surprised Nuyens by telling him, 'If it's snowing, you can't train. If you can't train, don't stress. It's not possible.' Nuyens went to Calp in Spain, just him and a masseur, to get the miles in: long rides during the day, then back for a shower, a massage and food prepared by his masseur. The routine was good for him physically and mentally.

Nuyens' tests showed he was in good form. He was ready to race. And then, when it came to the first race of the year, the Tour of the Mediterranean in February, Riis gave the team talk. He listed the objectives for the seven other riders in the team, and gave them instructions. Then he came to Nuyens. 'You're here to train, Nick,' he said.

The same thing happened at his second race, Tirreno–Adriatico. But the instructions were slightly different. Nuyens was to continue training, relieved of team duties, but he was to do a test on a 15-kilometre climb which came two-thirds of the way through the fifth stage to Castelraimondo: the 1,455-metre Sassotetto. Only 30 riders were left at the top, and Nuyens was one of them. Two days later there was a 9.3-kilometre time trial and Riis left it up to Nuyens whether he wanted to ride it at full bore. Cancellara won but 28 seconds behind – in tenth place, ahead of some extremely experienced time-triallists and stage racers – was Nuyens. A Belgian journalist, Chris Picavet from *Sporza*, texted Nuyens: 'Nobody's talking about you, but I think you're going really good.'

Four days later, Nuyens rode Milan–San Remo for Saxo Bank and he got caught behind a split midway through the race, along with Cooke, who was the team's leader on the day. On the team bus afterwards, Riis gently rebuked Cooke for falling asleep at a dangerous moment. Nuyens expected a similar criticism, but all Riis said was, 'Next Wednesday it starts for you.' Wednesday was the day of Dwars door Vlaanderen, which he won ahead of Geraint Thomas. E3 was less positive. When Cancellara dropped everybody on the Oude Kwaremont, Nuyens hesitated. He suspected he wouldn't be able to follow Cancellara's pace, but he regretted not sitting in for as long as possible, just to compare himself with the strongest rider in the race.

Tristan Hoffman, the Saxo Bank directeur sportif, knew Nuyens was good. The cycling world had taken little notice of Nuyens' 39th place in Ghent–Wevelgem, his final race before the Ronde a week later, but Hoffman had watched as Nuyens spent 30 kilometres on the front of the peloton, helping to pull things back together so that Cooke could have a go in the sprint. It had only resulted in a tenth place for the Australian, but Nuyens and his team knew he was ready.

Over the Valkenberg, the only problem Nuyens can see is the 35-second gap to Cancellara and Chavanel, though he's sure they'll come back.

Ahead, Cancellara waves Chavanel through, and Chavanel doesn't budge. He's been told not to work.

The Valkenberg has seen the Ronde shift into an entirely new shape. The initial earthquake was the attack by Boonen, Cancellara and Pozzato on the Leberg, but the aftershocks carried on until the top of the Valkenberg, when the landscape settled into position. At the front: Cancellara, with Chavanel sitting behind him. Then a 35-second gap to the peloton. That's it. Since the Paddestraat, at least 50 riders have attacked at one point or another, and the sum total of all that effort and enterprise, all that disruption, all that ambition, is two riders holding a gap of half a minute over the bunch.

Three hills left. Boonen thinks Cancellara and Chavanel will come back. The plan in the morning was not necessarily for Chavanel to be out at the front, but now it suits Quick Step. He'll sit in and try to follow Cancellara all the way to the finish, while the team is relieved of any obligation to chase the move down. The team's general manager Patrick Lefevere thinks that asking Chavanel to sit in is going against the rider's nature, but as Cancellara had shown the previous year, if you work with him he'll kill you.

In 2002 I went to a post-Tour de France criterium in Montmarault, a tiny town in the middle of nowhere in central France between Moulins and Montluçon, the kind of place where nothing much happens, the kids leave as soon as they are old enough, and the shutters go up at 8 p.m. I was there to watch Laurent Jalabert, then the most successful French rider in the world, on his farewell tour. Following a second win in the Tour de France's king of the mountains classification and a glittering career, he had announced his retirement at the end of the season. Races like the Montmarault criterium are exhibition events, raced on circuits and usually following a script and pre-arranged winners – more a chance for a communion between riders and fans than actual races, but still run off at a fast, exciting pace. Jalabert would be one of a number of famous French pros, alongside a handful of second-string international pros, ambitious semi-pros and strong locals.

The race headquarters was a small office in the mayor's office. Riders signed on, picked up numbers and race information; the French champion at the time, Nicolas Vogondy, sat in the corner to pin his race numbers on. Jalabert passed through almost unnoticed. Then Jacky Durand showed up.

Durand was a moderately talented French rider who rode as a professional between 1990 and 2004. I always thought he was a lucky bastard – he wore the yellow jersey at the 1995 Tour de France when he was one of the early starters in the prologue and a deluge opened after he'd gone to the top of the leaderboard. The course was technical, so even the best riders in the world were unable to beat his time in the apocalyptic conditions. Or maybe he was the living proof of the adage that you make your own luck. Durand used to spend so much time on long-range attacks, many of them fruitless, that *Vélo* magazine used to run a graphic called the 'Jackymeter' through the season to log how many kilometres he spent off the front of the field. One year it was reportedly 2,270.

When Durand appeared in the mayor's office in Montmarault, his personality filled the room. He has a loud voice and he laughs at his own jokes. He flirted with the women, gave crushing handshakes to the men and was the centre of attention, effortlessly. I was both appalled and impressed by his presence.

The attacking tactic he used in races worked very well for Durand in two ways. First, it made him famous, popular and marketable in a way that his talent never could. Second, he won some big races: that Tour prologue and another stage; the French championships (twice); Paris–Tours; and, in 1992, the biggest of all – the Tour of Flanders.

Long-range attacks don't work in Flanders unless it's the work of champions. Magni, Merckx and Cancellara might have succeeded with comparatively early breaks, but generally the winner plays a waiting game, relying on superior endurance in the final hour of racing when other riders are more fatigued. And it's important to draw a distinction between a suicide attack and one that kills others, no matter where it happens. Durand's looked very much like it belonged to the former category.

Durand had ridden the Ronde once already, and he hadn't liked what he'd seen. He'd packed at the second feed, but he already knew that if he was to achieve his ambition in the race in 1992 – to come in the top 20 – he'd have to be off the front of the peloton when the fighting began. His team, Castorama, wasn't much interested. The manager, Cyrille Guimard, had gone with the A team to the GP Rennes in Brittany – a smaller race in the grand scheme of things but more important to a French team in a parochial sort of way insofar as they might win it, whereas they had no chance at the Ronde. There had been two French winners at the Tour of Flanders in the 76 editions up to 1992: Louison Bobet in 1955 and Jean Forestier in 1956. Thierry Marie was going to be the Castorama team leader but he had crashed and cracked a rib in the Three Days of De Panne, so the team orders given by the directeur sportif on the ground, Bernard Quilfen, were, in Durand's words, 'to do our best'. When I interviewed Durand for a piece in *Cycle Sport* on the race, he told me that most of the Castorama riders were sent to the Ronde for punishment. 'The management sent them to the Tour of Flanders to learn about racing,' he said.

The early break went at the third attempt: Durand, Thomas Wegmüller, Patrick Roelandt and Hervé Meyvisch. Wegmüller was crucial – he rode for Sean Kelly's Festina team and was under orders to get into the break to take the pressure off Kelly, who'd already won Milan–San Remo that year. But he was renowned as a strong and aggressive rider – he'd come second to Dirk Demol in the 1988 Paris–Roubaix and might have won if a plastic bag hadn't blown into his back wheel as the finishing sprint was beginning.

For 20 kilometres the peloton chased, and the lead was no more than 20 seconds – Wegmüller was considered too danger-ous. But eventually the Panasonic and Buckler teams decided they were doing everybody else's dirty work for them, and called off the chase. Somehow, the lead ballooned to 22 minutes at the first hill, the Tiegemberg.

Even then, there was no panic. Roelandt and Meyvisch weren't seen as dangerous, and Durand was an unknown quantity. Wegmüller, on the other hand, thought the race had turned in their favour. He knew that chasing through the hills was hard – breaks are caught in the Ronde as much due to the fatigue of the escapees as the organisation of the peloton. The weather was also relatively pleasant, with no wind.

The lead at the second climb, the Oude Kwaremont, was 15 minutes. They crossed the Paterberg, Hotond, New Kruisberg and Taaienberg, and at the seventh climb, the Eikenberg, their lead was 11 minutes. They dropped Roelandt two climbs later, after the Volkegemberg and Varent. At 60 kilometres to go, Durand had a crisis and was unable to contribute for 20 kilometres, sitting behind Wegmüller and apologising for his inability to help. Wegmüller tried to keep the pace going but without going too hard on the hills, which would quickly tire all of them out. Meyvisch disappeared with an hour to go, leaving Durand and Wegmüller alone at the front.

They crossed the Leberg, the Molenberg and Berendries, and as they entered Geraardsbergen, with 18 kilometres to go, their lead was four minutes. Wegmüller felt strong enough to drop Durand, but he figured the Frenchman would be useful to him between the Muur and the Bosberg. Durand, for his part, was coming round. On the Bosberg, Wegmüller wanted to attack, but instead it was Durand who powered away. Behind, defending champion Edwig Van Hooydonck and Maurizio Fondriest – who'd won the 1988 World Championships just down the road in Ronse – set off in pursuit. The lead at the top of the Bosberg was still two minutes.

Durand rode alone to the finish. With three kilometres to go, Eddy Merckx leaned out of the race director's car and said, 'You've won the Tour of Flanders, young man.' Durand was ecstatic; the crowd were underwhelmed. After the finish, he could hear people asking, 'Jacky *who?*'

CHAPTER 15

Tenbossestraat

If it were situated 100 kilometres earlier in the race, Tenbossestraat would barely register with the riders of the Tour of Flanders. Andreas Klier said to me, 'If you did it in training, or with a tourist group, you wouldn't even feel it was a climb. But in the race, it's a really hard climb.'

Tenbossestraat comes 230 kilometres into the Ronde, in Brakel. It's a smoothly surfaced ramp closed in on both sides by red-brick terraced houses all the way up, a residential suburban climb with none of the higgledy-piggledy charm of the rural bergs, but which developed a reputation as a perfect place to launch mid-range race-winning breaks when the finish was in Meerbeke. Museeuw, Van Petegem and Vanderaerden all attacked here in one or other of their Ronde-winning years.

The climb is close to the town centre, a Y-shaped street with a small offshoot near the bottom which confuses the numbering system. It used to be a bit of a rat run, before the authorities closed off access from the main road meaning that there's a convoluted route in. If it stands out in any way, it is for its blandness. It's just an ordinary street, where ordinary people live. On race day, however, it was a riotous alley of support – the closest the Ronde got to the feeling of the Tour de France's mountain stages. On the bergs, the race organisation and police keep the crowds out of the narrow roads. There's no doubting the intensity of the atmosphere, but the fans generally stay back from the action. However, on Tenbossestraat it's wide enough that fans encroach on the riders' line, jumping back when they get near. A lot of people used to stand here because – like the Kruisberg in Ronse and the Muur in Geraardsbergen – it's situated in a town. Fans could watch the race pass and be back in their front rooms to watch its finish before the riders even got to the bottom of the Muur.

The Moeder Agnes restaurant is at the very top of the climb, a converted farm with a courtyard set back from the road and a very nice-looking menu indeed; it's not actually on Tenbossestraat – by this point, the road has turned into Olifantstraat, which in the race will lead the riders to the main road between Brakel and Geraardsbergen. The owner, Audrey, came here from Paris 11 years previously. 'It seemed that when I came to Brakel, everybody was related, and knew each other. It was like a village,' she told me.

Brakel is a small town sitting right in the Flemish Ardennes between Geraardsbergen and Oudenaarde. The Zwalmbeek flows north through the town, following a pleasant valley north past Zottegem, then through Zwalm before joining the Schelde north-east of Oudenaarde. The population is officially just under 15,000, although this includes several villages around the periphery – Everbeek, Parike and Elst (near the top of the Leberg), for example. Nederbrakel, which is the main centre of the municipality, makes up just under half of the total population.

The Australian cyclist Robbie McEwen, who spent his career living in Parike and whose wife is from Brakel, told me it was a typical Flemish rural town. 'Everyone knows everyone, and conversation revolves around football and cycling. It's grey, wet, windy and freezing in winter, then changes to beautiful shades of green in the spring. The people took it badly when the Tour of Flanders no longer passed through Brakel in the final. It was like a funeral when the course change was announced.' He also pointed out how proud the locals are of the town's favourite son, Peter Van Petegem. 'People didn't say, "He won the Ronde." They said, "*We* won the Ronde."'

Audrey pointed out the demographic realities facing a small town like Brakel, which doesn't have much industry. 'We suffer from our proximity to bigger places. People go to Oudenaarde, Ghent or Geraardsbergen for the shopping. The kids leave school and go to university in Ghent, Kortrijk or Brussels. The houses are expensive, so young people aren't buying them. In Brakel it seems the people are well dressed, chic and over 50,' she said.

Audrey misses the Ronde. 'It's a shame it doesn't come here any more. It's not for the money, but we miss the atmosphere of the day. This is a quiet road, calm every day except the day of the race,' she said. 'In France we only know the Tour de France, but for the Flemish, cycling is part of their culture. Life stopped on the day of the Ronde. People talked about it for a week before and a week afterwards, even people who aren't interested in cycling.'

I got talking to the father in a family of four sitting in the bar area. Guy worked for a software development company in Brussels, which meant a hard commute to and from the capital, but he pointed out that has always been the way for people in Brakel. 'My grandparents went to the mines in Wallonia,' Guy said. 'There were special trains from Brakel to Charleroi or Mons to work. It was a hard life. Now I'm doing the same thing, except I'm going to Brussels. I was born here and want to carry on living in the country. The closest highway to here is the E17, which is 40 kilometres away. This means there is no industry here, but it also means it stays small and charming.'

Guy follows cycling closely enough to know that he likes it less than before. He senses that the Ronde is getting more commercial. 'It's not the same as before,' he said. 'Real sports fans preferred it in the past. You can't chase the race any more, and you get these big party tents on the route where it costs a lot of money for people to simply exchange business cards. I think the race is now more for industry than the people.'

Something that I've noticed in my time as a cycling journalist is that the demographic of cycling fans in the 'traditional' cycling countries is predominantly older and male. It's something that's pointed out to me by race organisers and other people in the industry, that the sport has to attract younger and broader audiences, if for no other reason than to replace the older fans one day. I asked Guy's two daughters – one at university in Ghent, the other at high school – if they followed the Ronde. Not at all, they told me. They and their friends were more obsessed with Tomorrowland, a dance-music festival held in Boom near Antwerp every July, where 350,000 tickets take 20 minutes to sell out when they are made available. 'It's the biggest thing in Flanders,' they told me.

There are about 50 riders left in the peloton and with Cancellara up the road, it's all hands on deck. Lotto manager Marc Sergeant orders Jürgen Roelandts to work to pull back the escape.

Cancellara, however, has a small problem, which could rapidly escalate. As he rides through an unofficial feed, he gestures at the soigneurs standing with their bottles that he wants a bottle. There is no Leopard soigneur there, because the team doesn't have enough staff on the race, and the other soigneurs ignore him. The Leopard team car has still not made it past the peloton up to the break (cars may only pass at the organisers' discretion, on wider roads, which is an issue at the Tour of Flanders), so Cancellara can't get a drink. *Don't expect nothing from nobody*, he thinks to himself. It's a comparatively warm day, with the wind coming more from the south than the west. This is another potential obstacle – the road from Brakel to Geraardsbergen heads south-east, so there'll be a cross-headwind after Tenbossestraat.

At the top of the Valkenberg, the Ronde route heads left, then takes another left to join the N8, which is fast here. It descends back to Brakel down a speed trap of a slope known as the Kleiberg, which has two sharpish corners illuminated by flashing red chevrons. The peloton is a shambles – Van Avermaet attacks again, though he has used too much energy now for it to be effective. He's followed by Voeckler. Then Flecha has a go, again followed by Voeckler, Leonardo Duque of Cofidis, BMC's Manuel Quinziato, Hushovd and then the rest of the bunch. A comparison between the speed and momentum of Cancellara and that of the bunch is telling: Cancellara is time-trialling steadily on, while the bunch accelerates and slows with each attack. At its fastest, the peloton is going faster than Cancellara, but the decelerations mean that there is a net deficit in speed. At the top of the Valkenberg, Cancellara's lead was 34 seconds. At the bottom of the Kleiberg, as Flecha freewheels and relents with no obvious reinforcements coming through to take his place at the front, Cancellara's lead is 48 seconds.

With 30 kilometres to go, Cancellara finally gets a drink from the neutral service car, but it's water rather than the energy drink he needs. He tries to convince Chavanel to ride with him – he thinks that if they work together, they have a 50-50 chance each of winning – but Peeters won't allow it. Chavanel fears contributing then getting dropped on the Muur, and everybody remembers 2010. His last reference point for the Muur was 2009, when he was unable to keep pace with team-mate Stijn Devolder on the climb, so he's arguably right to be pessimistic, though he's riding better in 2011 than he was two years previously. But Cancellara has a secret – he's left his best form at E3 Prijs, nine days before the Ronde. He can't work out if he has a mental block or is just having an off day, but he feels less good than he would have hoped. Plus, he's dehydrated.

Nevertheless, the lead creeps up. It is 53 seconds as the leading pair reaches the Fietsmonument Ronde van Vlaanderen, a circular sculpture made of hundreds of old bikes in the middle of the N8 roundabout in south-west Brakel. The route will head all the way through the town on the N8, then turn a hairpin bend and ride almost parallel back in the opposite direction before another Z-bend of roads brings them to the bottom of Tenbossestraat. Another kilometre, and the gap rises to 55 seconds.

Geraint Thomas leads the bunch through the Fietsmonument roundabout, followed by four BMC riders. This is a sign of trouble for Cancellara – he'll rely not just on his own strength to win the race, but also on the peloton not finding common cause to chase him. Saxo Bank have been extremely circumspect about committing to chasing, Garmin are running out of riders, and Thomas is theoretically Sky's last line of defence before Flecha. But BMC putting four riders at the front means a coherent chase. Fifty-seven seconds. Around the hairpin back into Brakel. One minute. And then, more reinforcements: the entire BMC team save Karsten Kroon, who crashed out before the Kwaremont, is at the front of the peloton. Seven riders in a line.

BMC's captain George Hincapie is marshalling the team. Really, they have no choice. He knows his riders are solid, and he knows it's their responsibility to chase, or Cancellara and Chavanel will not be caught. Their leader, 2007 winner Alessandro Ballan, is feeling good, and with the numbers they have BMC are the only obstacle standing between Cancellara and a probable victory to be taken in even more spectacular fashion than 2010.

The lead peaks at 63 seconds, just before Cancellara and Chavanel turn left on to Tenbossestraat, half a kilometre at an average of seven per cent. The Leopard team car finally makes it to Cancellara in the final 100 metres of the climb and passes him two bottles.

Van Avermaet leads the chase up Tenbossestraat, followed by his team-mates Hincapie, Marcus Burghardt and leader Ballan. The short chase and the climb have already pushed the other three BMC riders – Michael Schär, Quinziato and Danilo Wyss – back down the peloton. Behind them Steegmans is still acting as policeman, tracked by Boonen. The gap is 53 seconds at the top.

Jonathan Vaughters picks up the radio and gives one of his last four surviving riders, Tyler Farrar, a message. 'No riding. No riding,' he says. 'You and Thor, do not ride. Just sit in, rest as much as you can. Do not ride. If it's a sprint for third, it's a sprint for third. If it's for first, it's first. But no riding. Just sit in and let the other teams do the work. No more riding. We're just surviving for the sprint now.'

It looks like a negative tactic but, the way Vaughters sees it, there is no other option. They have two riders left; BMC have seven. Klier and Haussler are about finished and Hushovd and Farrar are leaders. Klier and Haussler can't work, and if Hushovd or Farrar works they will not win. Though on the surface of it, racing for third looks like a concession, the real choice is actually working and definitely losing the race, or not working and – if BMC succeed in pulling Cancellara and Chavanel back – having a small but greater-than-zero chance of winning. He thinks maybe they have a two per cent chance of winning if they don't chase, but that's better than zero.

There's one more reason to make the order. Vaughters is well aware how the peloton works, and he knows that the Garmin riders – as representatives of one of the more prominent and, on paper, stronger teams in the race – will be getting asked by the others in the group to contribute to the chase. By giving the order, Vaughters has given them a ready-made excuse to turn down the request.

The road from Brakel to Geraardsbergen, the N493, is a wide road of sweeping curves that first drops down, then climbs up an ascent known as the Parikeberg. It's not an official *helling*, but it's steeper than a drag and its position in the race makes it hard. The official stats list 600 metres at an average of five per cent, which means it's longer than Tenbossestraat but not quite as steep. BMC are now receiving help from Stijn Devolder, who is killing his own chances of winning (which had been reduced significantly when he chased in front of Nuyens between the Oude Kwaremont and Steenbeekdries). He needn't contribute, but his team-mate Leukemans will at least benefit if it comes back together.

Between the two groups, the Leopard team car has drawn up alongside the Quick Step car. They want to know if Chavanel can help Cancellara, to which the answer is no. 'Too strong. Your boy is too strong. It's not possible,' replies Wilfried Peeters. 'Chavanel has made a break of 60 kilometres. He's too strong.'

Peeters has a point. The gap moves back out to a minute as they climb the Parikeberg. BMC's Burghardt has punctured and it has taken the momentum out of the chase, though Vacansoleil's Thomas De Gendt has arrived to give Devolder some help. The chase is two Vacansoleil riders and two BMC riders – Van Avermaet and Hincapie – with Ballan sitting behind. When the Italian won in 2007, he attacked on the Muur; he is currently in a good position to do the same.

Ballan's win was a shock to Belgian cycling. Boonen was

on a hat trick, having won in 2005 and 2006, and as he lined up for the 2007 race he'd already won eight times in just over two months. Four stage wins at the Tour of Qatar and a stage of the Vuelta a Andalucía were the warm-up, but the ominous news for his rivals were wins in Kuurne–Brussels–Kuurne, Dwars door Vlaanderen and E3 Prijs. He looked unbeatable, and Belgium expected a third win.

However, on the Muur, Boonen came unstuck. He couldn't match Ballan's acceleration there and dropped back, with only Leif Hoste able to bridge the gap to the Italian over the top of the climb. Hoste was the local favourite and the fans' allegiance quickly switched to him. He looked faster in the sprint, accelerating away from Ballan, but Ballan just found enough to come back past Hoste metres before the line, almost silencing the vast crowd at the finish. He's rarely been that good since, but the way BMC are riding suggests that he's dangerous, and he's one of the few favourites who has not shown himself in any way. Cancellara, Boonen, Gilbert, Langeveld and Flecha, for example, have all made attacks, big or small. Ballan has been sitting tight.

As Cancellara and Chavanel crest the Parikeberg, Geraardsbergen appears across the valley. The town is built on a steep-sided hill. At the top, the Muur waits.

The day I went to meet Johan Museeuw in Ypres, the wind was pushing in strongly from the North Atlantic. It swung round an area of very low pressure centred on the southern tip of Greenland, from where it blew in a more or less straight line to Belgium. I'd had to get out of my car earlier because I was stuck behind a lorry inching along a one-lane road and the wind was so strong it had flung my door open, pulling it from my grip. As I checked the width to see if I would be able to pass between the lorry and a steep bank dropping into a field where a piece of farm machinery was harvesting carrots, I saw smashed carrots making bright blobs of orange against the dark, thick mud. The heavy clay soil around Ypres is a permanent characteristic of the region. André De Vries, in his book *Flanders: A Cultural History*, explained that in the Tertiary era, 35 million years ago, when this part of Belgium was under the sea, the seabed was a 350-foot-deep layer of clay. When Belgium emerged from the sea, floods deposited more clay and this part of West Flanders didn't get the wind-blown sand and loam deposits that covered the rest of Belgium. The land here is old and unchanging, and the thick clay is stubborn and hard to work.

The landscape around me stretched flat in all directions; war cemeteries with names like 'Track X', 'No Man's Cot' and 'Minty Farm' interrupted the straight line of the horizon, but there was nothing but an occasional building to stop the wind. I shivered as I waited for the lorry to pass. My meeting place with Museeuw was at a bike wholesaler in a very new concrete building on an industrial estate at the northern edge of the city. I'd had trouble finding it, and it was only the silver Volvo with the decals of the Johan Museeuw Cycling Academy parked outside that gave it away. The stairwells weren't finished yet, and they smelled of fresh cement; the main selling space – a hangar-like area with bikes, tables and chairs and a coffee bar in the corner – had the characteristic strong bike-shop odour of tyre rubber. The atmosphere was cold and sterile. When I arrived, I'd bumped into Museeuw and he greeted me with an extremely firm handshake and suggested we go up in the lift. There was no small talk: he turned around and made a call on his phone.

Johan Museeuw grew up in Gistel in West Flanders, just inland from the Belgian coast between Ostend and De Panne. He won the Ronde three times, came second three times and third twice. His consistency and results might be the best in the history of the race, and though he didn't match Briek Schotte's record of participating in 20 Rondes, he rode it for 17 consecutive years – every season between his debut as a professional in 1988 and his final year in 2004. His former manager at Mapei and Quick Step, Patrick Lefevere, said to me that with the physical assets he had and his ability in the Ronde, Museeuw should have won the race five times. He also found success elsewhere: he won Paris–Roubaix three times, the world championships road race and several other major one-day events, plus two Tour de France stages taken early in his career when he could use his strength to turn out a good sprint.

In 1991, at the age of 25, he came second behind Edwig Van Hooydonck at the Ronde. He was 14th in 1992, when everybody got caught out by Jacky Durand. And then his first win came in 1993. He attacked on Tenbossestraat with Dutch rider Frans Maassen, towed him almost all the way to the finish in Meerbeke and still outsprinted him. He was caught out in 1994, when he was ambushed by Gianni Bugno in the finishing sprint and came second. In 1995 he won with a solo attack over the Muur van Geraardsbergen but it would be another three years before he won his third, with another attack on Tenbossestraat and solo ride to the finish.

His wins were spectacular – based on unplanned long-range attacks, two of them made on his own. He should have won more, but injuries, crashes and circumstances conspired against him. When he was third in 1999, behind Van Petegem and Vandenbroucke, he was hampered by his recovery from smashing his kneecap in the previous year's Paris–Roubaix; in 2000 he suffered serious head injuries in a motorcycle accident. He had the form to win in 2002, but came second after Andrea Tafi escaped in the closing stages. I asked him if he was the best ever rider at the Ronde. 'Maybe, if you look at the results. I think so,' he said. He is the most matter-of-fact and unemotional man I have ever met.

There's one more thing. His press officer had asked me not to talk about drugs. That was fine – Museeuw has made two confessions since his career ended. In 2007 he said euphemistically that he'd 'not been completely honest' in his last year as a pro. Then in 2012 he expanded somewhat, implying that not only he but many riders routinely took performance-enhancing substances over the course of their careers. This wasn't news, and Museeuw is not the only Tour of Flanders winner or rider to have allegedy taken drugs. In his memoir *Breaking the Chain*, the ex-Festina team soigneur Willy Voet, whose arrest on the Franco–Belgian border before the 1998 Tour sparked the Festina doping affair, claimed that a past Tour of Flanders winner had used a not-for-the-squeamish method of cheating the doping control involving a condom and substitute urine. Museeuw had assumed that his 2012 confession might lead to a cathartic opening of the floodgates, with others following his lead, but nobody did. People who know him have told me he's frustrated that cycling turned its back on him while colleagues who – reading between the lines of his confession – also doped but stayed quiet, kept their jobs in cycling.

Following Museeuw's half-confession in 2007, he gave an interview to Lionel Birnie for *Cycle Sport* which started badly ('What would you like to say?' 'I don't have anything to say.'), continued awkwardly ('Are you prepared to tell us what substances you took?' 'No.') and ended no better ('Do you understand people will think you cheated earlier?' 'All I can say is that I did something wrong at the end of my career.'). Those looking for resolution to cycling's long doping saga will not find it in the testimony of Johan Museeuw; nor have they found it with many other riders, which makes Museeuw no more or less responsible than them.

When I record interviews, I remind subjects that they are being taped and that if they change their mind about or want to clarify something they've said, to tell me. Before I even finished my spiel, Museeuw talked over me: 'I never change my mind.'

Museeuw never stopped cycling, though his racing days are long past. He still takes groups out for rides in the Flemish Ardennes and, from what I've heard, he's a good-natured guide. He's the go-to guy for magazine journalists who want to be shown around the climbs of the Tour of Flanders. The many hours spent with the wind in his face have etched deep lines on his forehead, along with a worried-looking kink between his eyebrows. He doesn't smile or gesture much, and he comes across as emotionally disengaged, though one of my contacts in the Flemish media says he's just shy and felt abandoned by the sport after his confessions. This has forced him to develop a carapace of defensiveness – he was happier to talk about the race and his racing than anything personal. Conversely, he is a positive and optimistic presence on Twitter, which is not at all how he is in person with most people and which suggests that the shyness is pretty ingrained.

'The Ronde van Vlaanderen is not exactly a cobblestone race,' he told me. 'It's a long race. You need a lot of experience. You need volume and a big engine. You have to take it easy in the beginning; if you lose too much power before the end, it's over. That's very difficult to do. You have to think about everything in the Ronde. It's very important to make good decisions, not the wrong decision. The champions have the physical ability but also the intelligence. You are born with it; you can't learn it. You have it or you don't have it.'

A text arrived on Museeuw's phone. We sat in silence for minutes while he read it, then laboriously composed a reply, while Jim Diamond's 'I Should Have Known Better' played over the sound system. Then he explained why he preferred long-range attacks. 'If I had the legs, I went. If you don't have the legs, it's not the right moment. The legs say okay, then you can make the decision.'

Another text. Another long silence.

When he won in 1993, Museeuw towed Frans Maassen all the way to the finish after they'd attacked on Tenbosse. There's always a risk of being outsprinted – as he was the following year by Bugno – especially if the work has not been shared equally. 'I was quite sure to win. In the sprint it was impossible to beat me,' he said. 'A hundred per cent.' When I asked if there had been the slightest bit of doubt, he looked at me, but didn't answer.

'It's hard if you are solo,' he said. 'You have to ride at 50 kilometres per hour. So I looked at my computer and said, "Okay, 50. Forty-nine, 48 are not okay. Fifty. Fifty-two okay. Forty-nine not okay." You ride at 50 and they can't come closer – they'd have to ride at 60, and that's impossible. So I rode at 50 until Meerbeke. On television it looks like it doesn't hurt, but it is not easy. It means that you have more than the others, a different engine. If you can ride at 50 kilometres per hour after 235 kilometres it means you are a champion. It means you are different from the others, but to be a champion you have to be different. That's the secret. If you're a Classics rider with a big engine you have the possibility to win the Ronde. I had a big engine so I could win it. I knew the roads. And I liked the cobbles and short hills. I was explosive. I had all the elements to win the Ronde.'

Johan Museeuw forces us to ask questions of ourselves about why we follow sport, and why we support one rider or another or enjoy one rider's victory more than that of another. When he was winning the Tour of Flanders, I found him hard to identify with because he didn't give the impression he was enjoying his victories and he never looked that happy on the podium. He made his wins in the Ronde – which were very impressive – look a little easy and inevitable, and for me the most compelling part of sport is uncertainty. He was matter-of-fact about his incredible physical gifts then, and he's matter-of-fact about it now. His ex-manager Patrick Lefevere described him to me as introverted, better in small groups than big ones, and reluctant to speak up in team meetings. Perhaps Museeuw's only form of expression or communication was through his racing and he needed nothing more complicated than that. We talked about *Flandriens*; he recognises himself in the stereotype. 'You have to be good in bad weather, good in the Flemish races and on the cobbles, and win in a special manner,' he said. 'A *Flandrien* looks not so nice. You don't have to be a very nice rider, but after a crash, if you come back, then you are a *Flandrien*. Now it's difficult to call riders a *Flandrien* – they all look nice on the bike with good clothing and sunglasses. Maybe I was the last.'

I asked him to describe his character. 'I was just focused for the race,' he said. 'It's difficult to say. I don't know.' There was a long silence. Then: 'I don't want to describe my character.'

He added: 'I am happy with everything. If I could go back, I would do everything the same. I am happy with what I have done and happy that I am still around and still cycling.'

As the interview finished, he asked me if I wanted to get a coffee, and we walked over to the café area to get the drinks. I had interpreted the offer of coffee as an invitation to prolong the encounter and I was expecting to chat a little more, but instead he offered me one last very firm handshake and went to sit with some friends at another table. I sat at the edge of the room, watching him talk and laugh.

CHAPTER 16

Muur

The chapel of Onze Lieve Vrouw stands atop the Oudenberg, 100 metres above the Dender river in Geraardsbergen, the only backdrop to a bicycle race that, in my opinion, stands aesthetic comparison to the Dolomites of the Giro d'Italia, or the high Alps of the Tour de France. The knoll the church was built on, a well-manicured and landscaped grassy dome around which the Kapelmuur – the final part of the Muur van Geraardsbergen – winds, was a pulsating, screaming mass of humanity on the day of the race between 1981 and 2011. It was a natural amphitheatre built at the crux of the Tour of Flanders; a perfect confluence of sport and atmosphere and the best spectator experience in cycling by a long, long way.

I'd seen the chapel hundreds, if not thousands, of times in pictures and on television before I ever considered going in. It's ironic that my perception of the Muur was of baying, partying fans, whereas the backdrop I enjoyed so much was actually a place of pilgrimage and quiet contemplation for 364 days a year. When I spoke to Allan Peiper about the race, he said the Muur was one of his favourite places on the route. 'I'd stop weekly at the top of the Muur, park my bike and even though

I wasn't Catholic by denomination or upbringing, I went into the chapel, sat there for a second and just had a moment. I felt that was part of my ritual,' he said.

The chapel is dedicated to Onze Lieve Vrouw (Our Lady). The main space is an octagonal space arranged around the altar, with about 50 chairs arranged in neat rows. The first time I visited, there was one person sat facing the altar, thinking or praying; after ten minutes or so, she went to a statue of an angel at the side, touched its feet, mouthing some silent words, then wiped her hands on a cloth set beside the statue and left. With just me in the chapel, the quietness was almost total and I could hear my own breathing and movements. When I shifted in my chair, the sound echoed around the space. A tinkling bell struck the hour, and the air was thick and warm with the smell of melted wax – in one alcove, there were 323 candles burning.

Every wall was covered with small plaques with messages on them – '*Dank aan OLV voor myne genezing*' (Thanks be to Our Lady for healing me), for example – with dates etched at the bottom. Some dated back to the 1920s – the chapel itself was built in 1906, though there had been a 17th-century version before that, which the congregation had outgrown, and the first mention of a place of worship on the hill came in 1294. Unlike the church on the Madonna del Ghisallo in Italy, which is on the route of the Tour of Lombardy and is full of cycling paraphernalia, there is very little evidence in the Muur's chapel of the place's connection with bike racing. The only reference to the sport that I could find was a picture of a smiling rider from the old Chocolade Jacques professional team on a panel of fading photographs, mainly face pictures. A legend above the photos read, '*Wij bidden voor hen*' (We pray for them). The Chocolade Jacques rider was the late Dimitri De Fauw, a rider from Ghent who committed suicide in 2009 while experiencing depression following his involvement in a crash at a track race three years previously which cost the life of another rider, Isaac Gálvez.

On the door leading to a small office, alongside a schedule for mass (every day at 7 a.m), there was a telephone number for the priest.

Father François Mbiyangandu was appointed priest of Onze Lieve Vrouw van de Oudenberg in 2007. He was born and grew up in Bulungu, in what is now the Democratic Republic of the Congo, where he studied and was ordained in 1978 in the Josephite order. He also taught in a seminary in Bulungu, with various visits to Belgium from the age of 20. 'I'd never seen a big town before – Bulungu is in the bush,' he told me. 'I came out of the country and saw the big city, Kinshasa, which was different. Then I took the plane and came here and everything was different again.' When he was called to Geraardsbergen, he was almost at retirement age but decided to go anyway. 'The previous priest was getting older and they didn't have a replacement here, so they asked me if I could do it,' he said. 'I worked for 30 years in my country. I considered I had done my work there, and could leave the way for others to take over.'

Now Father Mbiyangandu has been here for ten years, he thinks he'll stay. He told me that if his superiors gave him orders to go back to Bulungu he would go, but he's happy running affairs in Geraardsbergen.

His days start early. 'I get here before six to be ready for people to arrive at Mass at 7 every day. In general there are a dozen people here during the week, then around 30 on Sundays and 50 on public holidays. Then I'm here if people want to confess or just need to talk. My number is on the door for anybody to call in case they need me at any time during the day. They call, and I can be here quickly.'

He told me about the changing attitude of Flemish people towards going to church. 'Religious practice is going down at the moment. But there are always believers. People used to fill the churches and go to all the celebrations but it happens less now. In spite of that, they still believe. The proof is that this chapel is never empty – somebody comes here every day. People don't show belief like before, but it is still there.'

The day of the Ronde, when it passed here, was no different from any other day, save for the regular attendees finding it difficult to park before morning Mass. But it happened at 7 a.m., same as always. Then the race took over. 'It was always a big day. A national holiday. From morning to evening, the road was full of people. And on the climb, when the race passed, it was as if God had descended from heaven. It really left me with an impression,' he said. 'But it's not religious, even if it looks like it. It's striking when the race passes, and it is as if the people are possessed by a force. But after the race has passed, just one second later, the feeling has gone.'

Oudenaardsestraat, the N493, descends into Geraardsbergen from the west, but before it gets into the town proper it climbs up a steep hump of a bridge that crosses six sets of railway tracks and sits above the town's station. Geraardsbergen station is at a crossroads of routes – the main line to Ghent via Zottegem heads out from the north; there's another line to the north-east towards Aalst; to the south there is a direct route to Mons in Wallonia; finally there's a line that heads south-east then east to Brussels. Commuters can get from Geraardsbergen to Brussels Midi in 42 minutes on a direct train.

I looked from the top of the railway bridge towards the Oudenberg. From here it didn't seem so imposing – just a wooded hillock behind the town with a tall television aerial on one side. From the bridge, I walked up Grotestraat, a busy and narrow street with shops, cafés and bakeries selling the Mattentaart (the local speciality of milk curd encased in puff pastry flavoured with buttermilk and almonds, which is protected by a European naming regulation). Five hundred metres from the railway, Grotestraat crosses a low swing bridge across the Dender river. Here the road starts to drag up into the centre of Geraardsbergen. The name changes to Brugstraat and the surface of the road changes to tightly packed stone setts. It's still narrow, and the buildings on either side are three storeys high, which makes it feel claustrophobic. Now that I was closer to the Oudenberg, it loomed up much taller behind the town.

Brugstraat opens up into the Markt, a cobbled square at the centre of the town. Two sides, the south and west, are lined by cafés and shops; the town hall, an ostentatious building with turrets and square battlements along the top, takes up most of the northern side. Just in case the town burghers ever start taking themselves too seriously, there's a *mannekin pis* statue standing above a two-level semi-circular fountain by the grand stairwell up to the front door. The *mannekin pis* is one of Belgium's most famous symbols – a statue of a young boy eternally peeing might not be as inspiring or galvanising a symbol as the Flemish lion or the Walloon cock, but it seems to be politically neutral, inoffensive and ridiculous enough that the country as a whole has collectively shrugged and allowed it to become one of their defining icons. The origins of the statue are unclear but the Brussels *Mannekin Pis* is generally thought to be the original. The people of Geraardsbergen, however, insist that their version – which, according to Alec Le Sueur in his book *Bottoms up in Belgium*, appeared in 1459 – pre-dates the one in the capital. (Geraardsbergen boasts of its 'three Ms': Mattentaart, the Muur and the *Mannekin Pis*.)

The eastern side of the Markt is dominated by the Sint-Bartholomeuskerk, a huge Gothic church. I walked up the Markt square, following the race route. On the stone setts here, opposite a chip shop called Frituur Obelix, somebody has painted the word 'Start', along with pictures of a couple of stopwatches. The road has already been dragging up along Brugstraat and across Markt, but the climb through the town gets steeper here. It's still another 300 metres before the Muur officially starts, however. At the top of Markt, I followed the route left on to Vesten, a wide and well-cobbled stretch of open street with a lot of car parking and one of those street-level fountains that tempt children in to play on summer's days. The two sides of Vesten are noticeably different: on the west side, the 'downhill' side, the houses are small, red-brick terraces; on the Muur side, the 'uphill' side, they are mansions. If there is a dividing line between the rich and poorer quarters of Geraardsbergen, Vesten might lie directly on it.

Somebody has erected a sign on the right-hand side of Vesten, about halfway along: *'Echt Flandriens rijden op kasseien!'* (Real Flandriens ride on cobbles.)

At the top of Vesten, just past a bar called 't Kapelleke (the little chapel), I turned right on to Oudebergstraat and saw a small brown sign with a picture of a bike on it, an arrow pointing up the hill and a single word: 'Muur'. This is where the Muur van Geraardsbergen officially begins. (The Muur goes to the foot of the hillock at the top, and then carries straight on to meet Oude Steenweg, where the Ronde used to pass. The Kapelmuur is the final diversion over the hillock, a loop up to the chapel and down the other side past the Kasteel Oudenberg wedding and function venue, an imposingly kitsch turreted chateau.)

The houses on this initial section of the Muur are neat but – unlike on Vesten – the cobbles are starting to deteriorate. They are still largely flat and uniform, but the mortar between them has eroded and so they aren't very well fixed – if I bent down and got hold of one, I was able to move it slightly. Once away from the town houses, the Muur becomes a little more wild.

Tall bushes and trees, choked with ivy, line the right-hand side as the Muur curves to the left. Above the town, the Oudenberg is home to a rare and protected purple flower, the devil's-bit scabious, which means the grass at the top can only be mown at certain times of the year. Just before the road ducks into the trees, there is a row of six one-room-wide houses. The seventh is completely derelict, with an overgrown garden out front. I knocked on the door of another house and the occupant, who'd lived there since he was a child, told me he mainly didn't miss the Tour of Flanders coming this way. The television companies used to come and park their lorries on his drive without asking, and getting in and out was impossible. 'But it was the pride of Geraardsbergen,' he said. 'The Eneco Tour and E3 come here and you get 500 people watching. For the Ronde, it was 5,000.'

At the top of this final row of houses, the Muur turns right, and a metal post in the road prevents cars going any further. There's a copse of very old-looking woodland, around which the Muur winds. At the bottom of a steep, stepped short cut to the top is a huge house behind locked gates. A sign reads that Jan De Cooman, a famous artist who made etchings of the local landscape and buildings, once occupied the house. Nobody was in when I visited but I got talking to the man who lived in the next house along, a ham-radio enthusiast called Hugo. Hugo has lived on the Muur for a long time, and he misses the race, though more for the atmosphere than for the sport. He showed me round to the front of his house, which perches on the edge of the Oudenberg, facing west with a panoramic view of the Dender valley and the *Vlaamse Ardennen* beyond. 'This is the most beautiful view in the world,' he said. Pointing down at the town, he added, 'We watched the riders coming through right there.' His house faced the Grotestraat in the town far below, which meant he could see the race coming in the distance, then watch them ride up through the town to the Markt. Then he could walk back across his garden to the Muur at the back, be on the climb with enough time to watch the riders go past, and then be back in front of the television in time for the Bosberg.

The Muur, once it reaches the trees – the most televisual and famous part – is best described as three sides of a rectangle (the fourth side is the steep footpath through the copse). From the car barrier, it rears up to 20 per cent for 100 metres, before a left turn, then 50 more very steep metres, then another left turn for another 100 metres to the foot of the Kapelmuur. The moves in the race used to go right here, conveniently for the fixed cameras the television companies put on each corner. I snapped my rear derailleur off here during the Ronde sportive one year and had to thumb a lift to the finish from a friendly local. This being Flanders, he was a friend of a soigneur in the Gerolsteiner team.

The trees were hanging over the Muur, so it was dark and mossy, and the road was covered in twigs and leaves. There was a constant thin stream of cyclists riding up the climb, and you could tell which were locals and which were tourists. The tourists used the racing line, up the left-hand side of the track, where the cobbles are slightly worn. The locals just hopped up onto the pavement for a much smoother ride. In the race, this option is barriered off.

The cobbles on these final steep sections look different in the television shots from those on the other *hellingen*. On the Muur, the cobbles have tipped back slightly in their settings, as if gravity is pulling them back down the hill, so their flat tops are facing diagonally up towards the sky and their edges are exposed. It gives the road surface a textured, dappled look that is unique to the Muur, but it makes the cobbles a lot more resistant to bike racing.

On the top corner of the Muur before the final straight section, there is another Willie Verhegghe poem, cast in iron next to a roadside bench, this time about Eddy Merckx which described the cyclist as 'A new god, a lightning storm on two wheels'. Just before taking the right turn to the Kapelmuur, I went for a drink in 't Hemelrijck, the bar at the top of the Muur.

The owner of 't Hemelrijck, Herman, was a childhood cycling fan, who still has the brown Molteni team jersey he bought in honour of his hero Merckx. Herman had pursued a career in banking in Brussels, following pressure from his parents, but his heart wasn't in it and in his spare time he went to hospitality school. In 1989 he stood on the Muur to watch the race go past. 'It was the year Edwig Van Hooydonck won. I saw the empty building, and thought, *"This is not normal,"'* he said. He told me that by the Wednesday, he'd made an offer to the brewery to buy it. 'I've got a lot of memories of the race. It used to be the best weekend of the year. The atmosphere was incredible – by eight or nine in the morning, you couldn't see the grass on the Kapelmuur any more because there were so many people. The Muur is like the Poggio in Milan–San Remo – when you are good on the Poggio you have a chance to win. Here, also, the first three or four riders over the Muur, you can say, "Okay, that one or that one will win." Now,' he added, 'it's the easiest weekend of the year.'

Herman told me he missed the trade but not the hard work. It took two weeks of preparation before the Sunday of the race, then three days of solid clearing up. 'In 22 years I never saw the race once,' he said. 'Now I have the time to go and watch.'

At the very top of the hill, higher even than the chapel, is an obelisk and a panoramic viewing table facing west. I tried to compare the view and the table, but it had eroded to near-illegibility. Before me, the land fell steeply away; Geraardsbergen was obscured by the trees but to the north-west there was a huge view of patchwork fields, a village – maybe Everbeek – in the valley and the southern ridge of the Flemish Ardennes stretching into the haze. It was quiet at the top. The only sign of anybody apart from me was two empty beer cans left at the foot of the obelisk by persons, presumably teenagers, unknown.

The Ronde has taken a variety of routes up and over the Muur in the course of its history. In the Muur's first appearances – between 1950 and 1952, and between 1970 and 1980 – the race didn't go through the town centre; it took the steep climb of Abdijstraat to the north, which brought the riders to the top of Vesten from where they could join Oudebergstraat – the Muur. Between 1953 and 1969, when Geraardsbergen was on the route, the riders started on Abdijstraat but instead of turning right on to Oudebergstraat they carried straight on, along Oude Steenweg, which continues behind the Muur – the descent from the Kapelmuur joins this road. During these years, the climb was known as Kloosterstraat. Between 1981 and 1997, they followed the same route as between 1970 and 1980 – up Abdijstraat and then the Muur, but the organisers added the Kapelmuur. The final tweak was made in 1998, which lasted all the way until 2011: the approach through the town centre, up Grotestraat and Brugstraat, via Markt.

When the Muur was taken out of the Tour of Flanders for 2012, there was widespread criticism, partly because the climb was seen as part of the fabric and iconography of the race. Some people in Geraardsbergen took it particularly badly – a group of fans staged a mock funeral for the climb, walking up to the top of the Muur carrying a coffin. Modernisers, unsentimental fans and contrarian provocateurs argued that the Muur was less traditional than some thought; after all, it had never appeared before 1950, and the established route at the end had only been used for 14 editions.

The decision was presented in financial and practical terms by the organisers. Meerbeke's contract for hosting the finish was up, and Oudenaarde was prepared to pay handsomely to replace it. Geraardsbergen is only 18 kilometres from Ninove, but further from Oudenaarde. The Muur wouldn't play the same part as before. The new concept of laps would give the organisers and police more control over the movement of fans – as the race had grown in popularity, more and more fans were haring around the countryside in their cars, gaming the route to see the race as many times as possible, which was feasible when the race was smaller but potentially dangerous as it grew. The Muur was reintroduced in 2017, and though it was the launchpad for a race-defining break that year, it was a long way from the finish.

The Ronde has always changed. The Ronde will always change. You can't, the organisers concluded, stand in the way of progress. Perhaps the race needed to change, just as Flanders itself has changed. Nostalgic people romanticise the stereotype of Flemish stoicism, along with the rural/industrial roots of the working classes, and in cycling this is even used as a marketing tool. However, if you go in search of a dividing line between new and old Flanders, you won't find it. Instead, the change exists along a continuum – a thousand decisions along the way nudged Flanders into what it is now; if any of these had gone differently, the result might be different to a small or large extent, but there would still be a progression.

The mistake, however, is to confuse inevitability with correctness. I think the race lost something unique when they sacrificed the Muur as the climax – on a sporting level and in terms of atmosphere even though on other levels (the bank balance of the organisers or the ease of logistics for road closures, for example) there were gains. The final 30 kilometres of the Ronde when the finish was in Meerbeke was one of the most serendipitously perfect pieces of race design in cycling. The gradual descent into Geraardsbergen, the very hard climb of the Muur, the quick descent to the Bosberg, that climb, then the schuss to Ninove with its short drags and swooping descents was perfect for both attackers and chasers. Attackers could always hope to hold off the chase; chasers could always hope to catch the attackers.

The new route is harder than the old route. Though the number of climbs is similar, riding the Kwaremont and Paterberg multiple times is physically tougher, which reduces the number of possible winners and turns the race into a purer test of strength without the tactical subtlety offered by the old route. This is not to say that there can be no exciting racing on the new route, nor that the old route was consistently exciting. The road from the bottom of the Paterberg descent to Oudenaarde is far less subtle than the road from the Bosberg to Meerbeke – just 12.5 kilometres of flat – but there was a finely balanced pursuit match on it between Peter Sagan and Fabian Cancellara in 2016, eventually won by the former. Yet the Muur gave the organisers their defining image, and the fans on the Kapelmuur's grassy hillock created cycling's greatest freeze frame. The new finish is a corporate imitation of the old one. It looks like it was designed in a committee room – a Powerpoint presentation of bullet points, while the Muur–Meerbeke finish was written in poetry.

Thomas De Gendt, from Vacansoleil, leads the chase up the Parikeberg. Right behind him, Gert Steegmans and Tom Boonen are trying to interrupt the rhythm of the chase, spoiling for Quick Step, while ahead, Chavanel is still sitting resolutely on Cancellara's back wheel. On the surface of it, the people who are in a good position are: Cancellara, probably the strongest rider in the race, with a minute's lead on all but one of his rivals; Quick Step, who have Chavanel ahead (albeit surely tiring, having been off the front for 60 kilometres), and Boonen, Steegmans and Dries Devenyns in the next group; BMC, who have numbers and a strong leader. Riders like Gilbert, Flecha, Nuyens and Langeveld are in a decent position – they're running low on team-mates but, with BMC and Vacansoleil willing to chase Cancellara, they don't need so much help. But they're less in control of their destiny than Leopard, Quick Step and BMC.

More teams are helping out at the front of the peloton. The seven-kilometre stretch from Parike to Geraardsbergen is the terrain most favourable to the chasers, with no real changes in gradient and no sharp turns or junctions. Luca Paolini of Katusha goes to the front, then Marco Marcato for Vacansoleil. The lead starts to tick downwards. With 19 kilometres to go, four after the top of the Parikeberg, it is 53 seconds. At 18 kilometres to go: 50 seconds.

Cancellara and Chavanel descend Oudenaardsestraat, and climb over the railway bridge. Forty seconds. Cancellara freewheels down the other side, stretching his legs. Behind the chase, riders are readying themselves for the Muur. Only the strongest riders will make it over in front, so the workers and leaders are auditing themselves to work out what their plan is.

Baden Cooke has fulfilled his own part in the Saxo Bank plan – he tried to go away in the final quarter but it didn't work so it's all for Nuyens now. He goes back in the bunch to find Nuyens and tells him he has one last effort left, which he will use to put Nuyens into position for the climb. Nuyens tells him he's feeling bad and to go for it himself, but Cooke knows he's got enough left to position Nuyens though not to get over the Muur. Nuyens tells Cooke again he doesn't feel good but Cooke says, 'We're 230 kilometres into the Tour of Flanders. Nobody feels good.' As Nuyens passes Cooke in Geraardsbergen, he's in about tenth place – not brilliant but at least near the front. That is the end of Cooke's race.

Geraint Thomas is having a conversation with his Sky

team-mate Mat Hayman. He tells the Australian he's still feeling good, so Hayman tells him to get to the front and keep fighting for position. In the Welshman's mind he is still working for Flecha, and he doesn't quite get as far forward as he wanted. It's only his second Tour of Flanders, and he's having more trouble than the more experienced favourites in the run-ups to the key points.

Leukemans is in a similar position, somewhere around tenth wheel. He's not panicking – he knows two key things about the Muur: first, that if you are strong, it will show; second, that the climbs up to the Markt and then up Vesten after the Markt are wide, so there is space to use that strength to move up. The approach to climbs like the Oude Kwaremont and Molenberg is only a few riders wide, but through Geraardsbergen to the foot of the Muur it's wide enough to pass a group.

Langeveld is in a very good position. Tom Leezer has put him right at the front up Brugstraat. He's not the most powerful over a climb like the Muur, but being on the front does give him a small head start. He doesn't have the explosive power to react to the attacks or to go clear himself, but his plan is to do a steady three- or four-minute effort at a very high pace so that the eventual attacks don't drop him. Gilbert, Ballan and Boonen are at the front, though Ballan's team-mate Hincapie is feeling destroyed. His plan is to ride up at his own pace, and not react to what the others do. Hushovd is there, as is Bernhard Eisel for HTC.

There is also a local rider, Staf Scheirlinckx, who is riding for the Veranda's Willems ProContinental team. Scheirlinckx is from Herzele, the next town over from Geraardsbergen to the north, and he trains on these roads almost every day. He may not be the strongest in the group but of all the riders there, he probably knows better than any of them what is coming up. Scheirlinckx is a journeyman pro who has been knocking around for years in a mix of teams – he was at Cofidis between 2004 and 2008, where he rode for Nuyens, then he rode for Gilbert at Lotto in 2009 and 2010. He's gone down a division for 2011, but paradoxically this gives him a much better chance to shine in races like the Ronde. When he was at Lotto, his energy was spent in the service of Gilbert. Now he's at a smaller team, he's free to do what he wants. Even through the years of being a domestique, he got top tens in Paris–Roubaix and E3, and he was 17th in the Ronde in 2007. He's perhaps not a potential winner, but luck and circumstances could put him in the top five.

Scheirlinckx has hidden for most of the race. His team are not capable of riding on the front in the last part of the race, so he sat back through all the early climbs, not even crossing the Koppenberg in the top 50. Tenbossestraat was the first key point for him. From there, he moved up and hung around tenth to 20th place, with the aim of moving up again into Geraardsbergen for the Muur. He is sceptical of Cancellara's chances, so he readies himself for the race coming back together over the Muur.

Through Markt, the lead is cut to 30 seconds. Cancellara visibly eases as he turns on to Vesten. Twenty-five seconds. Langeveld goes to the front of the group in Markt, ahead of Filippo Pozzato, Leukemans, Ballan, Gilbert, Boonen and Van Avermaet, who looks strained. Flecha and Nuyens are just behind. And as the chasers turn on to Vesten, they can see Cancellara and Chavanel for the first time.

The chasers are riding very fast, so it looks like they are doing the hard work of closing the gap, but Cancellara has sat up. He has known since coming into Geraardsbergen that he's not safe so – rather than try to stay away and tire himself irrevocably– he has eased off, with the aim of being able to match the others over the Muur.

Halfway up Vesten, the gap is ten seconds. Then the riders turn onto Oudebergstraat. The Muur.

The chasers, led by Gilbert, are in a long line, with those at the back of what is left of the peloton starting to lose touch with the race. Gilbert leads Leukemans, Nuyens, Boonen, Ballan, Langeveld, Scheirlinckx and Flecha. A small gap has opened behind these seven riders – Hincapie, Thomas and Hushovd are on the wrong side of it. Pozzato is dropped. Boasson Hagen is fighting but can't cross the gap.

Gilbert reaches Chavanel's back wheel at the right turn at the start of the Muur's rectangle. The break is over. But Cancellara, unbelievably, surges, dragging Chavanel with him up the first steep section.

Round the first bend, and the list of possible winners is: Cancellara, Chavanel, Gilbert, Leukemans, Nuyens, Ballan, Boonen, Flecha, Scheirlinckx, Langeveld, Hincapie, Grégory Rast of RadioShack, FDJ's Guesdon and Geraint Thomas. On the second straight, Langeveld is falling backwards, Scheirlinckx has begun to stall. Gilbert can't hold Cancellara's surge and is struggling round the final bend up to 't Hemelrijck.

Cancellara turns onto the Kapelmuur, with Chavanel. They are five lengths clear of Gilbert, Leukemans and Ballan. These are the five strongest riders in the race. Nuyens is just a few lengths back on his own, with Flecha and Boonen and Scheirlinckx together behind him. Then there is a gap to Langeveld and another gap to Hincapie and Thomas. Over the top and down the other side of the Kapelmuur, the Gilbert trio closes the gap to Cancellara and Chavanel: five at the front. The next four – Nuyens, Flecha, Boonen and Scheirlinckx – are together, with Langeveld desperately pursuing on his own. The Dutchman could be in trouble – the Nuyens quartet will be chasing the leaders, so they won't slow, and he won't be able to share the work of catching them, so he has to sprint to close the gap. Hincapie and Thomas are ten seconds back. The rest are nowhere. The winner of the Ronde will be one of these 12 riders.

Every cycling fan and aspiring cyclist, at some point, has an epiphany that the sport – far from being just the colourful, exciting, fun pursuit it seems from the Tour de France – is predominantly rooted in pain, discomfort and physiological and mental endurance. For me, as a teenage cycling fan, it was the stories about Eddy Planckaert that made me realise the sport was not glamorous. Planckaert was an East Flandrian, one of a family of cyclists. His oldest brother Willy won the green jersey in the Tour de France in 1966 and his next brother Walter won the Ronde in 1976. Their father died following a car crash when Eddy was young, and success in cycling was less to do with ambition or glory than the necessity of financial survival with no other source of income for the family.

Allan Peiper was a racing contemporary of Eddy and was invited to live with the Planckaert clan when he was 17. I read a story Peiper wrote himself in *Winning* magazine about his first encounter with the family. 'After one race Eddy offered to drive me home,' he wrote. 'First he took me to his mother's house. I remember walking into this 100-year-old house with a pump in the wash basin and the cast-iron stove burning strongly. As we walked into the kitchen, all heads turned from their card game in the dimly lit room.' This story was what made me realise that cycling was a gritty, unromantic, working-class sport, and when I interviewed Peiper about the Ronde for this book, he still used the Planckaerts to illustrate how he felt about the race and its people. 'The Planckaerts were all about the Ronde and Paris–Roubaix. That was all they ever talked about,' he said. 'For me, they epitomised the sense that the Ronde was a way of stepping out of mediocrity and doing something great. Living with them, hearing about Flanders and feeling how important it was to them instilled the same feeling in me. This is a family that was really as hard as nails. They had to fight for survival and fight to get ahead.'

Peiper remembered watching Walter Planckaert training himself to deal with cold conditions. 'Everything they did was about being tougher and stronger. Walter had a training circuit of 100 kilometres and he did it one day when it was snowing. After one lap his wife came out with a warm bidon, and he set off to do a second lap. No gloves on.'

But Peiper has seen the change in culture around the Tour of Flanders, even if some things have remained the same. 'The days when the coalmines were open and men from Flanders used to travel to work in the fields – that has all changed. There's an overlay of old and new. The weather is milder, the finish of the race has changed and now it's controlled. The Briek Schotte era is gone, but cycling in Belgium is still strong and it's more open than it was. You still have to love everything about that race, whether it's the mud or the shit on the road or the cold and rain, or whatever you are confronted with.'

Eddy Planckaert won the Ronde in 1988. He'd already won Omloop Het Volk twice, and E3 Prijs, as well as a couple of Tour de France stages. Though he'd previously ridden with the Panasonic team, he'd signed for the ADR team in 1988. His timing was good – Panasonic had a disastrous race, missing the break of 18, instigated by Sean Kelly, that went on the Oude Kwaremont. There were four PDM riders in the break, which would be crucial on the Muur van Geraardsbergen. Their rider Adrie van der Poel, who won the Ronde in 1986, attacked on the Muur and took Planckaert and Phil Anderson, also an ex-Panasonic rider. Kelly tried to react, but was sat on by van der Poel's three PDM team-mates and was marked out of it. Van der Poel cracked on the Bosberg, and though Anderson attacked a lot on the run–in, knowing that Planckaert was the better sprinter, he couldn't shake Planckaert. 'Phil was really pissed off,' Peiper told me. 'I remember him driving past my house in Ninove after the race, winding the window of his car down and saying to me, "Tell Planckaert I'm going to kill him."'

CHAPTER 17

Bosberg

By the time I pulled up at the top of the Bosberg, having spent far too long at the Muur, it was dark and raining. It was also a winter's Sunday, so I was surprised to see that El Faro, the bar-cum-restaurant at the top, was packed. The car park was full, so I had to park some distance down the road, scraping the bottom of the car on a grass bank. There were at least 50 people inside, not including the staff. My experience of off-the-beaten-track Flemish bars is that they are quiet and dark and that not many people visit them, but at El Faro it looked as if business could not be any better. It took me so long to count heads that the owners, seeing me looking around and writing down numbers, assumed I was from the local council, checking that health and safety limits on the number of customers weren't being exceeded.

It had struck me after speaking with Father Mbiyangandu at the Kapelmuur that the twin institutions of church and bar – the two gathering places of local communities over decades – are enduring a slow diminuendo into obscurity, for different reasons. But this didn't apply here.

El Faro's restaurant area is more functional than homely and the evening I visited there were several screens showing Ostend leading Standard Liège by one goal to nil in their Belgian First Division match. The menu suited families and the atmosphere was informal, sociable and noisy. The impression I got was that it's the kind of place where you're paying for convenience, for relaxed interactions with the waiting staff, for people not to mind how much noise your kids are making and for somebody else to be doing the washing-up. El Faro wasn't corporate, however – they served Tongerlo and La Chouffe (Tom Boonen's favourite beer) on tap, and had several locally produced beers available. They urged me to try the Spartacus, which was named after Fabian Cancellara. 'Much better than Kwaremont,' said the owner, Nancy.

Seven years ago, El Faro modernised itself out of the danger of obsolescence. 'It used to be a real old Belgian bar,' Nancy told me. 'We looked for a different concept, something that was good for all people; people with kids.' The bar – then called Uitkijktoren – had been owned since 1987 by Guido Debleser, Nancy's father, who has also been organising bike races and looking after cyclists for years. When Nancy and her partner Danny took over they rebuilt it to broaden the customer base. It's a family affair – Guido was around, they told me, and Danny's daughter Kimberley was helping out behind the bar.

Cycling culture runs deep at El Faro. When the building was renovated, they also included storage facilities and showers so cyclists could use it as a base for rides. The bar's position at the top of the Ronde's final climb made it one of the liveliest spots on the race route up to 2011. Almost too lively, by the end. Kimberley told me about the huge number of camping cars and buses that arrived in the days before the race. 'The atmosphere was great but some people weren't interested in the race, only in going drinking for the whole day and it got a bit too much. One year a couple of people got into a fight,' she said.

Like most people from Geraardsbergen and to its east, they

miss the Ronde, but the absence seems to be harder here. It's not just the business – on Ronde day they sold beer from four different temporary bars and had television screens up to watch the race. 'People who aren't from here don't understand how we feel about it – we have grown up with it,' said Kimberley. The Eneco Tour has come past a couple of times but it hasn't brought anything like the same numbers.

Guido has been a fixture on the Flemish cycling scene for many years. He used to have a soft spot for the Kazakh riders who came over to Europe in the 1990s, and Alexander Vinokourov – not a Ronde rider but who won Liège–Bastogne–Liège twice and came third in the Tour de France – used to come and sleep on his floor. He also organises the Zellik–Galmaarden race, which is a couple of divisions below the WorldTour but is a proving ground for young Belgian riders. 'The winner often turns pro,' Kimberley explained. 'Tom Boonen won and Greg Van Avermaet won, and they turned pro.'

Guido himself told me he wouldn't go to Oudenaarde. 'Too stubborn,' he said. He used to love the race coming past. 'Whoever gets to the top of the Bosberg first, they can win the race,' he said.

The Bosberg proves the point that context is everything in bike racing. Pound for pound it's one of the least interesting of the *hellingen* – it's pretty straight, with one right-hand curve halfway up, not hugely steep, wide enough for cars to pass each other in each direction, and short. The official stats make it a kilometre long, but a lot of that is a steady drag of *betonweg* out of the village of Atembeke to the bottom of the cobbled section. It's never steeper than ten per cent, with cobbles that don't shake the riders up too much.

However, as much as the Muur, the Bosberg was the crux of the old route of the Tour of Flanders because it was so close to the end and came only a few kilometres after the Muur, so riders were shattered by the bottom. George Hincapie told me it was one of the hardest climbs in the whole sport. 'It's brutal,' he said. 'The Muur is right before and your legs are shot. It's probably only a minute or a minute and 30 seconds long, and if you've made it that far, you know you have to stay in the group. Everybody knows that so everybody puts everything they have into that climb. Once you start climbing you can basically see the top, and that little false flat is the worst false flat in all of cycling. It's only about 100 metres long, but you get to the top and you've still got that to go. It's just painful. It probably hurts more than any other climb in the whole WorldTour.'

From Oude Steenweg, below the Muur, the Ronde heads east down a false flat on Onkerzelestraat, then downhill on Brusselsestraat to Atembeke. There's a kink left and then a sharp right through the village, then left onto Kapellestraat, otherwise known as the Bosberg.

Down the hill, it's five versus five versus two. In the front group, Cancellara, Gilbert, Leukemans and Ballan are rotating, while Chavanel – as he has been doing ever since the Valkenberg – is still sitting on. Initially, it looks like the gap will close behind them – they start the descent with a 20-metre lead but Gilbert is going hard on the front, and since he is evidently stronger than anybody in the second group, the gap starts to go out. Quick Step's race is hanging by a thread. Chavanel is probably the weakest link in the front group and is sitting on; Boonen is chasing at the front of the group behind.

Cancellara goes to the front of the first group; Flecha goes to the front of the second group. Ballan takes over from Cancellara, but it's Boonen who has to work again in the second group. Nuyens, Scheirlinckx and Langeveld won't work – to do so will make them vulnerable for the final part of the race. The lead goes above 100 metres, and Nuyens berates himself for his stupidity – if the gap goes out too far now, his race is over. He stops sitting in and starts contributing.

As the race hits Atembeke, Hincapie and Thomas are closing the gap on the Boonen group. *Full gas*, thinks Thomas. *No holding back and trying to make Hincapie do more work, because now it is all or nothing.* Each has a team-mate ahead – Ballan for Hincapie and Flecha for Thomas – and they are almost sprinting through the village.

Thomas and Hincapie are the oldest and youngest riders of the dozen riders at the front of the race. All are between 29 and 33 years old, except Langeveld at 26, Thomas at 24 and Hincapie at 37, who are the outliers. Hincapie is riding his 16th Ronde – he's participated every year since he turned pro in 1994 except 2003 and 2007 when illness and injury kept him away. His best result was third in 2006, when Tom Boonen and Hincapie's team-mate Leif Hoste attacked on the Valkenberg, but he's had five other top tens up to this point. He was dependable and resilient, always there, and yet he lacked the spark to convert his proven podium potential into a Ronde win. 'Pizza Margherita,' his long-time team-mate Frankie Andreu once said. 'Every freaking meal. Pizza Margherita. He'd never waver or vary his order. It was maddening. We'd point out other things on the menu and insist he order something else. Nope. Not George. He'd simply say, "No, I like this." He knew what he liked and he stuck with it.'

Hincapie has made two parallel careers for himself. He is defined for ever as Lance Armstrong's domestique de luxe at the Tour de France, the only rider to have ridden in all seven of the Tours Armstrong won before the Texan was stripped for doping. And he's been a perennial challenger in the cobbled Classics, though Ghent–Wevelgem in 2001 has been his only victory in any – he's a consistent placer but not a winner.

He's also tough. On the first page of his autobiography, *The*

Loyal Lieutenant, Hincapie wrote, 'The way I looked at it, boiled down to its essence, cycling could be simplified to an equation of who could train the longest and the hardest, and once in a race, who could best withstand the intensity of the pain.' He occasionally used to race hard enough that he couldn't stand up for an hour after the finish.

If Hincapie has learned one thing from his years of racing the Ronde, it's that he knows there's always a chance to come back. He has seen riders dropped and then go on to win, like Rolf Sørensen in 1997. He's been dropped himself and then finished in the top ten. If he can fight back into the front group, he's still in the race – especially with a team-mate up there.

Coming out of Atembeke, Thomas and Hincapie make contact. Five against seven. Sky now have two riders in the second group; BMC and Quick Step have a man in each group, which means they can try to sit on in each case. Chavanel and Ballan, in the front group, can skip turns and tell their companions that they can't work with riders behind; Hincapie and Boonen can skip turns and tell their companions that they can't work with riders ahead. As the front group starts the drag up to the foot of the Bosberg, sure enough Ballan and Chavanel melt to the back of the group, Chavanel looking back to check on Boonen's progress. Nuyens thinks Boonen is playing games; over the radio Riis tells Nuyens not to do any more work and to sit tight at the back – the Saxo manager can see that the race is going to come back together. With two riders in the second group, it's up to Sky to work, and the others know it. Thomas goes to the front of the group and chases. The gap is starting to reduce below 50 metres again, with the front group realising they are going to get caught and relenting.

Just as Thomas closes the gap, and the group becomes 12 for such a brief moment that it hardly counts, Gilbert hits the cobbles at the front and attacks.

Leukemans follows; he loses a bike length. Cancellara tries to slot in behind Leukemans but is having trouble holding the pace. Ballan and Chavanel sit behind him. Gilbert goes five metres clear, and Cancellara has to pull out of the line because he can't hold Leukemans' wheel. Gilbert doubles his lead again, while Ballan takes over from Leukemans, and at last Gilbert's lead stops growing. The group behind is starting to disintegrate.

At this point, there are no tactics other than to ride up the climb as fast as possible: the order of riders over the top will give the group a very basic hierarchy, from strongest to weakest. From 50 metres down the hill, Langeveld can see Gilbert going away, but he's not convinced the Belgian can win – he's the most explosive rider on steep climbs but he's less good at time-trialling, so it'll be hard for him to stay away on the rolling descent to the finish. Scheirlinckx started the climb near the back but he is picking off his rivals slowly. He sees Cancellara coming back to him, which gives him confidence as he feels his legs are better than those of the Swiss rider.

At the end of the cobbles, Gilbert leads Ballan by 20 metres. Then come Chavanel and Leukemans, another 10 metres in arrears. Scheirlinckx, next, overtakes Cancellara and draws away from him, 20 metres behind Chavanel and Leukemans. Then come the rest, a similar distance behind: Nuyens, Langeveld, Thomas, Boonen, Hincapie and, last in line, Flecha. It's not just the climb and its position that makes the Bosberg such a difficult part of the race. The top drags on and on, and there is no descent, just a flat and exposed road.

Gilbert is grinding his pedals round at the front of the race, 12 seconds clear of Ballan, who is just ahead of Chavanel and Leukemans who are, in turn, just ahead of Scheirlinckx and Cancellara. Then there's a gap to the next six. It's now one against one, against two, against two, against six. Quick Step and BMC's riders are split up, but Sky's two men are both in the group of six at the back, which may help bring them back. Sergeant, in the Lotto team car, thinks, *This is going to have to be the time trial of Philippe's life.*

There are 11 kilometres to the finish. Gilbert looks back, which suggests he's not confident in himself, and Ballan is already eating up the road between them. Chavanel and Leukemans are a pair, and can therefore work together to chase down Ballan, so they are gaining on him. Cancellara and Scheirlinckx are coming back to Chavanel and Leukemans. The road drags slightly down.

Cancellara and Scheirlinckx catch Leukemans and Chavanel exactly as that pair catches Ballan. It's one against five against six. Scheirlinckx isn't working – to be there is enough. He thinks it is looking good: just six riders left in the race and he is one of them. He's daring to think of the podium and he can hear people calling his name by the roadside. But he's aware that Sky are chasing behind. With ten kilometres to go, Gilbert leads by ten seconds and, ominously for him, he is struggling and fighting while the five behind are sharing the work in a smooth rotating paceline. Nine kilometres; the gap is six seconds, and the next group is a similar distance behind.

The catch happens outside the church in the village of Nieuwenhove, with just over eight kilometres to go. Six against six. And by the outskirts of Nieuwenhove, the two groups have come together.

Nuyens is very happy. He thinks Gilbert has killed his own chances with his attack, which was too early; that if he'd gone closer to the top, he'd maybe have had enough left in his legs to hold the gap on the flat following the Bosberg. And when the groups come together, with the 12 best riders of the day now in a single line at the front, Nuyens thinks, *Finally, we get to the fun part.*

*

Guido Debleser, the former owner of El Faro, remembers when Edwig Van Hooydonck did his training ahead of the 1989 Ronde. 'He had a training lap of six or seven kilometres on the Bosberg and back round Onkezelen,' he said. 'The circuit had two climbs and he did it 12 or 15 times through winter on a big gear. He knew every stone of the climb.'

Van Hooydonck won the Ronde twice, in 1989 and 1991 at the age of 22 and 24. Both times, he attacked to win on the final climb of the race, so fans called him 'Eddy Bosberg'. One of his team managers, Hilaire Van Der Schueren, lived at the foot of the climb and Van Hooydonck, who came from Ekeren near Antwerp, stayed with him during his training periods on the Ronde's roads.

Van Hooydonck is a complicated character. 'He's a shy guy, but he has authority in his ways,' Guy Fransen told me. I texted Van Hooydonck to ask if I could interview him for this book, and he replied very early the next morning: 'Sorry no interest. *Groeten*, Edwig'. He is rumoured to be tired of journalistic intrusions about the subject of doping – when he retired, early and having not lived up to the promise of his early years, the story went that he'd refused to join many of his peers in taking EPO (which would also explain the dip in his results). He was initially outspoken about it but avoids the subject now – from what I heard, rightly or wrongly, his criticisms didn't go down well with his peers. He became an aluminium door and window salesman after retiring from the sport, and also pursued a political career, getting elected to his town council in Wuustwezel for the Open Vlaamse Liberalen en Democraten, an economically liberal right-wing party.

My first memory of him was seeing him in *Winning* magazine having won the 1989 Ronde. The photos showed a rangy red-haired boy, caked in mud and tall enough to apparently need large extensions on his frame at the handlebar and seat tube. On the podium, he had burst into tears, which struck me as interesting at the time. Cyclists were supposed to be tough, and Flemish cyclists tougher, and this one had just won one of the hardest races of the year in terrible conditions. I suspected, wrongly, that he was a boy in a man's body. But though it was only his third Ronde, the pressure he'd been putting on himself to win it had already been building for many years. He'd decided at the age of seven that he wanted to be a cyclist and, since children weren't allowed to race in Belgium until they were 15, he regularly crossed the border to Holland, where he won the Dutch schoolboy championships for his age group five years in a row. He'd also won the under-23 version of the Ronde in 1986, so 1989 had been a long time coming.

He'd been underestimated in the race. His two previous appearances had resulted in top 30s, and he'd won Kuurne–Brussels–Kuurne earlier in the spring, but he was not a favourite. So when he got away in a group of B-list but very strong leaders and co-leaders – including Rolf Sørensen (who would win eight years later), Allan Peiper, Marc Sergeant and three others – on the descent from Berendries, the favourites weren't too concerned. But they took well over a minute's lead into the Muur and maintained it afterwards. Van Hooydonck knew where he was going to attack – at a rehearsed point by the second telephone pole on the left-hand side of the road on the Bosberg.

Two years later, he was a watched man, but he was able to do almost exactly the same. In a break with Sørensen again, Museeuw and a German rider, Rolf Gölz, Van Hooydonck approached the Bosberg with the same plan. Gölz and Sørensen were team-mates, but numerical superiority counted for nothing as the Belgian attacked at exactly the same point on the Bosberg, with the inevitable result. It looked far more authoritative the second time round, and Flanders anticipated more Ronde wins from their local hero.

From the perspective of the mid-2010s it's easy to forget that when Van Hooydonck won the Ronde for the first time, it had only been 11 years since Eddy Merckx retired, and the pressure on the younger rider in his home country was enormous. But in the end it wasn't the pressure that got to him; it was the speeding-up of the peloton in the 1990s as EPO took hold. If he had really cared about the pressure, he'd have joined in.

CHAPTER 18

Meerbeke

The 12 riders at the front of the 2011 Ronde van Vlaanderen with seven kilometres to go will not finish the race together. If they do, Tom Boonen will win. The Belgian is the best sprinter in the group by some distance; Cancellara and Gilbert are fast, Nuyens also, but they won't beat Boonen, especially as he has a team-mate with him.

But circumstances have changed too recently for anybody to have formulated a plan – they are still getting used to the new shape of the race. Nuyens' mind is working quickly. The first thing he does is look at who's riding at the front, which teams are there, how do they look, which gear are they using. First plan of action: if the three teams with two riders get into any moves, he must go with them.

The stronger riders on paper are Cancellara, Boonen, Gilbert and Ballan, though Cancellara will be tired from his long escape, Gilbert from his attack on the Bosberg and Ballan from being the main chaser behind him. Boonen seems not to be going so well, judging by the fact that he could not follow Cancellara on the Leberg nor Gilbert on the Bosberg. Of the others, Flecha, Leukamans and Langeveld are dangerous but they are not sprinters. Their hope will be to get away and for others behind to be reluctant to chase for fear of bringing Boonen up. Chavanel will be tired from his day off the front, Hincapie is past his best, Thomas is too young and Scheirlinckx is a second-division rider. But the race has had a levelling effect on everybody – the winning break may be as much down to luck as timing. Since nobody is strong enough to ride away on their own, the success of an attack will depend more on riders not chasing it.

Cancellara drifts from the front to the back. So does Chavanel. Flecha accelerates to the front. Then when Ballan takes over, he's not just going through, he's attacking, up a short drag, making the first attempt to break up the group. Flecha chases, which is strange because he has a team-mate, Thomas, to do that for him. The Spanish rider can't finish closing the gap because Ballan's attack, though seated, is strong, and Gilbert attacks to go after Ballan. Flecha lets Gilbert's wheel go and Langeveld, next in line, has to try to close up to Gilbert, with Ballan still hanging off the front.

Six kilometres to go. Gilbert closes down Ballan, Langeveld closes down Gilbert, and the group is together again. This would be a good moment for Hincapie to attack (he will later realise that – with everybody having seen him getting dropped on both the Muur and Bosberg – he may be seen as less of a threat) but he hesitates. His mind is telling him to go, but his body needs more recovery, and the moment is lost.

Nuyens attacks. He is immediately followed by Chavanel, Thomas, Flecha and Hincapie. Nuyens knows he has failed to make anything happen, and immediately sits up. It's the first time in the entire race that he has been on the front.

Five kilometres to go. Chavanel rolls through past Nuyens, and then Thomas attacks. It's pure instinct – he hadn't expected to be here and he hasn't had time to formulate a plan. Chavanel chases and catches the Welshman, just as the riders turn left off the minor roads on to the Edingsesteenweg, the N255 to Ninove. They will spend 3.8 kilometres on this road, turn right on to Brusselsestraat for 400 metres, and then on to Halsesteenweg in Meerbeke, which is the 500-metre finishing straight.

Flecha attacks. Leukemans chases, with Cancellara and Boonen close behind. Every time there's an attack, the order is reshuffled and the balance of power shifts. Flecha relents, leaving Cancellara on the front. Boonen rolls through. He is benefiting the most from the stalemate, and every failed attack increases his chances of winning. Cancellara goes through to the front again, but the pace is not high. The order is Cancellara, Boonen, Flecha, Leukemans and Langeveld at the front. Cancellara leads the group through the left-hand side of the road around a traffic island with just over four kilometres to go. Langeveld waits until Cancellara has almost gone through then attacks hard on the opposite side of the road. Everybody has gone to the left, so there is nobody on his wheel. It's not planned – he has just seen the opportunity with the traffic island and he can see the long drag ahead. His legs feel okay and if nobody chases, he thinks he can build a good lead. He gives it everything – this is his attempt to win the race and the effort will either succeed or kill his chances. If he's caught, he won't have enough left for another attack. Nuyens, sitting at the back, thinks this could be dangerous and starts to move up.

Initially nobody chases. Cancellara doesn't think it should be him, and Boonen yells into his race radio for Chavanel to chase. The Dutchman already has a 20-metre lead. It is Flecha, who used to be Langeveld's team-mate at Rabobank, who sets off in pursuit, but he can't close the gap. He drifts across the road, and Ballan takes up the chase, easily closing down Langeveld.

Close to the top of the drag, Cancellara attacks. Chavanel reacts. So does Nuyens.

This is different from the previous attacks. Every previous attacker since the group came together – Ballan, Nuyens, Thomas, Flecha and Langeveld – has gone alone. This time, three riders have a gap.

Hincapie watches. Ballan watches. Both think the other is going to react, and Hincapie thinks: *We've fucked it up; we've got the legs to follow but we've missed it.* Langeveld is cooked after his effort so can't chase. Thomas takes up the pursuit but there is a gap. Ahead, Chavanel is sprinting desperately to reach Cancellara's back wheel and Nuyens is doing the same for Chavanel's. Cancellara is in full flight and the gap is already 30 metres.

Chavanel gets to safety first. Then Nuyens, as they pass the three-kilometre-to-go mark, starts to squeeze the gap closed. At one point, he thinks he is not going to be able to do it, but he tells himself that if he joins Cancellara and Chavanel, he will be on the podium. The final two metres take a long time to cross, but he manages it. He also knows that if he is having to fight this hard just to close a two-metre gap, the riders behind will not be able to close 40 metres. *This is the podium*, he thinks. Then: *I'm the fastest here.*

The group behind has split up a little under the pressure of the pursuit. Thomas, Ballan and Leukemans are ahead of the others, and holding the gap at 30 metres. Gilbert is next, then the rest of the group.

By the time Chavanel has recovered enough to come through, Cancellara has done an entire kilometre on the front. The Frenchman does a small turn, then Nuyens goes to the front. There is no time for tactical manoeuvring – the trio must work together until they know there is no danger of being caught by the others. Ballan and Thomas are swapping at the front of the nine-rider group behind, but it's two against three, and the gap is starting to go out. Chavanel has to miss a turn, and he gives

Cancellara a small hand-sling to push him up to the front. The Swiss rider does another long turn, relayed by Nuyens.

Behind, Flecha attacks, countered by Boonen. Scheirlinckx sees them go and hesitates, immediately kicking himself – if he'd followed, fifth place was realistic. Perhaps even higher if the front trio slowed. Boonen is policing Flecha – he won't work, because his team-mate Chavanel is ahead, but fatally he doesn't even realise there is a gap behind him. If he worked with Flecha now, they could make it to the front group, but Flecha will find it difficult to close the gap on his own.

As the riders turn on to Brusselsestraat, with 1,200 metres to go, the leaders are four seconds ahead of Flecha and Boonen, and another four ahead of the rest of the group. Chavanel takes a turn. Then Cancellara again. Nuyens leaves the Swiss rider on the front as they turn into the finishing straight.

Boonen tears himself clear of Flecha and chases hard on his own now. He is only 20 metres or so behind, but Cancellara, left on the front, turns and sees him. Panicking, the Swiss rider opens up the sprint, Nuyens behind him, then Chavanel. Nuyens is not worried about Boonen – he thinks his compatriot has done his sprint already to close the gap, so he won't have enough left to beat Nuyens. Nuyens knows Cancellara is not so much fast as extremely strong, but he thinks the Swiss rider has spent so much energy and is starting the sprint in the lead, so he should beat him. Chavanel will also be tired. But Nuyens also knows that Cancellara won't want Boonen to win, after having spent so much of the race with a Quick Step rider sitting in his wheel.

When the sprint starts, with 300 metres to go, Nuyens is in too small a gear, so Cancellara initially moves further ahead of him. Nuyens changes gear, and at that moment he thinks he is going to win. He accelerates hard and moves sharply across the road to the right-hand side with 150 metres to go, passing

Cancellara. Chavanel doesn't react, getting first into Cancellara's wheel and only then moving across to Nuyens.

With 50 metres to go, Nuyens' legs feel awful. He sits down. Stands up again. Chavanel is pressing hard on his right-hand side. Nuyens was taught as a sprinter to never push somebody into the barrier. But at the same time, don't open the door. Just make yourself a little bit bigger. That's enough.

When Nuyens crosses the line, his arms are thrown high and wide in the air.

EPILOGUE

When I went to meet Nick Nuyens in Leuven, I'd texted him the evening before, telling him that I was brushing up on the 2011 race and watching the DVD: '17km to go. Cancellara's going to win . . . surely?' A few minutes later my phone pinged. 'Keep on watching . . . ' he wrote back, with a smiley emoji.

When I was researching the Tour of Flanders for this book, I was in search of some kind of grand unifying theory of the race and its relationship with the region. The one that developed – and it isn't perfect – was that Flanders is caught in a tension between its past and its present. There is a difference between what it was and what it is, which makes me curious about the region's self-image. Is Flanders the land of hard-working, stoic, unemotional farmhands, or is it a forward-thinking, modern and cosmopolitan service economy? Old Flanders was all around me as I travelled around the *Vlaamse Ardennen*. Some of the views or the nooks and crannies around the bergs probably haven't changed much in the last 100 years. But New Flanders was everywhere to be seen too. When I visited El Faro at the top of the Bosberg, I could see a living example of how the old evolves into the new. The same family used to run the more traditional bar that was there before El Faro, but they've adapted to the 21st century while keeping continuity with the past. You could try to find the line between old and new, but it keeps shifting.

There's a new Tour of Flanders as well as an old Tour of Flanders, which found expression in the 2011 race. It wasn't just, in my opinion, the most exciting and tense edition of the race (with a side helping of hubris and downfall, in the form of Fabian Cancellara, and heroism in the form of Sylvain Chavanel). It was also a convenient dividing line between new and old. It was the last to finish in Meerbeke, after almost 40 years. The modern Ronde – the one that has existed since 2012 – is a more corporate entity, growing every year, attracting more foreign fans and even seeing comparatively less success for the home riders. There was a run of four years between 2013 and 2016 with non-Belgian winners – the longest in the history of the race, though Philippe Gilbert brought that to a halt with his impressive win in the 2017 race. (Belgian riders have always been there or thereabouts, however – there have been only five editions in history without a Belgian on the podium, the last in 2001.)

I also felt that the winner in 2011, Nuyens, illustrated the difference between old and new Flanders perfectly. He's no *Flandrien*. He has a degree in media science and communication from Leuven university, and he told me one of the courses he enjoyed the most was commercial psychology.

I'd asked him what his parents did. 'They were working in the diamond industry. But now my dad is working in the garden of a castle because he really likes to be outside,' he said. 'His parents were farmers so he likes to be out in nature.'

I hadn't necessarily intended for Nuyens' family background to illustrate so perfectly the lineage and connection between old and new Flanders, but I explained to him that I didn't think he was a Flandrian in the sense of the stereotype. I told him I saw him as a modern Belgian. I told him I thought he represented modern Belgium far more than, for example, Stijn Devolder, who I saw as much more representative of the tradition of

Flandriens and working-class culture. Only two years separated each winning the race – Devolder in 2009 and Nuyens in 2011. But you can look back from Devolder's win in 2009, compare him to a winner from the 1930s, and understand the similarities between the two. Meanwhile, Nuyens has less in common with winners from the past, but look at his grandparents and there is a link. 'I consider it as a compliment,' he said. 'I'm not a typical Flandrian. If a Flandrian is a guy who is pushing all the time, in bad weather and bad circumstances, that's not me. Cycling is developing. You get more and more guys with university studies, and that is a good thing for cycling in general. I didn't think I was a guy like the old guys.'

It's possible to get nostalgic for the aspects of the race that are no longer the same. I preferred the atmosphere and tactical finesse of the Muur–Bosberg–Meerbeke finish to the sledgehammer Oude Kwaremont–Paterberg–Oudenaarde iteration. The race organisers are resolute that this has been a positive development; at the same time the marketing of bike races in Flanders relies heavily on the history and stereotypes of the past. Then again, as a new generation of fans gets used to the Oudenaarde finish, it's easy to imagine outrage, ten or 20 years down the line, when the finish is moved to Ronse or somewhere else.

Behind Nuyens, Chavanel was second in the 2011 Ronde. He had been on the front of the race from the Oude Kwaremont onwards and was still strong enough to be within half a bike length of the win. 'I take pleasure, and disappointment from it,' he told me. On Nuyens: 'He did a negative race. Always hidden. I made a small mistake not waiting for Tom when he attacked behind. And in the sprint I had to touch the brakes twice, which is what stopped me from winning. The moment I remember most is the moment I passed the line, and realised I had lost the Tour of Flanders.'

Cancellara was third. I think his ambition and confidence got the better of him, and there was just enough stacked against him to stop him from pulling off a similar exploit to that of 2010. Small things like his new team not quite gelling from a logistical standpoint, and Chavanel being able to sit on his wheel. It was hubris, but him being able to do what he did, get caught and *still* make the race-winning attack with four kilometres to go, was heroic. He told me he'd been suffering cramps from the Bosberg onwards.

Boonen was fourth. For Quick Step, second and fourth was simultaneously proof that they were the strongest team, and a disappointing defeat. Even a few years later, when I spoke to Boonen about the race, he was scratching his head about it. 'Nuyens was never, ever in the front of the race,' he said. 'He was dropped, he was suffering. There were some attacks, he reacted one time and that was it. When we went after them, I didn't realise we were 100 metres in front of the others. I looked back and thought, fuck, if I'd done one turn we'd have been with the front guys. It was a strange day.' It was a lesson in how bike races work: the fastest rider over the last 1,500 metres of the race was Boonen, but he'd started those 1,500 metres just too far behind the leaders to catch them.

Most of the rest of the group sprinted for fifth, and Langeveld led them in. I met him at the Tour of Britain to talk about the race and he remembered it well. 'I wasn't one of the top three guys in the race, I think I was a little behind that level. I think fifth place was my spot,' he said. Hincapie was sixth. He's still rueing either him or Ballan not following Cancellara's move, but one of the first things he remembered about the race when I spoke to him was that it was BMC who chased down Cancellara in the first place. The 15-kilometre shift they put in at the front of the peloton was the turning point of the race, every bit as defining as Cancellara's two attacks. When we spoke, Hincapie mentioned he might still have his power files from the race and he emailed a couple of days later with a link to a graph of his output in watts, and the explanatory note: 'Did some digging and found it. 339 normalized power !!' Without getting bogged down in the physiology, what that number means is that the effort required to be at the front of the race was monstrous – Hincapie's average over more than six hours was 269 watts, while the algorithm that calculates 'normalized power' takes into account the time spent freewheeling and gives a wattage that better reflects the physical work he did. You can go out and see how long you can hold 339 watts for, but I can save you the effort by saying that unless you're very well trained, it won't be very long. A few minutes, perhaps.

Leukemans was behind Hincapie, in seventh. As a non-sprinter, his best chance was to be in a smaller group at the finish and he'd ridden cannily from the Bosberg onwards, not making the attacks nor being forced to chase any of them. But he still missed the last move. 'You can't react to everything,' he admitted ruefully to me on the phone. 'I always thought I had the podium in my legs, but never did it. I think Nuyens was on that day not in the best ten riders. If you did the race ten times more, it would not happen like that.'

Staf Scheirlinckx was eighth. He'd been the odd man out in the finale – the only man riding for a smaller team, and his memories of the race were both disappointment and the ecstasy of being a local rider who'd made it into the finale. 'I hesitated a fraction when Tom Boonen attacked. I really wanted to go and I don't know why I didn't. After the race I was so angry at myself. The mind wanted to go, but the legs didn't.'

Gilbert was ninth – having made his move on and after the Bosberg, his part in the race was over. At his peak, which actually came in the three weeks following the 2011 Ronde, he was the finest hilly Classics rider in the world, but the fact he always targeted Amstel Gold, La Flèche Wallonne and

Liège–Bastogne–Liège (all of which he won in 2011) meant that he was undercooked going into the Tour of Flanders. However, he signed for Quick Step in 2017, focused on the race and won it.

Thomas was tenth and Flecha 11th. Both riders could have done less work through the race – they were both visible throughout, which meant they were on the front, though this added hugely to the spectacle. However, bike racing is not about being at the front, it's about being at the front at the right time - Nick Nuyens didn't hit the front until one small dig in the final five kilometres, and then again at the finish. For his part, Thomas has great memories of the race because it was only his second big run-out in a major Classic, and considering the amount of work he'd done for Flecha through the race it was amazing he was there at all. Ballan didn't sprint – having watched the DVD as often as I have, I would say he was probably the strongest rider after the Bosberg, but was unable to convert it into a win. He could have joined the Cancellara move, but I imagine he would have finished third or fourth in that sprint.

I think the Ronde is the best bike race in the world. The Tour de France grabs me in a different way, and the Ronde van Vlaanderen can't compete with its size. But a lot happens in the Tour that doesn't surprise me very much, whereas I can watch the entire six-hour broadcast of the Ronde and, once the hills start, be gripped the whole way. It's hard, tactically fascinating, unpredictable and engaging. Riders have spent entire careers trying to learn and master the twists and turns of the event, even as the organisers change the route either subtly or in major ways every year. And while the current route has tipped the balance a little away from brains towards brawn, the challenge of winning the Ronde still comes down to who can be physically and tactically good, and maybe lucky. Nick Nuyens told me, 'I realise I was not the biggest rider. I was not the strongest rider. Of course, to win, everything has to fit, like a puzzle.'

I asked Andreas Klier, possibly the most diligent student of the arcane subject of the Ronde in the peloton, to sum up the race. He replied immediately: 'If you can, enjoy it. If not, just pedal as hard as you can.'

It's hard to distil the Tour of Flanders down to its essence. It's too complex for that. Everything is there, in the Ronde: geography, history, culture, meteorology and humanity, and every new edition forces me to rethink what I thought I knew. While I was writing at length about Philippe Gilbert missing his best opportunity ever to win the race in 2011, he won the 2017 race in spectacular style, attacking with 55km to go, which was even further out than Fabian Cancellara in 2010. Somebody – it could be Peter Sagan, the 2016 winner – will win it four times. Each new edition of the race changes my perception of the Ronde.

The more I've found out about the Ronde, as with life, the more I've realised there is to learn.

BIBLIOGRAPHY

Cycling

Backelandt, Fredrik, et al – *Koarle!* (Uitgeverij Lannoo, 2006)

Barry, Michael – *Shadows on the Road* (Faber & Faber, 2014)

Bouvet, Philippe, et al – *The Spring Classics* (Velopress, 2010)

Cossins, Pete – *The Monuments* (Bloomsbury, 2015)

Fontecchio, Chris – *For the Love of the Cobbles* (lulu.com, 2016)

Foot, John – *Pedalare! Pedalare!* (Bloomsbury, 2012)

Fotheringham, William – *Merckx: Half Man Half Bike* (Yellow Jersey, 2012)

Fotheringham, William – *Put me Back on my Bike* (Yellow Jersey, 2002)

Friebe, Daniel – *Eddy Merckx: The Cannibal* (Ebury Press, 2012)

Henderson, Noel – *European Cycling: The 20 Greatest Races* (Vitesse Press, 1989)

Hilton, Tim – *One More Kilometre and We're in the Showers* (Harper Perennial, 2011)

Hinault, Bernard – *Memories of the Peloton* (Springfield Books, 1989)

Hincapie, George – *The Loyal Lieutenant: My Story* (HarperSport, 2014)

Hoban, Barry – *Watching the Wheels Go Round* (Hutchinson, 1981)

Kelly, Sean – *Hunger* (Peloton Publishing, 2013)

Maertens, Freddy – *Fall From Grace* (Ronde Publications, 1993)

Magowan, Robin – *Kings of the Road* (Human Kinetics, 1987)

Millar, David – *The Racer* (Yellow Jersey, 2015)

Nicholson, Geoffrey – *The Great Bike Race* (Velodrome Publishing, 2016)

Ollivier, Jean-Paul – *The Giants of Cycling* (VeloPress, 2002)

Peiper, Allan – *A Peiper's Tale* (Mousehold Press, 2005)

Thirion, Stéphane – *Tout Eddy* (Jourdan Editeur, 2006)

Thomas, Geraint – *The World of Cycling According to G* (Quercus, 2015)

Van Den Langenbergh, Guy – *Fabian Cancellara* (Hannibal, 2016)

Van Gucht, Ruben – *Museeuw* (Uitgeverij Kannibaal, 2013)

Voet, Willy – *Breaking the Chain* (Yellow Jersey, 2002)

Watiez, Laurent – *Day of Glory or Day of Pain*

Wielaert, Jeroen – *Het Vlaanderen van de Ronde* (De Arbeiderspers, 2013)

Woodland, Les – *Get Away by Bike* (Pelham, 1990)

Woodland, Les – *Tour of Flanders, The Inside Story* (McGann Publishing, 2014)

Wuyts, Michel & Jose de Cauwer – *Honderd Jaar de Ronde* (Manteau, 2016)

Belgium

Aronson, Theo – *The Coburgs of Belgium* (Thistle Publishing, 2015)

Deschouwer, Kris – *The Politics of Belgium* (Palgrave Macmillan, 2012)

De Vries, André – *Flanders, A Cultural History* (Oxford University Press, 2007)

Elliott, Mark – *Culture Shock! Belgium* (Marshall Cavendish, 2010)

Hermans, Theo, Ed – *The Flemish Movement, A Documentary History 1780-1990* (Bloomsbury, 2015)

Hicks, Carola – *Girl in a Green Gown, The History and Mystery of the Arnolfini Portrait* (Chatto & Windus, 2011)

Le Sueur, Alec – *Bottoms up in Belgium* (Summersdale, 2014)

Santc, Luc – *The Factory of Facts* (Granta, 1998)

INDEX

Aalst, 63, 243
ADR, 257
Ag2r La Mondiale, 56
Aimar, Lucien, 148, 149
Albert I, 170
Alcyon, 64
Ali, Muhammad, 202, 206
Altig, Rudi, 149, 216–17
Anderson, Phil, 98, 99–100, 257–8
Andreu, Frankie, 263
Anquetil, Jacques, 209
Antwerp, 43, 62, 87, 136, 159, 163, 164, 165, 166–7
Ardennes, 8, 30, 35, 39, 43, 44, 47, 57, 76, 115, 123, 124, 199, 226, 248–9
Ardennes Classics, 110, 112
Argentin, Moreno, 97
Armstrong, Lance, 39, 76, 108, 263
Arnolfini, Giovanni, 48
Astana, 52, 56
Ausenda, Tino, 49–50

Bak, Lars, 127
Bakker, Ruud, 94
Ballan, Alessandro, 21, 53, 55, 72, 74, 109, 140, 187, 202, 217, 230–1, 232–3, 253, 254–5, 262, 263, 264, 265–6, 270–1, 272–3, 279, 281
Barbé, Koen, 19–20
Barry, Michael, 142
Bartali, Gino, 48
Basso, Marino, 210
Bauer, Steve, 6, 45–6
Bavikhove, 79
Becca, Flavio, 213
Beheyt, Benoni, 45, 216–17

Belgium:
  and Brabant Revolution, 165
  and Catholicism, 25, 163–4
  coalition governments in, 160–1
  densely populated, 43
  as federal state, 159–60
  feudal states of, 163
  first constitution of, 169
  and Flanders name, 162
  German forces overrun, 169
  German occupation of, 27
  isolated, under Spanish rule, 164
  and languages, 41, 61, 64, 75, 162, 165–6, 167–8, 169
  and last ice age, 161–2
  and Marshall Plan, 170
  millionaires in, 19
  and nine *départements*, 165
  and Talleyrand Plan, 166–7
  in Tertiary era, 234
Bettini, Paolo, 189
Birnie, Lionel, 39, 178, 192–3, 236
Bitossi, Franco, 211
BMC, 21, 52, 55, 113, 128, 230, 232, 251–2, 264, 265
Boasson Hagen, Edvald, 55, 135, 152, 153–4, 156, 185, 187, 188, 203–4, 215
Bobet, Louison, 118, 222
Bonjour, 75
Boom, Lars, 41, 55, 75, 93, 153–4, 185, 187, 188, 201, 203–4, 215
Boonen, André, 136
Boonen, Tom, 15, 18, 21, 40, 53–4, 55, 66, 72, 74, 75, 78, 81–2, 83, 84, 85, 92, 104, 108, 109, 110, 121, 122, 128,

287

Boonen, Tom – *continued*
129, 131–2, 136–44, 152, 153, 185,
186–7, 192–3, 199, 200–4 *passim*, 213,
215, 216, 217, 220, 231, 232–3, 251,
253, 254–5, 261, 262, 263, 264, 265,
270, 272, 274, 279, 280
Borg, Björn, 206
Brabant, 159, 160, 162, 163, 165, 167
Brakel, 35, 39, 125, 141, 178, 184, 215–
16, 225, 226–8
Braun, Gregor, 151
Breaking the Chain (Voet), 236
Brel, Jacques, 209
Bruges, 48, 63, 87–8, 105, 115, 163
Brugstraat, 244–5
Brussels, 35, 43, 62, 159, 161, 227
Bruylandts, Dave, 184
Buckler, 223
Bugno, Gianni, 235, 238
Burghardt, Marcus, 231
Buysse, Achiel, 143, 262
Buysse, Marcel, 64

Caethoven, Steven, 19–20, 22
Cancellara, Fabian, 18, 21, 33, 53, 54, 55,
65–6, 68, 72, 93, 109, 113, 122, 128,
132, 135, 143, 186–7, 188, 189–98,
200–4 *passim*, 213, 215–16, 217,
219–20, 222, 228–33 *passim*, 251–2,
254–5, 262, 265, 270–6 *passim*, 277,
278–9, 282
Caput, Louis, 50
Carlos II, 164
Castorama, 222–3
Cavendish, Mark, 189, 192
Cervélo, 21, 23, 28, 33, 38, 55, 213–14
Charlemagne, 163
Charles V, 163–4
Chaucer, Geoffrey, 17
Chavanel, Sylvain, 55, 74, 75, 76–8, 82,
83, 85, 90, 91, 92–3, 107–8, 109, 113,
126, 127, 128, 132, 135, 152–5 *passim*,
185, 187, 188, 198, 199, 200, 202,
204, 213, 215–16, 217, 220, 229–30,
230–1, 232, 251, 252, 254–5, 262,
264–6, 271, 272–5, 277, 278–9
Clarke, Simon, 58, 71, 90, 91, 92–3,
107–8, 109, 113, 126, 127, 128, 132,
135, 152–5 *passim*, 185, 187, 188, 201
Cofidis, 56, 77, 218, 254
Contador, Alberto, 189
Cooke, Baden, 74–5, 108, 109, 120–1,
188, 192, 194, 201, 203, 219–20, 252
Cookson, Brian, 88
Coppi, Fausto, 48, 143, 209
Criquielion, Claude, 45–6, 110, 111, 112

Critérium du Dauphiné Libéré, 6
Critérium International, 6
Cycle Sport, 26, 178, 180, 191, 192, 222,
236

Dave Rayner Fund, 205
Davitamon, 73
De Cooman, Jan, 246
De Fauw, Dimitri, 241–2
De Gendt, Thomas, 232, 251
De Kempen, 135
De Keulenaer, Ludo, 98, 99–100
de Kort, Koen, 32, 52
'*De Molenberg*' (Verhegghe), 172–3, 174
De Vlaeminck, Roger, 104, 105–6, 107,
129, 143
De Vries, André, 17, 234
Debaets, César, 50
Debleser, Guido, 260, 261, 267
Declerck, André, 117
Decock, Roger, 115–19
Defilippis, Nino, 130
Defraye, Odile, 62
Deman, Paul, 63–4
Demeyer, Marc, 104
Demol, Dirk, 79, 83–5, 108–9, 136–7,
142, 143, 194, 195, 223
Devenyns, Dries, 251
Devolder, Stijn, 53–4, 56, 69, 72–3, 75,
79, 80–6, 93, 107, 108–9, 112, 113,
135, 138, 139, 143, 188, 201, 230,
232, 277–8
Dhaenens, Rudy, 97
Dierickx, André, 211
Discovery Channel team, 39, 142
Docker, Mitchell, 22, 74, 90, 91, 93, 113
doping, 53, 76, 105, 107, 151, 189, 236,
267
Driessens, Lomme, 106–7, 210
Duque, Leonardo, 229
Durand, Jacky, 221–4, 235
Dwars door Vlaanderen, 15, 55, 77

Eddy Merckx: The Cannibal (Friebe), 207
Eisel, Bernhard, 31–2, 37, 56, 72, 186,
253
E3 Prijs, 29, 54, 68, 98, 105, 233
Europcar, 52, 56
Euskaltel–Euskadi, 56

Fabri, Jos, 106–7
The Factory of Facts (Sante), 159
Fall from Grace (Maertens), 105
Farm Frites, 28
Farrar, Tyler, 21, 28, 29, 33, 34, 55, 74,
92, 108, 214, 231

FDJ, 56
Federer, Roger, 189–90, 206
Festina, 223
Flanders Classics, 133
Flanders: A Cultural History (De Vries), 234
Flanders locations, *see Contents on p. v*
Flanders, Tour of, *see* Ronde
Flecha, Juan Antonio, 21, 40, 54, 55, 72, 91, 109, 127, 128, 132, 134, 153, 185, 187, 202, 229, 230, 233, 252, 254–5, 262–3, 265, 270–4 *passim*, 281
Fondriest, Maurizio, 45–6, 224
Foot, John, 48, 49
Foré, Noël, 209
Forestier, Jean, 222
Fransen, Guy, 27–8, 66, 115, 138, 183, 208, 267
Friebe, Daniel, 207
Froome, Chris, 189

Gálvez, Isaac, 242
Garmin, 21, 23, 28, 33, 55, 71 2, 113, 213–14, 215 16, 230, 232
Géminiani, Raphaël, 80, 129
Geraardsbergen, 24, 50, 81, 123, 124, 149, 182, 233, 240, 243–51
Get Away by Bike (Woodland), 159
Ghent, 22, 29, 38, 43, 50, 63, 64, 87, 105, 115, 123, 132, 135, 160, 163, 172, 173, 208, 227
Gilbert, Philippe, 21, 54, 55, 92–3, 107–8, 109, 110–11, 112, 113, 132, 185, 198, 200, 201, 202, 215, 217, 233, 252, 253, 254–5, 262, 264–6, 270, 271, 277, 280–1, 282
Gimondi, Felice, 105, 209, 210
Giro d'Italia, 63, 143, 207, 240
Glasser, Adam, 26
Godefroot, Christophe., 146
Godefroot, Urbane, 147
Godefroot, Walter, 103, 146–52, 209, 211
Gölz, Rolf, 268
Goris, Rob, 32
Greipel, André, 37
Grivko, Andriy, 37, 39, 40
Guesdon, Frédéric, 155–6, 184, 185, 255
Guimard, Cyrille, 222
Gustov, Volodymir, 191

Haaghoek, 198–9
Hainaut, 57, 162, 163, 165, 167
Hammond, Roger, 22–3, 28–9, 38–9, 55, 74, 90, 91, 93, 113, 127
Harelbeke, 29, 43

Haussler, Heinrich, 21, 28, 29, 55, 112, 214, 216, 231
Hayman, Mat, 74, 75, 91, 156, 185, 188, 201, 203, 204, 253
Herrada, Jesús, 19–20
Heylen, Rudy, 14
Hilton, Tim, 94
Hinault, Bernard, 76, 77, 102, 202
Hincapie, George, 30, 55, 74, 75, 93, 108, 109, 113, 141–2, 216, 230, 231, 232, 253, 255–6, 262, 263–4, 265, 270–1, 279–80
Hoban, Barry, 66, 207, 209, 211
Hoffman, Tristan, 120, 219
Horebeke, 36
Hoste, Leif, 56, 79, 95, 141–2, 216, 233, 263
HTC, 56
Hulsmans, Kevin, 137–8
Hunt, Jeremy, 22, 38, 39, 74, 90, 91
Hushovd, Thor, 21, 28, 29, 54, 55, 109, 128, 132, 185, 187, 199–200, 202, 214, 229, 231, 253, 255

Icarus on my Knee (Verhegghe), 173–4
Indurain, Miguel, 7

Jalabert, Laurent, 221
Janssen, Jan, 130, 149
Jørgensen, Jonas, 72

Katusha, 56
Kelly, Sean, 95, 96, 100, 111, 112, 223, 257
Kings of the Road (Magowan), 9
Kint, Marcel, 117
Klemme, Dominic, 33
Klier, Andreas, 28, 41, 69, 71, 72, 87, 109, 110, 113, 127, 140–1, 177, 180, 214, 225, 231, 282
Kluge, Roger, 19–20
Köchli, Paul, 202
Koksijde, 35
Kortrijk, 19, 26, 29, 35, 61, 62, 63, 115, 227
Kristoff, Alexander, 47
Kroon, Karsten, 73, 230
Kübler, Ferdi, 116
Kuiper, Hennie, 99

Ladagnous, Mathieu, 32
Lampre, 52, 53, 56
Landbouwkrediet, 56
Langeveld, Sebastian, 40, 55, 109, 128, 132, 134–5, 152, 180, 201, 233, 252, 253, 255, 262–3, 265, 270–1, 272–3

Laver, Rod, 206
Le Sueur, Alec, 244
Leezer, Tom, 108, 153, 156, 185, 188, 201, 253
Lefevere, Patrick, 83, 139, 220, 235, 239
Leie river, 29, 79, 145
Leman, Eric, 143, 211–12
LeMond, Greg, 77, 99, 202
Leopold I, 167
Leopold II, 168
Leopold III, 170
Leukemans, Björn, 56, 75, 109, 187–8, 201, 203, 215, 253, 254, 255, 262, 265–6, 270–1, 272, 273, 280
Liège, 143, 162, 163, 165, 166
Limburg, 95, 136, 159, 162, 163, 165, 166
Liquigas, 56
Lloyd, Daniel, 71–2
Lodewyck, Klaas, 32
Lotto, 21–2, 23, 33, 52, 55, 71–2, 73, 112, 181, 215, 266
Lotz, Marc, 80
Louis XIV, 164
Louis, Joe, 206
Lowe, Trent, 214
The Loyal Lieutenant (Hincapie), 263–4

McEwen, Robbie, 30–1, 73, 135, 226–7
McGee, Brad, 191–2
McQuaid, Pat, 88
Maarkebeek, 37
Maassen, Frans, 235, 238
Madiot, Mark, 111
Maertens, Freddy, 23, 104–5, 106–7, 151, 210, 211
Maes, Nikolas, 120, 121–2, 126
Magni, Fiorenzo, 48–50, 118, 143, 173, 186, 222
Magowan, Robin, 9
Marcato, Marco, 52, 252
Marciano, Rocky, 206
Marie, Thierry, 222
Martini, Alfredo, 48
Marycz, Jarosłav, 19–20
Mattan, Nico, 184
Mbiyangandu, Fr François, 242–3, 259
Meetjesland, 105
Mercator, 56
Mercer Quality of Living survey, 197
Merckx, Eddy, 10, 23, 24, 53, 66, 100, 103–6, 108, 119, 129, 130, 138, 143, 149–50, 152, 186, 205–12, 222, 224, 248, 269
Mercury, 121, 184
Meyvisch, Hervé, 223–4

Millar, David, 21–2
Minardi, Giuseppe, 116
Molteni, 23
Montmarault, 220
Mortensen, Martin, 154, 155, 156, 213
Moser, Francesco, 104
Movistar, 56
MrBookmaker.com, 38
Museeuw, Johan, 69, 112, 129, 138, 143, 181–3, 211, 218, 225, 233, 234–9, 268

Namur, 162, 163
Napoleon, 165
Nicholson, Geoffrey, 97, 104
Ninove, 28, 35, 44
Nuyens, Nick, 13–16, 19–20, 27, 30, 33, 36, 39, 54, 55, 69, 72–3, 77–8, 92, 93, 107, 108, 113, 114, 133, 151, 202, 215, 217–20, 232, 252, 254–5, 262–3, 264, 265, 266, 270, 271, 272–3, 274–6, 277–8, 279, 280, 281–2
Nygaard, Brian, 192

Ocaña, Luis, 105
O'Grady, Stuart, 33, 72
Oliver, John, 159
Omega Pharma, 21–2
Omloop Het Nieuwsblad, 131, 132, 133–4
Omloop Het Volk, 20, 21, 77, 98, 105, 106, 110, 131, 133–4, 218
Ostend, 60, 63, 234
Oudenaarde, 23, 35, 37, 42, 44, 47, 89, 124–5, 249–50, 278
Ovett, Steve, 5

Paddestraat, 29–30, 31
Panasonic, 22, 97–8, 99, 257
Paolini, Luca, 252
Paris–Nice, 6
Paris–Roubaix, 22, 38–9
PDM, 181, 257
Pedalare! Pedalare! (Foot), 48
Peeters, Jos, 42
Peeters, Wilfried, 85, 156, 229, 232
Peiper, Allan, 53, 94, 95, 97, 111, 179, 240–1, 256–7, 268
A Peiper's Tale (Peiper), 53, 94
Pélissier, Charles, 104
Petito, Roberto, 140
Petrucci, Loretto, 118
Pettersson, Gösta, 148
Picavet, Chris, 219
Planckaert, Eddy, 66, 79, 80, 97, 98, 99, 104, 256, 257–8

INDEX

Planckaert, Josef, 79
Planckaert, Walter, 66, 79, 104, 107, 257
Planckaert, Willy, 256
Pollentier, Michel, 151
Post, Peter, 97, 99
Poulidor, Raymond, 80
Pozzato, Philippo, 93, 109, 200, 201,
    203, 204, 215, 220, 254
Procycling, 184

Quick Step, 21, 22, 23, 52, 53, 55, 74,
    75, 77, 78, 84, 85, 113, 119–20, 128,
    132, 137, 142, 194, 200, 220, 251,
    252, 262, 264, 265
Quilfen, Bernard, 222
Quinziato, Manuel, 229, 231

Raas, Jan, 96
Rabobank, 32, 33, 55, 128, 200, 201,
    218
The Racer (Millar), 21–2
RadioShack, 30, 56
Rast, Grégory, 30, 255
Redolfi, Attilio, 118
Renaix, *see* Ronse
Reybrouck, Guido, 149
Riis, Bjarne, 151, 213, 217, 218–19, 264
Rodenbach, Georges, 17
Roelandt, Patrick, 223
Roelandts, Jürgen, 195, 228
Roeselare, 19, 63
Ronde:
    and bergs, 8
    centenary of, 10
    climb concentrations in, 124–5
    culture changes around, 257
    and diversions, 29, 58
    ever-changing nature of, 250
    first edition of, 63–4
    fluidity of route of, 11
    and German war occupation, 27
    increasing number of climbs in,
        123–4, 125–6, 208
    increasingly corporate identity of,
        277
    Klier's summing-up of, 282
    local knowledge needed for, 36
    modern, route of, 7–8
    new circuit-based, 11
    Nuyens's defining descriptions of, 14
    point of start of, 18
    reflecting social change, 170–1
    route locations, *see Contents on p. v*
    Schotte's 'ten commandments' for, 27
    significant route changes to, 87
    transition for, 148
    TV audience for, 24
    tweaked route of, 65
    yearly location of, 7
Ronse, 39, 40–5 *passim*
route locations, *see Contents on p. v*
Ruta del Sol, 38

Sagan, Peter, 87, 122, 133, 195, 251
Sampras, Pete, 206
Sante, Luc, 60–1, 159
Saxo Bank, 14, 33, 52, 55, 58, 72, 74,
    120, 192, 213, 215
Schär, Michael, 231
Scheirlinckx, Staf, 253–4, 255, 262,
    265–6, 270–1, 274, 280
Scheldeprijs, 134, 181
Schleck brothers, 213
Schmitz, Bram, 37
Schotte, Briek, 26–7, 49, 50, 82, 106,
    115, 116, 117, 118, 211, 234–5
Sels, Ward, 150
Selvaggi, Mirko, 37
Sergeant, Marc, 111–12, 228, 266, 268
Simpson, Tom, 130
Sint-Niklaas, 63, 87, 94
Skibby, Jesper, 98, 181
Skil, 56
Sky, 21, 22, 23, 38, 52, 55, 91, 113, 128,
    200, 230, 264, 265
Sørensen, Rolf, 264, 268
Sorgeloos, Edgard, 174
Spruyt, Jozef, 211
Stannard, Ian, 91
Stauff, Andreas, 40
Steegmans, Gert, 32, 73, 74, 75, 108,
    109, 127–8, 193, 199, 200, 231, 251
Stevens, Julien, 211
Steyaert, Carolus Ludovicius, *see* Van
    Wijnendaele, Karel
Sunderland, Scott, 9–10
Suter, Heiri, 49
Sykes, Herbie, 48

Tafi, Andrea, 184, 235
Tankink, Bram, 54
Terpstra, Niki, 68
Thomas, Geraint, 9–10, 15–16, 40, 55,
    91, 92, 108, 109–10, 113, 127–8,
    185, 187, 202, 217, 219, 230, 252–3,
    255–6, 263, 264, 265, 271–2, 273,
    281
Tiegemberg, 123, 145, 223
Tielt, 19, 115
Tirreno–Adriatico, 6
Tjallingii, Maarten, 32–3, 34, 36–7, 52,
    152, 199

Topsport Vlaanderen, 55, 77
Tour of Britain, 6
Tour of Flanders, *see* Ronde
Tour de France, 5, 6–7, 30, 62, 63, 64,
   73, 74, 76, 77, 80, 104, 117, 118, 130,
   133, 143, 151, 171, 190, 192, 202,
   206, 207, 208, 209, 220–1, 240, 281
Tour of Italy, 5
Tour of Lombardy, 25, 106, 110, 116,
   143, 241
Tour of Morocco, 117
Tour of Qatar, 192, 233
Tour of Romandy, 6
Tour de Suisse, 6, 202
Tour de Trump, 6
Tour of Tunisia, 148
Trek, 21, 22, 33, 34, 52, 55, 79, 128, 193,
   194, 213
Trident, 257
Truyers, Noël, 180
Turgot, Sébastien, 22, 74, 90, 91, 93,
   113
TVM, 28
Tyson, Mike, 139, 206

US Postal, 79, 84

Vacansoleil, 33, 54, 56, 188, 252
Valverde, Alejandro, 189
Van Avermaet, Greg, 74–5, 93, 109,
   128, 132, 135, 153, 156, 185, 188,
   195–6, 201, 203, 204, 217, 229,
   231, 232, 254, 261
Van Damme, Tom, 88–9
Van De Kerckhove, Bernard, 211
Van Den Haute, Ferdi, 179
Van den Haute, Léon, 63
Van Den Langenbergh, Guy, 27
van der Poel, Adri, 111, 257
Van Der Schueren, Hilaire, 267
van Dijk, Stefan, 22, 74, 90, 92
van Est, Wim, 117, 118
Van Eyck, Jan, 17, 48
Van Gils, Lieven, 16
Van Hauwaert, Cyrille, 62
Van Hooydonck, Edwig, 186, 224, 235,
   248, 267–9
Van Keirsbulck, Guillaume, 45
Van Looy, Rik ('Rick II'), 45, 106,
   129, 130, 136, 149–50, 207, 209,
   216
Van Petegem, Peter, 28, 30, 108, 121,
   138, 140–1, 176, 177–85, 198, 214,
   215, 216, 225, 227, 235

Van Steenbergen, Rik ('Rick I'), 66,
   106, 129–30, 136
Van Wijnendaele, Karel, 59–64, 86, 133,
   134, 145, 158
Vandenbergh, Stijn, 121, 195–6
Vandenbroucke, Frank, 181–3, 184, 235
Vanderaerden, Eric, 10, 94, 95–6, 98,
   99–100, 111–12, 136, 225
Vanderjeugd, Tim, 196–7
Vanmarcke, Sep, 74, 75, 195–6
Vansevenant, Johny, 149–50
Vanwalleghem, Rik, 23–5, 70
Vaughters, Jonathan, 28, 29, 110, 180,
   214, 231, 232
Veelers, Tom, 58, 71, 90, 91, 92
Velzeke-Ruddershove, 29–30
Veranda's Willems, 56
Verbeeck, Frans, 212
Verhegghe, Willie, 172–4, 176, 247–8
Verhoeven, Nico, 99
Vinokourov, Alexander, 261
Voeckler, Thomas, 109, 135, 198, 217,
   229
Voet, Willy, 236
Vogondy, Nicolas, 221
Vuelta a Andalucía, 233
Vuelta a España, 5, 20, 149

Wallace, David Foster, 189
Wallonia, 8, 40, 52, 56, 57, 159, 160, 161,
   162, 165–6, 168, 170, 227
Waregem, 15, 19
Wattez, Omer, 8
Wegmüller, Thomas, 223–4
Wevelgem, 29
Weylandt, Wouter, 33, 72
White, Matt, 214
Willems ProContinental, 253
William I, 165, 166
Wilson, Matt, 32
Winning, 96, 256, 267
Woodland, Les, 64, 129, 130, 159
World War One, 64, 123, 169
World War Two, 27, 116, 133, 147, 170
Wuyts, Michel, 95, 195
Wyss, Danilo, 231

Yates, Sean, 6
Ypres, 63, 182

Zabel, Eric, 140–1
Zandegù, Dino, 209
Zberg, Markus, 182
Zoetemelk, Joop, 96